WAYALESHI

WAYALESHI

Peter Fraenkel

*' If God can do anything, why does He not
broadcast so that we can hear His voice and
know how He wants us to live?'*

Listener's letter to the
Central African Broadcasting Station

50622

WEIDENFELD AND NICOLSON
7 CORK STREET LONDON WI

For my parents
who often disagree with my ideas
but always tolerantly

MADE AND PRINTED IN GREAT BRITAIN
IN 11PT IMPRINT
BY WYMAN AND SONS LIMITED
LONDON, FAKENHAM AND READING
R. 6399

CONTENTS

1. Out of the Saucepan 11

2. Can you Grow Mealies on Mount Everest? 28

3. Of Mikes and Men 40

4. People Pose Problems 62

5. Copper Towns 74

6. Lion Mane and Spectacles 92

7. Men Between 117

8. Keeping in Step 135

9. Impact 146

10. Vultures High and Low 161

11. Leaders? 179

12. Vampire-Men 196

13. Up-hill Struggles 209

14. White Men have no Sympathy 222

ILLUSTRATIONS

Listening family   *facing page* 64

Michael Kittermaster at Victoria Falls   65

Ha-hi-ha Mlongoti   80

Nkhata's Quartet   80

Conducting a play-rehearsal: *Mfumfumfu* Kateka   81

Unscripted play on the air   81

Godwin Mbikusita Lewanika on the river Zambesi . . .   144

. . . by the river Thames   144

Knitting lesson in Barotseland   145

Luunda Chief Kazembe XV and Labour Chief Clem Attlee   160

Blind minstrel in Nyasaland   161

Author recording in Nyasaland   161

ACKNOWLEDGEMENTS

MY THANKS are due to Mr M. Esslin who first suggested this book; to Professor H. Powdermaker and Miss N. Cleak for permission to consult unpublished research-papers and to several friends in the Rhodesias who supplied information and checked facts. I shall not name these as it might embarrass them.

I have had valuable advice and criticism from Miss V. Manoukian, Dr A. L. Epstein, Dr and Mrs V. Turner, Mrs P. Smith, Messrs M. Horne, D. Smollett and J. Smulian, and from Merran, who read the first chapters I wrote as Miss McCulloch but by the last had changed her name to mine.

I am indebted to the following for permission to reproduce the photographs in the book; Mr George Carder for the picture facing page 161 (bottom); to the Northern Rhodesian Information Department and their photographers Nigel Watt, 64, 65, 80 (both) and 160, Theo Gorecki, 81 (top), and Mike Potgieter, 81 (bottom); and to the Central Office of Information of Great Britain, 144 (bottom). The remaining photographs are my own.

The map was reproduced by kind permission of the Federal Information Officer at Rhodesia House.

My thanks are due to the following for permission to quote extracts from their publications: Reginald Reynolds and Messrs Jarrolds (Hutchinson) for *Beware of Africa*; Evelyn Waugh and Messrs Chapman and Hall for *Black Mischief*; and M. G. Marwick and the International African Institute for *Africa*.

P. J. F.

RHODESIA AND NYASALAND

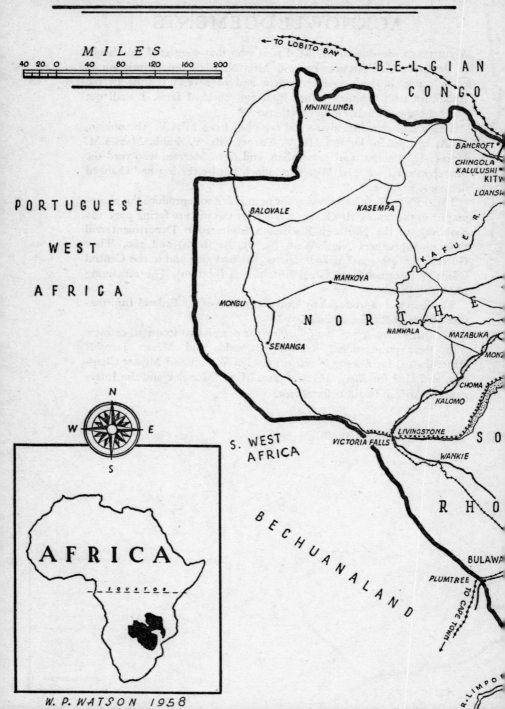

MILES

40 20 0 40 80 120 160 200

TO LOBITO BAY

BELGIAN CONGO

MWINILUNGA

BANCROFT
CHINGOLA
KALULUSHI
KITWE
LUANSHI

PORTUGUESE

WEST

AFRICA

BALOVALE

KASEMPA

KAFUE R.

MANKOYA

MONGU

NORTHE

NAMWALA

MAZABUKA

SENANGA

MONZ

CHOMA

KALOMO

S. WEST
AFRICA

VICTORIA FALLS

LIVINGSTONE

SO

WANKIE

RHO

BECHUANALAND

BULAWA

PLUMTREE

TO CAPE TOWN

AFRICA

IQUATOR

N
W E
S

W. P. WATSON 1958

R. LIMPO

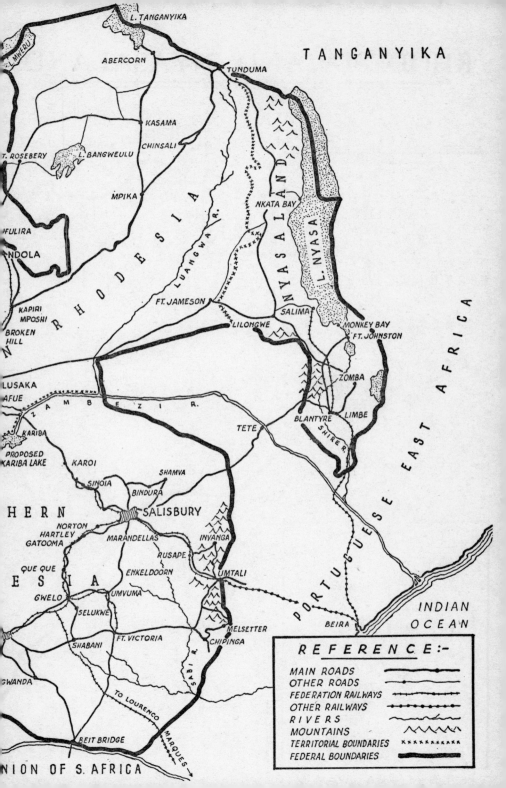

1. OUT OF THE SAUCEPAN

THE AFTERNOON SUN beat down on the iron roof of the office of the Registrar of Co-operative Societies and was reflected by the aluminium prefabs next to us. They were temporary, war-time offices—still standing in 1952. I drew the faded green curtain to shut out the glare and thought,

'All of this will be changed next week. I'll have a tile roof over my head.'

The African office-orderly came in and stood to attention.

'Please, sir, I want to know something.'

'Now what, Albert?'

'Is it true . . . about the Northern Rhodesia Regiment? People say they are all die on way to Malaya.'

I sat up.

'Drowned? Good God, no. Not that I know of. Where did you hear that?'

'Everybody talk. Everybody in compound say steamer drown in sea.'

'Can't be. I would have heard of it by now.'

Just then Edwin Kapotwe, our senior African inspector of co-operatives walked past the open door.

'Mr Kapotwe,' I called, 'have you heard about the NRR?'

'I have. Lusaka is full of it. People say they heard it over the wireless, but I was listening last night and I heard no mention.'

But Albert was still unhappy. 'Please, sir. I'm very worry because of my elder brother. They know you at Broadcasting House. You work for them. Please, you ask them.'

I knew there was no point in ringing up. It always took hours to get through at Lusaka. I felt I had to get on my high horse.

'No, Albert, I do *not* work there. Not yet. I'm going there on transfer next week, but this week I'm still with the co-ops, full-time.'

He was not shaken off so easily.

'But you broadcast for them. I hear you explaining trouble in Korea.'

'That is done after hours, in my own time. I promised that to the Registrar. But I'll tell you what Albert, when we knock off we'll go over together.'

He looked puzzled.

'Knocking-off-time,' I explained, 'the time when we finish work.'

'Ah, yes.'

'Only half an hour to go.'

So I went back to my work on the salary lists for African co-operative inspectors: cost-of-living allowance on a salary of twelve pounds ten shillings per month was seventeen and sixpence; Mwamba was going up to thirteen pounds this month. Now, had his incremental warrant been signed?

At five to four I checked that the door of our stationery-room was properly locked, that the keys for the departmental vehicles were on the keyboard, that the cars were parked in their right places. Then at four, Albert and I walked across the grass towards the little red-tiled building that housed the Central African Broadcasting Station.

It was a distance of only a few hundred yards, but we had to pick our way between mountains of earth and to balance on gangplanks across deep ditches. The whole of the small, but rapidly growing capital of Northern Rhodesia was criss-crossed by trenches for the new sewerage scheme. Many of them carved up roads that had only been tarred a few months previously. They would have to be done again.

At the broadcasting station we walked into more chaos. The whole of the African staff seemed to be crowded into the small space that had been designed as a waiting-room, but now served as the office for the bosses. They seemed to be engaged in an argument with Michael Kittermaster the head, and with Dick Sapseid his second-in-command, whom everyone called Sapper. I stopped by the glass door.

'There he is,' called Kittermaster from behind his desk; 'You're a fine one.'

'Why, what have I done?' I asked.

'Causing fear and despondency. Riot and revolution.'

Sapper joined in, 'Weeping women are besieging every district commissioner in the territory.'

A fat African standing nearby took up the joke, 'A chief at Mporokoso has died of heart-failure.'

I was not yet used to the tone at Broadcasting House. I grinned sheepishly and Sapper saw my discomfort.

'We think you're responsible for those rumours about the Northern Rhodesia Regiment.'

'Me?'

'That's right.'

'But I haven't even mentioned the regiment. You—you've both seen the scripts I've done. There was one last week about the constitutional changes in Tanganyika, and one on General Eisenhower's candidature . . .'

'What about the one about that ship,' asked Kittermaster, 'you know, the one that almost sank but the captain stayed on board?'

'The *Flying Enterprise*? You suggested that, sir. We were short of a suitable subject. *I* didn't think it was worth all the fuss. Anyway it had nothing to do with the regiment.'

'No, but it's the only broadcast we've done that mentions ships or sinking. Have you got the script there, Zulu?'

I was handed a copy of the script I had written. It was annotated with the dates on which it had been broadcast in each of seven languages: Bemba, English, Nyanja, Lozi, Ndebele, Tonga and Shona, the official languages of the two Rhodesias and of Nyasaland. I read the paragraph they had marked:

> 'The wind has blown up waves as high as six or seven men, one on top of the other. Ships have been sunk and men have been drowned. These ships are not just little open canoes such as we have on our rivers. They are far bigger even than the boats on Lake Nyasa and Lake Tanganyika. They are so large that the goods they carry would fill six railway-trains. . .'

'Several of the reports we've had attribute the rumour to this broadcasting station,' Kittermaster explained. 'Kateka and Mlongoti here think your script must be at the bottom of it. But of course, one never really finds out what starts these rumours.'

'So I'm fired before I've started?'

He laughed, 'No, but you're getting your initiation early. You'll need a sixth sense in this job. Not that any of us foresaw *this* one.'

He saw that I looked crestfallen.

'Never mind, not to worry. It all helps to keep our listeners tuned in.'

'What about drafting a denial?' I asked.

'It's already going over the air in all languages,' and he turned to one of the Africans, 'Asaf, have you finished your translation?'

'Not yet,' said Asaf, and rushed away.

'You're on the air in ten minutes,' Kittermaster called after him.

A little later I had an idea. 'Couldn't you get some interviews recorded when they land at Singapore?'

'We've already sent telegrams to Colombo and Singapore.'

'Oh good. Are they stopping at Colombo?'

'We're not sure. I phoned the adjutant at the barracks and he's making inquiries, but that will take years so I wired on spec.'

It was characteristic. In other government departments where I had worked facts were checked first, then someone made a draft, sometimes a second official polished it, then authorization was requested to dispatch it. But broadcasting and Michael Kittermaster could never wait that long.

'So it is all lies?' It was Albert, the office-orderly. I had quite forgotten him.

'Yes, Albert. It seems your brother is quite safe.'

'People tell plenty lie. Why for?'

'I don't know.'

'You should tell us,' Kittermaster turned to the orderly. 'And also why people believe them and spread them.'

Another African chipped in, 'Our people are very ignorant. They have very little education. When all of us have proper education there will be no more of this.'

Another said, 'They have never seen the sea. It seems very fearful.'

Another added, 'They are afraid of Europeans.'

'Why should that start this sort of rumour?' Kittermaster wanted to know.

A wizened little African with a humorous glint in his eyes started to explain to us Europeans, slowly, as if to children,

'The hare caused the death of the lion. It need never have happened if the lion had heeded the warning of the bird.'

All the Africans roared with laughter. Only we three Europeans looked puzzled. Albert could not stop laughing.

'He's full of these stories,' explained Kittermaster to me. 'You'd better tell us what it means, Mlongoti.'

'You Europeans are few, but you are very clever, like the hare. Oh very clever, even though you don't understand our stories. You know how to make aeroplanes. But we Africans are many and we are strong, like the lion. We dig ditches and build railway embankments. Can a European dig a ditch? Have you ever seen one? Of course not, they are weak, yet they always win over us, just like the hare tricked the lion in the legend. The little bird warned the lion but he would not listen.'

'Who is the bird?'

'Our forefathers. They said beware . . .'

'I don't get it,' I interrupted. 'If the NRR had really drowned, who would have got the better of whom?'

A short silence.

'Some said the European officers got away in a little boat.'

'Are—are you trying to tell us that the rumour says that the Europeans drowned the regiment on purpose?'

'That's what some of them say.'

Now we Europeans were roused. 'Well of all the . . .'

'Why the hell should they . . .?'

Albert the orderly became talkative in the Broadcasting House atmosphere.

'One Congressman I know, he say, "Europeans get frightened because many black people very good soldiers now. So Europeans give them all good pay to go to Malaya. They go and then . . .!"' He made the gesture of slitting a throat.

'And you believed that, Albert?'

He looked a little abashed. Then he said,

'No. I say to him, "Why they training more Africans to shoot machine-guns even now?" But he say, "You join Congress and you'll understand. They want our land. They are very clever."'

The free-for-all discussion went on, but eventually the Africans drifted back to their various tasks, some went home and only we three Europeans continued. After my two dull years as a clerk I was too animated and excited to stop, and pestered Kittermaster and Sapper with questions about broadcasting to Africans. We discussed how bewildered many Africans were by all the new facts they were expected to assimilate in so short a time.

'As bewildered as I am by their legends!'

But the other two thought that was different because it did not cause me any real anxiety. I could live quite happily without know-a thing about the world of the Africans. Most of the whites in the Rhodesias did. But it was not so the other way round.

'And their anxiety is worse these days,' suggested someone, 'because of all this confusing talk about Federation and so on.'

We agreed on that one. I asked about the best way of dispelling false rumours.

'It's not a question of scotching *one* rumour,' said Kittermaster. 'It's a long-term business. There isn't enough faith in official channels of communication. It's slow work building up such faith. That's our job here at the CABS, and I think we're succeeding.'

Before I left they loaded me with pamphlets and scripts and programme-schedules to browse through, so that I should get to know more about the organization I was about to join. It was, for me, the first of many such discussions and the beginning of five exciting years with what a BBC executive had called 'the most fascinating broadcasting station in the world'.

It had taken me a long time to get in. I had first heard of what was then called 'Radio Lusaka' when I was still a schoolboy, a refugee from Nazi Germany just starting to take an interest in the country of my adoption. One day when I was 13 or 14, some friends and I had gone and asked shyly to be shown over the tiny station then operating from a borrowed room at the Lusaka airport. It was a very Heath Robinson affair. If the equipment did not give in and if the power supply did not fail, it came on the air for half an hour every evening with war news in various African vernaculars. On Sunday mornings and other days if the information officer could spare the time, there were also short programmes for European listeners. I took part in one such programme as a member of a children's choir, just before my voice broke. Our singing was so lusty that we overtaxed the equipment, and in the end Harry Franklin, the Director of Information, had to make us stand in the yard outside while he held the microphone at the open window!

Franklin[1] was then running the station in his spare time, aided by a signals-sergeant from a local regiment. Some translators from

[1] Subsequently a member of the Legislative Council representing Africans and Minister for African Education and Social Services.

the government newspaper that came under his department did the announcing, and white volunteers occasionally put on a radio-play for European listeners. Such Africans as listened did so at community receivers put up by the Government at mission-stations, at chiefs' courts and at *bomas* or administrative centres.

At the end of the war Franklin put up a scheme proposing that 'Radio Lusaka' should be developed into a fully-fledged station broadcasting exclusively to Africans. In one of the pamphlets I had been handed he had written:

> 'We believed that formal educational methods, taking per-
> haps two or three generations to produce a comparatively
> civilized African people capable of working reasonably well
> in the development of the territory, were too slow in the
> face of the obvious possibilities of rapid advance in Central
> Africa. We believed that if broadcasting could reach the
> masses, it could play a great part in the enlightenment . . .'

But Northern Rhodesia alone could not afford such a scheme and an agreement was made with the neighbouring territories of Southern Rhodesia and Nyasaland by which African broadcasting was to be centralized at Lusaka, while European broadcasting was conducted from Salisbury, Southern Rhodesia. The British Government in London donated money for transmitters and a studio, and the Central African Broadcasting Station got under way to broadcast to an area five times as large as the United Kingdom. It was the first station in Africa to broadcast exclusively to the native peoples.

While all this had been happening, I had been away at boarding-school and then at university in the south, but back at Lusaka during my vacations I had admired the tallest wooden transmitter aerial mast in the world, several tree-trunks lashed together. There was no steel in those days just after the war, but that did not daunt Franklin; he used local materials.

I had heard of his five year plan for education by radio. It appealed to my temperament, for even as a schoolboy I had dreamt of bulldozing Burma roads through mountains, or making the peasants of Anatolia literate, or building Dnieper dams. But this seemed quite as exciting, and it had the advantage of happening on my doorstep, in my adoptive country. Once I applied for a

B

vacation job there. I saw Harry Franklin in his improvised shack
of an office and noticed a poster with bold Chinese characters and
the interpretation below, 'One symbol is worth a thousand words.'
These were the sort of people I wanted to work with, but there
were no vacancies and I was shunted off to the Price Control
Department to work out the permitted price of cotton goods.

Back at university I occasionally read snippets about the progress of the little station. Community receivers had not proved a
success and Harry Franklin had started to search for a suitable set
that Africans could afford to have in their homes. It made a good
success story and it often got into the papers. For three years he had
inquired all over the sterling area, had circulated wiring-diagrams
and had written letters even to faraway Australia, to explain his
requirements.

They were unusual. He needed a set that worked off a battery
because only the larger towns in the Rhodesias have electricity,
and even there most of the African 'compounds' are not connected.
It had to be a dry battery set because charging accumulators is too
difficult in a land of bad communications. It had to work on short-
waves because only short-wave transmissions can cover the vast
areas of Central Africa. It had to be sturdy enough to withstand
days of jolting on the back of transport lorries. But above all, it
had to be cheap.

Such a set did not exist and manufacturers were not interested
in producing one. Franklin spent his overseas leave in Britain going
from one manufacturer to another, trying to persuade them to
build it. But they insisted on asking awkward questions, and when
they found out that Northern Rhodesia was a vast, empty land
with less than two million people, the majority of whom were subsistence farmers who saw little or no money all the year round,
and that even the workers in the towns and on the mines seldom
earned as much as three pounds a month, they lost interest. It was
not worth while setting up a production line, not unless the Northern Rhodesian Government would guarantee to buy a few thousand.

There was not much chance of that. Many of Franklin's
superiors looked upon his schemes with disapproval. They knew
the African, they grumbled, and the African would never want such
a set or understand what was broadcast, or if he did he would
listen to Moscow. If there had to be wireless sets for Africans they

should be pre-set to one station only. However in those post-war years of Labour government, new ideas of colonial administration were gaining ground and in the end permission was grudgingly given, even to Franklin's insistence that Africans should be free to listen to any station they chose. But there was very little chance that the old administrators would allocate tens of thousands of pounds of public money for the purchase of wireless sets.

In vain Franklin tried to persuade the manufacturers that there would be a market for such sets throughout the poorer areas of the world. They were not interested. Franklin had for many years been a district commissioner, and he had seen the Africans' thirst for new knowledge and their need for some brightness in lives now deprived of the old excitements of cattle-raiding and hunting. He was convinced that Africans would gladly pay a large part of their meagre wages to buy such a set, and he persisted.

Then, through a personal acquaintance, he met one of the directors of the Ever Ready Company who specialize in batteries. Franklin put his case. Ever Ready were not uninterested, and thought the matter was worth investigating. Even if they sold the wireless at cost price, it might open up a new market for their batteries. What was more, it would be doing a useful service and they were prepared to try. They set their engineers on to making some prototypes. One of these they mounted in an old biscuit-tin, another in a bakelite box, a third in a circular container, a pressing scrounged from a next-door saucepan factory, the first run of a saucepan in fact. The round set seemed to be the most satisfactory and Franklin, a BBC adviser and the Ever Ready director chose it. One of them suggested that it should be called the 'saucepan set'. Another improved on it 'The Saucepan Special', and that was what it became.

Twenty sample sets were sent out to Rhodesia and within a few days they had been snapped up by Africans who paid without complaint five pounds for the set and one pound five for the battery. Ever Ready sent their manager out to investigate further, and when he and Franklin visited the new owners unexpectedly they were met with such overwhelming enthusiasm that the Ever Ready Company decided to go into mass production.

At the end of 1949 the sets started to come on the market in large numbers. They were bought up faster than they could be

produced, and not long after there started to arrive at the new
Broadcasting House letters from listeners, some typed neatly,
others scrawled painfully in one of the many vernaculars of the
land. At first it was a trickle, then a stream, then a torrent:

'I have pleasure in telling you that ever since my life I have
never had anything which could please my life better than
the wireless I have got.'

'Many do not believe that the news came from Lusaka.
They think the set is just an ordinary gramophone made in a
different way. To convince them that the news is really
broadcast from Lusaka, I should be grateful if the names of
those I have mentioned could be broadcast . . .'

'Nowadays I will be enjoying a lot if I don't die quickly.
I do enjoy very much listening to my set although I don't get
satisfied (satiated) as I do when eating *nsima* (maize-meal
porridge). If you spend your six pounds five on buying a
cheap wireless set then you know that it will always keep
you happy.'

'I thank you very much for your work of making our
country progress. Through your help we learn many different
kinds of things by hearing them through our wireless set. . . .
Therefore I am thanking you and the Government who chose
you to work for us we Africans. And you do your duty
heartedly for love for Africans.'

'Many people, men, women and children, came in large
numbers as if they were entering a church, all desirous to
hear the news. . . . Then they said: "These Europeans are
wonderful people and the wisdom which God gave them is
incomparable."'

'Broadcasting is to Africans as the great invention of
printing was to European countries in the Renaissance
era. . . . We are no longer isolated. When I buy a radio set I
bring a teacher into my family.'

'I hear . . . some important events happening in Europe . . .
I listen to interesting talks on agriculture, veterinary and
English. The reading of the Bible is not excluded. . . . I feel
proud when I switch on my Saucepan Special and have the
whole world in my hut.'

Before many weeks had passed the vernacular languages of Central Africa had been enriched by a new word—*wayaleshi*—the local way of pronouncing 'wireless'.

It was a success story with few parallels in Central Africa. When Franklin retired not long after and was awarded an OBE, nobody in the Secretariat made the usual gibe about 'Other B's Efforts'.

But I grew up in Rhodesia among traders and farmers, not among civil servants, and I knew that among the European settler element not all were enthusiastic. Like some of the older administrators they grumbled that the wireless receivers should have been pre-set to the Lusaka station only, and that Franklin had been wrong to insist on the freedom of the ether. God knew what ideas Africans would pick up. Some thought that the money donated by the London Government would have been better spent on broadcasting to people who could appreciate it. Often I heard settlers scoff when having strayed upon the Lusaka wavelengths they picked up the 'barbaric' music and then heard request-programme announcers address African listeners as 'Mister'. That sort of thing was not done, except by a few of the officials.

One irate farmer, standing for election to the Legislative Council, demanded that the Lusaka broadcasting station 'should be brought under more impartial control as they are doing irreparable harm in building up a quite unjustified sense of importance among the native community'.

But such extreme Blimpish views were not common. The irate farmer was not elected. On the credit side a Rhodesian transport firm had allowed Franklin to persuade them to deliver 'Saucepan Specials' to the rural areas free of charge and a chain-store company decided to sell them at virtually no profit. The majority of Rhodesian Europeans were not ill-disposed towards Africans, so long as they were clean, modest and knew their place in the scheme of things.

My early childhood as the underdog in Germany and my student days among the liberal minority of Johannesburg did not fit me very well for this atmosphere. I was on the side of the CABS and wanted to work for them. I applied again after graduating, but again there was no vacancy. I had to accept a junior clerk's post with the government department organizing

co-operative societies among Africans. I spent almost two years
there always hoping to get a transfer, but my time was not wasted.
Watching the progress or otherwise of the co-operative enterprises
I gained some practical experience of the difficulties of Colonial
Governments. Some of my youthful idealism became mellowed
there. It was a slow, uphill task to convince Africans of the benefits
of these co-ops. They were so suspicious: '*Bwana*, why do you
want us to contribute ten shillings for share capital? How do we
know the inspectors will not steal it?' And they were so dishonest!
I filed away report after report that told the same sad tale of co-op
committee-members who stole goods and browbeat the salesmen
into silence. Salesman after salesman had to be dismissed for theft
or for giving unauthorized credit to his kinsfolk or to committee-
members.

Nevertheless some of the farmers' co-ops (producers', not con-
sumers') grew to be big and successful enterprises, though often
their members and committees had little idea of what was being
done in their name. While the European 'advisers' were wrestling
with problems of price-stabilization, or were considering what
proportion of the big trading profits should be invested in gilt-
edged and what proportion should go into new storage silos or
mills, the members had not yet grasped that there were any sur-
plus funds. When they did, they loudly demanded that these
profits be distributed amongst them. It was slow work teaching
Central Africans the workings of a money-economy for they have
no trading traditions.

But despite the great difficulties I kept feeling that the European
'advisers' were far from blameless, that they were not doing
enough to take their members with them and to give them a sense
of participation. Too many decisions were simply taken by the
advisers. I realized that they had other work to do: that the poverty
of their areas was so great and the benefits once an efficient market-
ing organization had been set up so astounding, that to many it
seemed a waste of valuable time to spend days expostulating, dra-
matizing, explaining and to let the African committees make decisions that the advisers could have made themselves in a matter of
minutes. Moreover the results of such persuasive efforts were not
tangible and would not go unrewarded. Annual reports did not
contain any column for 'Numbers of Co-op Members who under-

stand the Principles Underlying Fluctuations in World Commodity Prices'.

Perhaps it was presumptuous of a junior clerk, but I sometimes wondered, when a trusted co-op secretary had made off with the funds once again, whether this would have happened if he had really been the secretary and not a figure-head and if his fellow members could have been made to feel that the secretary had robbed—not one of the government's pet schemes—but *them*.

Gradually I drifted over into broadcasting, first doing occasional scripts, then applying and being accepted for a vacancy that arose. There I noticed a very different atmosphere. It is true that in broadcasting there are few financial temptations, but there are many of other kinds, none of which were ever succumbed to. For here there was boundless enthusiasm for the work, an enthusiasm that showed itself in the resourcefulness and energy of almost every African on the staff.

It did not take me very long to find out who had succeeded in generating it. It was Michael Kittermaster, the Broadcasting Officer. Harry Franklin had done well to appoint him.

Kittermaster was a man in his early thirties when I met him. He had an unruly mop of hair and dressed untidily. He walked with careless, almost sloppy movements, as if his every gesture were an unconscious protest against the disciplined, military bearing of some forebear of his. Actually he came of a family who had long provided teachers for the most famous old schools of England. He was really a shy person, but hid it under what looked to outsiders like haughtiness. He was energetic, impatient, often tactless. He cut through red tape. He got things done. His pet aversion was pomposity, and there was plenty of that among the secretariat officials with whom he had to deal. But most loudly he fulminated against the Sanders-of-the-River old-timers there who 'hadn't had a new idea in twenty years and were probably wrong even twenty years ago'. Nor could he stomach the timid liberalism of many of the younger generation.

He created around him a team among whom colour-discrimination was completely unknown. But more, he seemed somehow unaware of the social pressures outside and did all the things that were simply not done in Rhodesia as if haughtily absent-minded.

He entertained Africans at his house and, oblivious of the reactions of white passers-by and neighbours, showed them over his garden, and served them drinks on his open veranda. When my predecessor as 'programme assistant' proved unable to get on with Africans, Kittermaster curtly asked him to resign or he would be fired. In Rhodesia it was more usual to reprimand the Africans for being 'cheeky'. When an official in another department insulted an African broadcaster, Kittermaster went over, grabbed the man by the tie and dressed him down in his crowded office.

Those who have not been in Southern or Central Africa cannot always appreciate what courage is required for such deviations from the norms of the white community, but visiting overseas journalists were astounded by it. Reginald Reynolds in *Beware of Africans* wrote:

> '. . . the real high-spot was my visit to the Central African Broadcasting Station . . . what gave me such a shock was the *sanity* inside the building. White and Black were actually behaving like human beings. It was hard to believe that there was a colour-bar just outside.'

If ever Kittermaster's superiors made a suggestion that went counter to these ideas or that interfered with the impartiality of his broadcasting service, he fought them with complete disregard for the effects that his stubbornness would have upon his future career. But he was permitted more latitude than is normal in bureaucracies because they all recognized the results he produced.

Kittermaster saw that it was essential to break down the distance between himself, the European government officer and his African listeners. There was never a visitor so humble that he did not consider him worth consulting about reactions to programmes. Few Africans had ever before been treated that way in a government office. They rightly came to look upon the CABS as something special.

I remember tuning-in of an evening and hearing Kittermaster on the air, obviously improvising, filling in a few minutes between programmes. He told listeners at Balovale that our recording-van was coming into their area the following week. It was at present in the Kasempa district. Would all musicians please practise their instruments? He told them what type of songs the record-library was particularly short of. Then, would anyone who heard this announcement please give his respects to Chief Ishinde and say the Broadcasting Officer was sorry that this time he could not come with the team himself; and further, would anyone in the Kasempa district please tell the touring technician that more recording-tapes were being flown to Balovale on next week's plane. Now about Mr Kamela's letter about repairs—no, the recording engineer could not undertake radio repairs. If he did, he wouldn't have any time left for recording music and then not only Mr Kamela but all the listeners in the Balovale district would have something to complain about. . . .

It was informal, friendly, intensely personal. It was very unlike the British and South African Broadcasting Corporations where Kittermaster had been trained. But he was anything but hidebound.

He went out to the African masses. He himself took our recording-van into the remotest parts of Central Africa. In northern Nyasaland he lost a trailer down a precipice. In remote Bemba country he tracked down centenarians who still remembered Dr Livingstone. He even took a recording-machine to Johannesburg while on leave and there got interviews with Rhodesian Africans who were dodging forcible repatriation by 'passing' as South Africans.

He and Sapper made thousands of recordings of folk-singers, the traditional music of the villages and the Europeanized new music of the towns. Broadcasting became very much a two-way affair. The listeners contributed most of the music and some of the ideas.

He had enormous energy and worked very fast. Technicians dreaded going on tour with him because he worked them from seven in the morning until eleven at night. Once, when he was learning an African language he worked sixteen hours a day and collapsed as soon as he got out of the exam.

He might have got as much done as he did with less work if he could have delegated responsibility and worked through a hierarchy, but that he could not do. He did not even use a stenographer. He did not like to play the boss and to be waited upon, and anyway he typed better than most, so he did his correspondence straight off the typewriter.

One day when the yard behind Broadcasting House was littered with paper, despite several previous requests to keep it clean, Kittermaster took a broom and proceeded to sweep it up. Within a minute a dozen shamefaced broadcasters were hastily picking up their litter. Other officials, had they seen it, would have disapproved strongly, but Kittermaster achieved more than just cleaning the yard: his staff never dropped rubbish there again.

He hardly ever corrected our work or reprimanded us. He merely showed by his example how scripts should be written, how news should be edited and radio-plays produced. I soon discovered that he did not like to criticize my scripts after I had done a draft. If I wanted the benefit of his sharp and inventive mind I would have to ask for suggestions before I started.

In his odd way he instilled in all of us, Europeans and Africans, a sense of participation, an enthusiasm that kept us working for ten or twelve hours a day without complaint.

According to a White Rhodesian stereotype, Africans are irresponsible. Everywhere else I have found much justification for the stereotype. But in the CABS I was to see African lads just out of school rise to the occasion and assume responsibility in a way that most European employers would have believed quite impossible. They came to identify themselves completely with the organization. So did the listeners who flocked in, not by the back door as is usual in Rhodesia, but by the main entrance asking to see 'their' station. It was refreshingly new to me. Nothing like it had happened among the co-op members.

True, the challenge to the CABS was immense and exciting, to bring education to seven million Africans by methods new, untried and experimental. There was no precedent we could follow. We were the first to try, and from as far away as Paris and the Polynesian islands broadcasters were coming to Lusaka to study our techniques. However, I have since seen broadcasting stations in other African lands where the challenge is just as great, but which were sluggish through lack of enterprise, with the slavish copying of unsuitable European techniques and with clock-watching.

No, it was Michael Kittermaster who generated this enthusiasm in the CABS. It is not surprising that he had become something of a legend at the age of 34.

It is now several years since he shook the dust of Central Africa off his feet, but to this day there are many Africans who believe that just as the principal of a school is called a headmaster, every controller of a broadcasting station is called a kittermaster. I regret to say there was only one.

2. CAN YOU GROW MEALIES ON MOUNT EVEREST?

THE MONDAY MORNING I arrived to start working full-time at Broadcasting House, a third desk had to be moved into the little office that had originally been a waiting-room. No 'boy' was called to do the furniture moving. Kittermaster, Sapper and I did it. Then my desk was piled high with files marked 'District News— Kasempa' and 'District News—Mwinilunga'—and so on.

'Your baby now!' they explained.

A few days later Kittermaster went off on a long tour to record music in Southern Rhodesia and Nyasaland, so it was left to Sapper to teach me. He was a kind, paternal man and did not hurry me.

'It's parish-pump news,' he explained. 'News of hunts and births and of development schemes in tribal areas and marriages and deaths. But don't think that makes it unimportant. For many of our listeners in the towns it provides an important link with the tribal areas from which they've come. And what's more, we hope they'll graduate to listening to our bulletins of Central African news and eventually to world news.'

'Sort of . . . widening their horizon gradually?'

'Exactly. Now we have news-correspondents all over, some are pretty good, others are very bad. We're trying to replace the bad ones as fast as we can. Your job will be to keep in contact with the correspondents, give them advice and criticism, and compile news-bulletins from their letters. After that our translator-announcers put them into the right vernaculars. Do you know which districts speak which vernacular?'

'More or less.'

Just then an African came in and interrupted. He was translating a talk on the conservation of forests and wanted to know what, exactly, a watershed was. Sapper explained it by constructing a ridge with some books and pouring a packet of office-pins over it. The translator went away satisfied. Sapper turned back to me:

'Originally we used to accept news sent in by anyone and in any language. But the standard of accuracy was low, so we had to get it on a proper footing. Now we've appointed one or two correspondents in each administrative district.'

'How do you select them?' I asked.

'Usually it's a clerk at the district commissioner's office. We insist that the letter be written in English and that it be counter-signed by the DC. The system has some disadvantages, of course. We may not get all the news, but what does get through to us is reasonably reliable. But in the old days . . . well, enough of the unsolicited stuff still gets through. You'll see for yourself.'

I did. There were reports about the woman who could bathe in a crocodile-infested river because she had strong medicine that kept the beasts at bay, about the hyena that was shot and, in death, turned back into a man, about the tree that fell, killing three people, and later rose again.

Often, however, I was to find an uncanny insight and a fine use of symbols displayed in correspondents' letters. For example, some years later a fierce struggle developed between two organiza-tions of African employees on the copper mines, the African Mine-workers' Union and the African Staff Association. The circum-stances were as follows.

The Staff Association, led by some moderates, was accused by its opponents of being a stooge organization of the bosses. It was alleged that the Chamber of Mines only recognized the Staff Association as the representative of the senior Africans in order to deprive the vigorous, radical Mineworkers' Union of its white-collar leadership cadre. The Chamber of Mines argued that they had to recognize a second organization to represent Africans pro-moted to supervisory posts. If they did not, foremen would have no authority because they would be under threat of disciplinary action by a union dominated by the very workers whom they might have occasion to reprimand. The Staff Association itself pointed out that there were similar organizations among the European mine-employees. Whatever the merits of the case, our official correspondent left us in no doubt as to what the *vox populi* said:

'. . . housewives and children are participating to aggravate the situation by publicly naming Staff-members. . . . Any member of the latter is nicknamed *makobo* and the Union-members call themselves *kabombola*.

'Makobo is a fresh fish, bream, now being imported into the
Copperbelt markets in large quantities from Lake Mweru.
It has a weak appearance and soon dies after it is caught in
the net. Kabombola, a bubble-fish, retains its flesh longer,
struggles when entangled in a mesh and attempts to resist
death after being caught. Because of the quality, dignity and
powerfulness of this fish, the Union-members compare
themselves to it.

'A Union-member was sentenced to a fine of ten pounds
or three months' imprisonment in default of payment for
calling a compound policeman *makobo*. The case was heard
in the urban court.'

Some of our correspondents wrote English well. Others wrote
it pungently:

'. . . An impala buck losts its way into Sesheke township on
Thursday 21st at two-thirty-five p.m. It was chased by some
boma messengers and was thereby quickly brought to meat.
'. . . The annual audit inspection of the native treasuries
has just been concluded. I am glad to report that this year
all the treasury-clerks escaped without scratch.'

Occasionally their style varied markedly from paragraph to
paragraph:

'. . . Mr Mukupo has been holding a very enjoyable tea-party
because he is with great pleasure at the arrival of his bonny
daughter Maliya who saw the light of sun on 21st January.
His friend, Mr Chibelu did perform the guitar and sing very
loud and interesting.
'Considerable progress has been made in rice-production
in the area of Chief C. and a record-crop is predicted. An
inspection of secondary roads and bridges has, however,
revealed widespread neglect. Remonstrances with the chief
have evoked his usual inebriate protestations that all would
be well before the onset of the buying season. Action has
been taken to ensure that his promises become sober reality.'

This indicated that part had been copied from the district-
commissioner's report to his superior which our correspondent

had probably had to type. It also indicated that the DC placed rather more reliance on the discretion of his clerk than seemed justified. In my edited version such a paragraph then became:

> 'There will be a good crop of rice in the area of Chief C. this year. The chief and his people are working hard to repair the roads and bridges. They do this so that lorries can come to fetch the rice so that it may be sold.'

This problem of what to publish and what to withhold became far more acute as I graduated from editing parish-pump news to Central African news and world news. I asked Kittermaster about it.

'We try to provide a free and independent news-service, as free as the powers-that-be will let us,' he said. 'What we've got to avoid like the plague, is that our listeners should come to think of us as a mere vehicle for official hand-outs.'

At the time I had some doubts about the wisdom of this. When I had got to know my bosses sufficiently well, I argued with them.

'That may be okay with the educated minority, but can you always tell the unadulterated truth to illiterate and unsophisticated listeners?'

'We try,' replied Kittermaster.

'But would it be a good thing,' I persisted, 'to broadcast news of the bankruptcies of co-operatives, and of the losses that members have suffered? It would harm the efforts of co-op organizers in other parts of the country.'

'Well, that's one of those difficult ones,' said Kittermaster. 'But it is far better that we should tell them about it accurately and soberly than that they should hear it through the grapevine, grossly distorted. Of course, there are situations where one has to use one's discretion, but by and large honesty is by far the best policy. What makes our listeners pleased that we now relay the BBC news? The same listeners often admit that they only understand a small part of the English, but although they're unsophisticated, they can see that the BBC is independent and outside the African political squabbles. We must strive to get such a reputation too.'

I came to see that he was right. The long-term advantages of a reputation for honesty far outweighed the short-term disadvantages in telling the whole truth to primitive listeners. This became an article of faith with me, as it was with Kittermaster. For years he put up a tenacious fight to keep his bulletins independent and after he left I tried hard to keep up the standard he had set.

We were to find that it became increasingly hard in the eventful years ahead. Immediately after I started we became involved in arguments about our coverage of the Mau Mau rebellion in Kenya. Many settlers and some administrators thought it was irresponsible to report such news at all. It would give the natives dangerous ideas. But Kittermaster insisted on frank coverage.

'The English-language newspapers cover it, don't they?' he argued. 'They're written for Europeans, but there's no law to stop Africans reading them. Thousands of them do, but many don't follow the English very well, and that's not surprising when you look at the journalese. God only knows what distorted versions filter down to the illiterates. But we can give them clear and accurate news in the vernaculars. Isn't that better?' Kittermaster got his way.

I graduated to writing news of the wider world. When I started I thought my main problem would be one of simplicity of language. I used the Basic English vocabulary, with some few variants. For example, *snow* is on the basic list, *adultery* is not, yet the latter word was very much more familiar to my audience. Later, as we checked and discussed bulletins with translators and with listeners, it became obvious that difficulties arose not over vocabulary, but over the European concepts that kept getting into the news.

Parish-pump news came from African correspondents and told of events taking place in an African society. But the news of the wider world concerned happenings in a different society, so needed reinterpretation. Take, for example, a news-item about the strikes triggered off by the introduction of automation in Britain. Incidentally, the terms *strike* and *trade-union* are now familiar in the Rhodesias.

'COVENTRY, ENGLAND. British workers in the factories that make motor-cars may go on strike tomorrow. Their trade union is asking the factory-owners to take back six thousand workers whom they dismissed recently. However, the factory-owners have refused. They say they had two good reasons for dismissing the men. One reason is that they have now started to use clever and complicated new machines in their factories. They say that these machines can do the work of the men better and more cheaply than the men could. The second reason that the factory-owners give is that they can no longer sell as many motor-cars as before. People are not buying as many cars this year as they did last year, so not so many workers are needed. For these reasons the factory-owners refuse to take back the six thousand men they dismissed recently and the trade union members have threatened not to come to work in order to force them to do so.'

Simple? But even here the words 'machines can do the work of the men . . . more cheaply' really call for many pages of explanation. Uneducated Africans coming from a background of subsistence agriculture without any knowledge of the laws of a money-economy do not have any idea of costing. The item meant little to them. Listeners visiting Broadcasting House often commented about the rising cost of living: 'Why are these shopkeepers so cruel?' They believed that the rapacity of shopkeepers was responsible for the increases.

These are of course the reactions of illiterates or semi-literate people, not of the educated minority. But even our comparatively sophisticated translator-announcers found many European concepts foreign to them. Their questions were most refreshing and made me revise many of my preconceived ideas.

'It is believed that the British Government . . .'

'Who believes?'

'People . . . probably newspaper reporters in London.'

'How do they know?'

'I suppose somebody who knows the government secrets has given them some inside information.'

'Who?'

'Probably a government official.'

'Why don't you say that a government official in London has said . . .?'

'Ah, but I don't know. . . .'

After they had finished with me, I could never again accept the impersonal organization, the 'machinery' of our modern state quite so meekly and unquestioningly. When I got to London in

c

1953, one of the first things I did was to ask to be taken to a Press conference at the Foreign Office so that I could see for myself just who 'understands', who 'believes' and what 'informed sources' and 'sources close to the government' look like.

We tried to interpret news rooted in Western culture in 'background to the news' talks, striving to explain strange events by reference to the known, the familiar. Russian enmity towards the Yugoslavs after the Tito-Stalin split I tried to explain by reference to the terrible hatred that Chaka, the Zulu king, had for Mziligazi, his commander, who branched off and founded the Ndebele nation. The coronation ceremonial we explained with frequent references to the scriptures, which mission-educated listeners would know well.

I always found figures particularly difficult. Probably only statisticians and big-business executives have a mental picture of large numbers. So how could one get across some idea, however vague, of budget-expenditure, to an audience such as ours? On one occasion I spent some time at a bank weighing wads of pound notes. Then I went on the air with the following clumsy attempt:

> 'Do you know how light a pound note is? It doesn't weigh very much, does it? A breath of wind and it flies away. But you know how heavy a full bag of maize is? Two men lift it up and put it on the shoulders of a strong man. But even a strong man can only carry it a short way Well now, if we were to find a big pile of pound notes, as heavy as two full bags of maize, then we would have about the same amount of money as our government will be spending on schools this year.'

Sometimes I tried to interpret not only the tools but also the underlying principles of our way of life. When the Dutch announced new plans for land-reclamation, I waxed enthusiastic over man's ability to overcome nature:

> '. . . we can see from this work that the Hollanders are doing that human beings *can* overcome the difficulties of the world around them. Many people, especially old people here in Central Africa, believe that the earth always remains the same. Because of this, they do not show much energy in

overcoming nature. They are slow to try out new ways of
agriculture, new tools, new crops, new animals, because they
do not really believe that it is possible to improve their lot.
They have never seen the results of changes that they themselves have brought about by their own hard work. But we
younger people know that human beings *can* overcome the
difficulties of the world around them by their own efforts.
We know that we *can* turn the infertile land of Central
Africa into very much better land. By using modern methods
of agriculture we can make our soil grow much bigger crops
than it does now. In this task we can get encouragement
from the hard, slow but successful work that the people of
Holland are doing.'

On the occasion of the five hundredth anniversary of the birth
of Leonardo da Vinci I extolled the Renaissance spirit. I could
not convey any idea of his work as an artist by speech alone, his
art is too culture-bound. But his versatility, his thirst for knowledge, his restlessness and inventiveness I tried to put over. The
Africans with whom I discussed the draft-scripts were prepared
to acknowledge that there was something to be said for creating
land where there had been sea, and for building bridges and
designing aeroplanes, but they often had serious and searching
doubts about the European spirit.

One of my colleagues did a background talk on the conquest of
Everest. His task was not made any easier by having to explain
what snow and ice were like. Shortly after, some of our announcer-
translators buttonholed me.

'It is not a pleasant place, this mountain?'

'No, terrible.'

'So why do they climb up there, these Europeans?'

'It is the highest mountain in the world. Nobody else has ever
climbed so high. They wanted to be the first.'

'Are they afraid of the Russians getting there before them?'

'Maybe . . . well, no. Not really.'

'I suppose there are valuable minerals up there?'

'No.'

'What then? Can you grow mealies on Mount Everest?'

'No, of course not.'

'So what is the point?'

'It's hard to say. I suppose we are a restless people. Anything that has never been done before we feel we ought to try and do.'

At this point Edwin Mlongoti, our senior broadcaster, launched forth:

'Yes. Restless, that's true. Never satisfied, always stirring up things. Do you ever see one of them just sitting in the shade and breathing air? Ah, these Europeans!' He shook his head as with an amusing but somewhat exasperating child.

'And watch out,' he continued, 'they're making us that way too. When I was a youngster the men from my village went to work for the Europeans for two months to earn a blanket. Then they came back to rest and were happy. To have a blanket was a wonderful thing in those days. But we? As soon as we have one thing, something new starts to worry us. We want a bicycle. And after that clothes, and then dresses for the wife, next, a wireless set. There are some already wanting motor-cars these days. Look at Nkhata there. He wants a motor-car. And are we any more satisfied? Are we any happier?'

At this point I escaped back to my desk.

I enjoyed doing these background to the news talks very much and the discussions that they provoked even more. But after some years and numerous conversations with Africans of all strata, we had to come to the hard conclusion that it was pointless to put most of these talks on world affairs into the vernaculars. The overlap between the culture and experience of a western European and an African who spoke a vernacular only, was too small. It is impossible for an African who knows no European tongue to have a frame of reference sufficient to understand world affairs. He had never seen an atlas, knew virtually no geography and no history beyond that of his tribe.

Often illiterate Africans said to me such things as 'Italians? Oh, yes, They live behind Nairobi', remembering the Abyssinian campaign. Others asked:

'You have your family in Rhodesia, why do you want to go to England for your leave? It is all desert.'

'Whatever gives you that idea?'

'Well, if their country was fertile, would they come to take ours?'

We decided to confine our world news and commentaries to our Simple English broadcasts. In the vernaculars we concentrated on local affairs or on such apparently clear-cut issues in world news as the terrorist campaign in Malaya and the Russians in Hungary, issues that could be simplified to the question, 'Are we winning or are they?'

The problem of communications was by no means one-sided. It was not only that Africans could not understand us every time. There was much that our African staff and contributors wrote and sang and broadcast that we Europeans could not understand fully. This became increasingly apparent as African producers became more proficient and independent.

There was, for example, a play in Shona, a Southern Rhodesian language which I do not understand. The play was called *Mumba and his Bicycle* and the producer translated the plot for me:

'Mumba has bought a new bicycle, a very elaborate one with three-speed and dynamo and other refinements. He is very proud of it and shows it off to all his friends. They decide to celebrate and go off to the beer-hall. There they get drunk. When they come out the bicyle has gone.

'Mumba and his friends notify the police and then set off to see whether they can find it themselves. After following various false clues, they eventually find the frame, but only the frame. The other parts have been stripped off and presumably sold. The friends laugh at Mumba standing there with the frame in his hand.'

I was puzzled.
'Don't they catch the thief?'
'No. No one knows him.'
So where is the point of the story?'
Our producer laughed at my ignorance.
'Why of course, Mumba should not have been so proud of his bicycle.'
Strange! I had known that these plays always have a simple moral, but to me only two possible ones had emerged; 'Don't drink' or 'Crime does not pay.' The one that had been obvious to the producer had not occurred to me. And to me it seemed in

very poor taste when the friends laughed at Mumba's misfortunes. Why this difference in attitude? Perhaps, I thought because the producer was a member of a tribal society undergoing rapid change. The traditional society discourages individuality, pride and personal effort. Man learns to think of himself in the first place as a member of the community. 'Only wizards walk alone.' Status in the community grows with age and experience. But now these people are plunged into an industrial economy. The members of the tribe no longer depend upon each other for food, shelter and safety. It is now safer to think of oneself, to be an individualist. Young men leave the shelter of the community to earn wages working for Europeans, and some acquire wealth by their individual efforts. They outpace their elders. Not unnaturally they want to reserve the benefits of their wealth for themselves; but guilt gnaws at their insides. The old moral code asserts itself in songs, in stories and in radio-plays. Mumba and his friends knew that he had done wrong to boast of his bicycle.

Some of these plots I could puzzle out, but it was not always so easy with the stories of Edwin Mlongoti, our story-teller. One afternoon I served as his producer when he was pre-recording a number of stories before going on tour. We worked in a small aluminium shack that our technicians had converted into a recording-studio. They had boarded up the windows and hung blankets on the walls to reduce the echo. No building could have been less suitable, there was no air-conditioning and in summer it became unbearably hot. But no other was available.

That afternoon the rain came down on the low aluminium roof making such a patter that we had to stop the recording and sit around for half an hour. When it cleared he recorded a story which I find mystifying to this day.

'I want to tell you about three friends,' he said. 'Once upon a time the Frog, the Hornet and the Pathrat were living together. The Frog had a mouth that kept moving all the time, the Hornet looked so thin as if he did not have enough to eat, and the Pathrat had a nasty smell which offended his friends' nostrils. They lived and worked together for many years, each not knowing what was the matter with the other. Each one wondered at his two friends, but did not ask and find out the truth. Then one day the Pathrat could bear it no longer and began to tell an imaginary story about talkative people who never said a word. The Frog guessed that the Pathrat was driving at him, and asked his friends if they would agree to hear his story. They agreed and this was the story he told.

'"My friends, you wonder at my ever-moving lips. Twenty years ago I went to live in a foreign land. All my relatives were left behind. After staying there a few years I received a message to say that my father had died. Another messenger arrived with the news of my mother's death. Then another told me that my brothers had died and yet another brought me news of the death of my uncle. Now because I had received such bad news at the same time, in trying to make the loudest mourning I found my voice quite gone, but my lips went on moving to this day."

'After the Frog had finished his story, the Pathrat said: "My friends, I know that you wonder at the smell on my body. My story is similar to the one you have just heard, but in my case I did the burying of all my people, and because I could not bury them all at the same time, some of them rotted and were smelling badly. After burying all my people I found that in spite of washing with hot water the smell still remained on my body."

'The Hornet then told his story: "I also know that you wonder at the thinness of my body. I see that we all have the same story to tell. Each time I received news of the death of one of my relatives, I tightened my mourning-belt (traditional sign of bereavement of the Chewa tribe) until I looked as if I would divide into two. This is my story."

'When the three friends had finished they were silent for a very long time. Each one was appreciating the stories of his friends. Each one found that he had suffered in the same way as his friends. In the end the Frog stood up and said:

'"My friends, I have found that we are all in the same trouble. All these years we have been living together, I thought I was the only person alone in the world. But our stories have shown us that each of us is alone. So my friends, I suggest that we separate, because if we live together our miseries will be multiplied by three and then my mouth would gain yet more speed in moving."

'The others agreed to this and next morning they said good-bye to each other, and so today we find the Hornet living in the tree-tops, the Frog in the water-pools and the Pathrat of course, near paths.'

3. OF MIKES AND MEN

GRADUALLY, as I settled in, broadcasting lost its novelty but not its excitement. Even the long afternoons of 'knob-twiddling', of working the turn-tables and microphones and switches in the control-room, were never dull.

At three minutes to four I started the signature tune disk and a band of drums and xylophones sounded in the air of Central Africa. As the second-hand approached the hour of four, they mounted to a finale. Then I turned up the microphone and tried to say in tones loud and confident: 'This is the Central African Broadcasting Station at Lusaka, Northern Rhodesia, calling on forty-one and sixty-two metres. Good afternoon everyone . . .' But often I did not feel very confident, especially on days when, looking through the double-windows, I could see that several of our staff were still scurrying about in the announcing-studio, carrying our heavy typewriters and files balanced on top of them. The studio was used as an office during the day and just before four those translators who had not yet finished their work moved into the record-library next door. They always seemed to leave it to the last moment and I was often afraid I might have to impro- vise into the microphone until the last one had left. But usually they were out as I finished my set piece, leaving only the announcer for that afternoon sitting in front of the microphone.

'. . . our broadcast this afternoon is in Bemba and here is your announcer, Edward Kateka.'

As soon as I gave him his signal, Kateka poured forth a torrent of rapid Bemba, greeting chiefs and commoners, commenting on his fan-mail and extolling the programmes of the day. He was a Falstaffian man and he had earned for himself the nickname *Mfumfumfu*—which he rendered into English as 'he from whom words pour unceasingly like a river down a waterfall'. A rapid series of jokes and anecdotes mainly about himself, came from him.

'I'm very well today, listeners. Hope you are too. Only my finances! This big body of mine is costing me too much money. Not only do I have to feed it, but bicycles . . . bicycles! I bent the third one today. It's quite useless now. The saddle is almost touching the ground. I had to walk from my home to the studio. You're lucky I'm here to introduce the first programme which is a series of new songs our van recorded at Chitimukulu's village. Are you listening there, my friends at Chiti's? What about Mutale the teacher? Is he there? And the treasury-clerk Chileshe? Better clear away the tables in the native authority hall because you'll be wanting to dance when you hear these . . .'

While he was speaking I opened the door and windows of the control-room to let in some air, but poor Kateka had to suffer in the hot studios with his windows closed because of the noise outside.

'. . . very thirsty work, this. Now I've had a letter from a man in Balovale who tells me that his little son Chizongo thought I must be getting thirsty with all the talking I have to do, and poured a cup of water over the battery. Now the battery is spoilt and the little wonder won't work until they get a new one.'

Often when I opened the door of the control-room there were inquisitive eavesdroppers sitting on our back-steps or standing on the grass behind the building. I explained to them that they could stay and peep in as long as they did not make too much noise. Kateka, in the meantime, would be drawing to a close,

'So here, now, we have Chilufya Chitimukulu's Trio singing *Nako Akatetye*.'

I started the record and my loudspeaker poured out sounds which were weird and strange to my European ears, but obviously delighted the eavesdroppers at the open door. Often the music was played on instruments I had never even seen, one-string musical bows or metal-plucking instruments with calabash resonators, or bottles struck with hoe-irons. Sometimes, if I looked particularly mystified, Kateka came out of his studio and explained,

'It is a friction-drum. They rub a stick against the stretched hide', and he puffed up his enormous cheeks and imitated the strange, bear-like noises until he burst out laughing and had to stop.

For the larger part of the next three and a half hours we sat facing each other, signalling through the glass windows that separated us. But whenever a longer recording, a pre-recorded play or church service was running, he came out of his studio into the cooler control-room and we talked.

'That song you heard, it was about urban court assessors. You know, the judges that the chiefs send to the towns to hear cases. The people are complaining about them. They are too proud. They think they are chiefs themselves. When they ride along the path they ring their bicycle-bells . . .'

Sometimes during the programmes the comments of the uninvited watchers at the open door became too loud and I would have to threaten to shut them out. In fact, observing their minute-to-minute reactions through the corner of my eye was a valuable first lesson in listener-reactions.

Around dusk a girl-announcer came to do the request-programme. That gave Kateka a chance to relax and chat to the eavesdroppers or to come and sit with me and discuss the state of the world. They were strange, disjointed conversations, interrupted while I changed records and watched out for cues.

The long afternoon sessions gave me plenty of opportunity to get to know Kateka and my other African colleagues.

The obvious leader among them was Edwin Mlongoti, the story-teller. He was the same age as Kateka, about 40, but looked older having suffered from diabetes for almost ten years. Most Africans in their forties think of themselves as elders, notables, and Mlongoti had the manner and speech of a kindly old patriarch. He had a wizened face and laughing eyes. His sense of humour was infectious and he had been nicknamed *Ha-hi-ha*. He spoke four African languages fluently and could give running commentaries on public events and football matches in one after the other, switching every few minutes. He knew the folk-lore and proverbs of many tribes intimately and his conversation was usually rounded off by some story of animals or ancestors from his enormous repertoire. He excelled in unscripted vernacular plays, thinking up the outline of the plot and then explaining it to his actors. Together they discussed it for about a quarter of an hour, then went on the air improvising their lines.

One afternoon I was on duty when his weekly play dealt with the exploits of a robber-band. He acted as their chief and before they set out on a raid he called the roll, improvising the most astonishing names:

'Sixpence?'

'Present, *bwana*!'

'Sevenpence?'

'*Bwana!*'

'Jailbird?'

'*Bwana!*'

'Stinkbug?'

'*Bwana!*'

'Piano?'

No reply. He had done the round of his actors. He pointed once more to the first who altered the pitch of his voice and replied hastily:

'*Bwana!*'

'Look snappy. What's the matter with you? Don't you want to go out thieving with us tonight?'

'Yes, master. I want to go.'

'Well remember, he who wants a piece of meat must hold on to it while they're cutting! Now, quietly everybody. Follow me.'

They crept in single file around the microphone, Mlongoti whispering complaints each time he passed the 'live' side:

'Sevenpence, your shoes creak. Jailbird, I told you not to wear that bright scarf.'

Then there were just creeping footsteps, halted suddenly by violent barking coming from Mlongoti. The barking stopped and the dog turned thief:

'Shhhhh, good doggie, good doggie.'

Barking.

'Shhhhh, nice doggie. I'll bring you a bone tomorrow, but you be quiet tonight.'

More barks.

'Come, come. I'm not going to steal *you*. Why should you worry about your master's money? Can you eat it?'

Violent barks.

'Your master doesn't even feed you properly!'

By now the eavesdroppers at the open door were in fits of laughter and even the fellow-actors in the studio had to turn away to stifle theirs.

'Blast you hound, I'll wring your neck.'

Angry growls, then hysterical barking.

Mlongoti, exasperated: 'Whatever shall I do?'

A pause.

'Hey, Piano!'

'*Bwana!*'

'You go first.'

I too was rocking with laughter, but was interrupted by an irate technician who rushed in to complain that the 'level' was all over and did I damn' well want to blast the transmitter off the air? When he saw what was happening he relented and also stopped to watch the proceedings.

Mlongoti had a way with Europeans. He was the firm friend of both European programme staff and technicians. In Rhodesia, European artisans often get on badly with Africans, but even those of our technicians whom I knew to be afflicted by strong colour-prejudice respected Mlongoti as a good and wise man. One day I found him talking to one who was to retire soon.

'Do not pity,' said Mlongoti, 'there are many good things in old age, to sit in the sun and to watch one's grandchildren playing, to remember happy days and to grumble at the way the world is going now, to watch the crops coming up, not to be chasing about madly like most of you Europeans . . . you'll see.'

His experience of life was more varied than that of any other African on our staff. He often told us about his career. He had been sent to school by his father's employer who recognized that the lad was bright. He had gone as far as Standard IV, the education of a child of eleven in other lands, which was the best that Northern Rhodesia could provide in the 1920s. At the time it would have qualified him for a teacher's job, but he went to work as a labourer on the railways.

'I used to lay sleepers. If you go from Kapiri Mposhi to Ndola at night and you're kept awake because the train shakes so much and the bags and the bundles and the cages full of chickens fall down from the racks above, and all the chickens go "tuk, tuk, tuk", then it's my fault. I laid that bit while my *bwana* foreman was drunk.'

And when the laughter had died down he added:

'And now you know why the Europeans call them "sleepers".'

Eventually he took a job as an office-orderly with the Government newspaper for Africans. His first salary was eleven shillings a month plus food. His employers gave him books to read. He became a translator, then editorial assistant, finally the assistant editor. From there he drifted into broadcasting.

'One day Mr Franklin, who was then the Director of Information called me and said, "Mlongoti, translate this talk into Tonga and come and read it over the air". It was something about the war in Abyssinia. I translated it, but I didn't know what was going to happen to it. Then they put me into a room all by myself and said, "When we wave at you, look at this little box and read it." Well, Europeans are full of crazy ideas. What for? I didn't know. But I read it and when I got home my friends said to me "We heard your voice in the wireless-box in the welfare hall," but I said, "How can that be? I was miles away." You know, it took me some days until I would believe that they could really hear me.'

But Mlongoti's career had not been without its interruptions. 'In 1931 they sent me home,' he said. 'No more work. I said: "Why, *bwana*? Have I made a mistake?" "No, you're redundant. Government economy drive. The mines have closed and the Government has no more money." So I went home shaking my head. No foresight. Why couldn't the Government say to me when I left school "You go home and grow kaffirkorn and drink beer. There's not enough work."'

On this occasion Pepe Zulu, our Nyanja announcer, joined the discussion.

'It's because of economics,' he said. 'I've been reading about it.'

'That's right Pepe,' said Mlongoti. 'You read plenty of books. You'll read so many you'll become just like a European, and you'll forget your people and their customs. But what is going to happen next time there is no work? Will the Europeans feed you? Can you eat books? No. You'll go back to your village but nobody will remember you. Ah, well, it's always the same: child only sits down properly after it has farted.'

Mlongoti was showing great insight into the character of Zulu. It was not until years later that I saw just how much. Zulu was a self-confident young man in his early twenties when I first met him, but he seemed younger. He was small and neatly built, his clothes were always ironed impeccably. He held his boyish head erect. His gestures were precise and elegant, perhaps a little too well-considered, as if he were watching his every movement in a mirror. He had not yet grown out of the teacher-baiting phase of

his youth. I was two or three years older but not very far removed
from that phase either, so I delighted in my encounters with him.
He did most of the baiting.

'You say the missionaries brought more good than evil, and
you say that they are well-intentioned and recognize no colour-
bar? I don't think you know very many. You should have seen the
priest collecting money in my village. My father would rush out
and carry the white man's bicycle across the river and yet my
father was an old man and the priest was younger. Why?'

'You must ask your father. It was very courteous of him, but
I'm sure nobody forced him.'

'Do you think the priest would have carried my father's bicycle,
ever?'

'I don't know.'

'You know . . . you know.'

I suppose he was right.

On another occasion I wrote a talk drawing attention to a new
Government pamphlet on child-care. He challenged this:

'None of us were brought up this way and it didn't do us any
harm. I was weaned when I was about two years old. And I was a
filthy child myself,' and he made a gesture of distaste, 'filthy.
Nose always running.'

I could hardly believe it for now he always looked immaculate.
I replied,

'What does that prove? Some of you survived. But the infant
mortality in Central Africa was among the highest in the whole
world. Over three hundred out of every thousand. The population
of Northern Rhodesia was more or less stationary in the last
century. Now it doubles itself every twenty-seven years. That's
modern medicine for you. There are twelve of you in this office?'
I gestured as if to cut the group into two equal parts. 'Half of
you would not be alive now but for the medicines and the peace
we brought. Some of us whites may be bastards, but that's a hard
fact.'

'Where do you get this figure from?' Zulu wanted to know.
'About the population doubling itself every twenty-seven years?'

'From the census.'

'And you believe it? Have you ever seen the census collected?
All the people in the village who aren't on the tax register and

evade the poll-tax disappear into the bush as soon as an official comes near.'

'Maybe,' I argued, 'but that was also true twenty-seven years ago and now they're counting twice as many people.'

I spotted that there was something wrong with my argument before I had quite finished. But would Zulu see it? He did. A triumphant smile lit up his boyish face:

'No, the number who escape is getting smaller all the time. A man who has once been caught can never get out again. Once his name has been written in the tax register, it stays there until he dies. The ones who escape are getting fewer each year. And that's why our population seems to increase so much.'

'But Pepe, you must admit it has increased. There are thousands of new villages all over the country.'

'Maybe, but not so much. And it isn't because we scrub our babies all the time, because we don't.'

I knew that if ever he married and had a child, it would be neater and more thoroughly scrubbed than most European children.

Zulu's method of argument was logical, unlike Mlongoti's who argued in the African manner, by analogy. One day during a staff discussion, Zulu was again holding forth about the disadvantages of European civilization:

'The big man is right,' he said, gesturing towards Mlongoti, 'you Europeans have just made us discontented. We were much happier in our villages, even if it is true that only half of us survived to grow up.'

Kittermaster tried to explain to him that the pains of industrialization were not confined to Africa, that we Europeans also had occasional doubts about its advantages, but that for us it was virtually impossible to contract out. 'But what's stopping you, Zulu?' he said. 'You could still go back to your father's village and grow mealies?'

'No,' said Zulu emphatically, 'we can't go back. We have already become too much like you.'

Mlongoti confirmed it:

'A tame animal forgets how to hunt. You cannot set it free in the bush.'

Over the years a change came over Zulu. When I first met him he was still confused and undecided, but then he turned away from the life of his people and towards the new ways, just as Mlongoti had predicted.

'I want to know about politics,' he said to me. 'Now Communism? Can you lend me any books about it? Proper books, not just books against it?'

I must have smiled maliciously: 'I'll lend you Marx if you like.'

I lent him a copy of *Das Kapital* but as I expected, got it back a few days later: 'I want something simpler.'

Then I gave him El Campasino's *Listen Comrades!*, a tale about a Spanish Communist's weaning from Communism and his experiences in the labour camps of Siberia. He brought it back, shaking his head:

'You are right. The Russians are worse than the British. Now I want to know about Conservatives. What do they believe?'

I lent him Quintin Hogg's *Case for Conservatism*.

'I don't understand it properly. How can we Africans draw on our past? It has nothing to teach us.'

'Nothing?'

'No, nothing.'

His inquisitive mind ranged far and wide. He plagued me for books on what the Nazis had believed and about the Industrial Revolution in Europe, for articles about the Balance of Payments and so on. Very few Northern Rhodesian Africans I have met ever read anything that was not a school textbook, but Zulu read widely and with some method of his own. Like most of his generation he also did correspondence courses, but unlike most of the others, he did complete his. He took courses in book-keeping and economics, and after office hours I sometimes found him in the record-library drawing precise and neat columns of figures upon lined paper. In his spare time he kept accounts for one or two African traders for practice. He tried to draw logical conclusions from his lessons in economics:

'The trouble with us Africans is that we don't think in economic ways. The traders give credit. They say, "I can't refuse Nyirenda. He's my sister's child." But they don't have enough capital to buy new stocks, so they can't cover the overheads and they all go bankrupt. It's these old-fashioned family duties. Why should I feed twenty of my relatives who do no work? They should work for their keep. Europeans don't do these things. Theirs is the way of the modern world.'

His bark was worse than his bite. Some years before he had done a night-school course in typing. He then went back to this night school, attached to a Lusaka church, and served as an instructor. One day I happened to hear that he was doing it voluntarily, without pay. He was giving up two evenings every week. This time I baited him:

'Hey, Pepe! I thought it was all wrong to do things without payment? Isn't that the way of the modern world?'

He looked a little abashed. Then he said with a trace of defiance in his voice:

'It pleases me!'

In his work he was as methodical as in his spare-time activities. He laboured over his translations to render them into precise and classical Nyanja, undefiled by neologisms. He would question us intensively until he understood the script thoroughly before he tackled his translation. He usually broadcast it himself, his musical bass voice rolling over his phrases lovingly. Although he was not a warm personality, he had a great and admiring audience, perhaps because he spoke with the clarity and authority associated with traditional chiefs. Visitors always expressed surprise that the powerful sonorous voice came from so young and dapper a little man. One listener wrote in to say that the great voice had shaken his set so much that all the valves had burnt out.

Zulu's behaviour had a compulsiveness which I found quite un-African. He was never happy-go-lucky, always reliable and efficient. They were qualities which I suppose he had learnt from the authoritarian Catholic fathers who had educated him. He repaid them with a fierce hatred which I could not understand. One day however, I came upon him entertaining his colleagues with a beautifully sung Mass in Latin.

'Zulu,' I said full of admiration, 'you're better than a priest.'

'No,' he replied sadly, 'I spent some years at a seminary in Nyasaland training to be one. They didn't think I was suitable.'

All the cockiness had gone out of him. I started to understand.

Some years later I was running a recording-studio in Zomba, Nyasaland. Zulu was to be sent to relieve me, one of the first Africans to be entrusted with this responsibility. However, he

D

was unhappy and tried to get out of it. I guessed he did not like
to go back to the scene of his failure. Eventually he came, but he
was still unhappy and grumbled that the travelling allowance paid
to Africans would not cover his expenses. This was true, but only
if he stayed in hotels or rest-houses.

'Come come, Pepe,' I said, 'You know yourself that you can
save the whole allowance. When Banda travelled with me he never
stayed at an hotel or rest-house anywhere and I don't think he ate
a single meal in a tea-room. There were a dozen people waiting to
invite him home at every stop. And you, you're much better known.'

'I know,' said Zulu, 'but I shall not accept their hospitality.
We Africans cannot go on living in this easy-going way. I myself do
not want to have to support hundreds of strangers, so in turn I
cannot accept the hospitality of these people. I shall not stay
privately at places where there are guest-houses.'

Nor did he, so far as I know, and though I thought he was over-
doing it, perhaps he was right, the break with the past had to be
made dramatically. Anyway, I respected his consistency and guts.
Nobody would thank him for refusing hospitality. Others I knew
grumbled incessantly about having to extend what they did not
hesitate to accept.

There was one invitation in Nyasaland however, that Zulu did
accept. The Roman Catholic bishop of one of the dioceses insisted
on putting him up, and fêted him as one of the brightest products
of the mission. Zulu came back feeling rather more charitable
towards the church.

Over the years Zulu grew out of most of his brashness and
cockiness, but I used to reflect that this development had only
been possible in the 'island atmosphere' that Kittermaster had
created. In most other offices I knew in the Rhodesias he would
have been dismissed after a week, perhaps because a semi-literate
white girl employed as a filing-clerk would complain that he was a
'cheeky kaffir'. He would then have become a malcontent, his
intellectual development might have been stunted and he would
have grown into an embittered and garrulous middle-age. Probably he would have ended up making a living by some shady
means. There are hundreds like that all over the country.

A very different sort of person was Alick Nkhata, an easy-going
artist of great charm and showmanship, a 'dreamer of songs', as

a traditional blind minstrel once called him in a praise-song. Nkhata had been a teacher before the war, then became a sergeant in the army. His talents as a guitarist, singer and composer attracted attention, and after the war he obtained an ex-service-man's grant to study music. He had attached himself to Hugh Tracey of the African Music Society in South Africa, and together they had studied and recorded traditional African music all over the continent. After this training Alick had joined the CABS.

He sang of the new Africa, not tragically and painfully like some others, but humorously. There was seldom a sting in his songs. And yet, away from his guitar he was not a funny man. Unlike fat *Mfumfumfu* or *Ha-hi-ha* he seldom made his colleagues laugh. He spoke seriously and in almost faultless English about preserving traditional African music, about the culture of his people and about colour problems.

He was extremely sensitive to colour-prejudice, exaggeratedly sensitive I thought. For example, he might say of one European, 'He pretends to be very friendly, but when he entertains Africans it is always on his veranda. He never allows us into his rooms.'

But I knew that the person in question entertained everybody on his veranda. This very thin skin was not unique in Nkhata. Almost every African who appears in this book had it. Unfortunately they were very often right. Once I introduced some of them to a European acquaintance of whom I knew full well that his liberal protestations were rather stronger than his feelings. After he departed they said promptly:

'He speaks nicely, but did you see how he hesitated before shaking hands with us?'

Behind his guitar and surrounded by his quartet, Nkhata became a different person. His eyes danced, his fine set of teeth flashed as he sang his snappy comic songs in Nyanja or Bemba, sometimes with liberal admixtures of town slang and corrupt English. He sang of the cook-boy Romeos who live in the little houses in the yards of their European employers. (The words in italics are in 'English' in the original.)

'Some young men of today have no sense.
When they see a girl with painted lips
they lose their heads.

Then they speak in English:
Yesh, good,
alas my beauty,
come live with me in the yards.
You're gonna get bread an' butter
I have everything.
New look in *plenty.*
You'll have so many dresses
you'll be changing clothes all day.
And every morning you'll be taking
Morning coffee, toshta an' butter
if you live with me.
You'll grow very fat.
If we two appear in public,
young men will be shaking
because of your beautiful clothes.'

('It is a very educative song,' said one of our listeners, 'it teaches us to look after our wives properly and to beware of domestic servants. They are morally weak.')

Nkhata sang of the joys of snuff-taking, of beautiful women and fine footballers, of strong alcoholic concoctions, of taxi-drivers who overcharge and of his lightning successes with the ladies. 'I am a whirlwind. I pass by and leave the spinsters weeping. . . .'

He did not know much about the technicalities of music. Although he made numerous attempts to learn to read scores he never did get very far. He also made some half-hearted attempts to improve his guitar-playing technique, but they never came to much. He lost interest if there was too much effort involved. He continued to play very simply but with inborn artistry. There was little incentive for him to improve, as he was already the most popular singer in Central Africa and his records sold in their thousands.

Left to himself Nkhata would have produced four or five original songs every year, but broadcasting required a much greater output. Sapper, himself an accomplished pianist and a former bandleader in Britain, organized a group around Nkhata's quartet. They called it the Lusaka Radio Band. Sapper played the piano and the electronic clavioline. The present Press attaché at Rho-

desia House, London, was bullied into playing the drums and
Pepe Zulu learnt to play the maraccas. A European electrician
played the double-bass. Kittermaster asked them to provide at
least one new tune every week for his Saturday evening variety
show. Nkhata could not compose so fast, but he could adapt. He
and Sapper searched our vast library of traditional African village
songs. They discovered many forgotten ones that lent themselves
to their treatment; they were hotted up and played on new instruments. Many a sophisticated townee in our audience was surprised
to find so much that was to his taste among the despised music of
the old fogies.

Sometimes these songs made a piquant study in contrasts. In
one the drums and maraccas had taken over the rhythm originally
provided by maize-pounding pestles, and Nkhata's quartet in
smart evening dress sang the plaint of bare-breasted Nsenga
women about the drift of men to the centres of European settlement:

> 'Kalindawalo is a good chief. Oh! Oh!
> Kalindawalo is a good chief. Oh! Oh!
> Only one thing is wrong with his reign,
> The loss of his people.
> They drift away.
> His people sing:
> "I want to see the railway line before I die.
> Before I die I want to see the line of rail."'

It was a sad little song, but sung to a boisterous tune. This
difference in musical conventions between Europeans and Africans
often forced itself upon my attention.

Sapper and Nkhata between them produced one glorious pas-
tiche. Nkhata composed a powerful and beautiful song in Bemba
about 'town-marriages'. These are unofficial liaisons, often long-
lasting ones which produce children, but have no legal standing.
None of the traditional payments have been made. Often they are
between a man from a distant tribe and a good-time girl from a
near-by one who has come into the town to seek her fortune. The
woman constantly demands gifts in return for her attentions and
when the man becomes tired of providing them she leaves him.

Sometimes the cause of the break-up is the husband's homesickness. He wants to go back to his village for a while, but the woman would not fit into his home environment. This rather unhappy situation set Nkhata singing in Bemba:

> 'Good-bye. Now I go back to my home where I come from.
> I'm tired of waiting.
> It seems you cannot change your ways.
> Go! Die alone.
> Now I go back to my home where I come from.
> Do not forget your duty: look after our children.
> Even though I go, I will help you to support them.
> It is you who have made the mistake.
> You want too much wealth which I can never possess.
> I, poor man, must return to my home.'

'Terrific!' said Sapper, who did not know Bemba, 'what's it all about?'

'Women and love and parting,' said Nkhata.

'Best thing you've ever done. This tune will sell on the European market. You must insert a few English lines into it. Something like "Be true to me."'

Nkhata dutifully did so and on the commercial record that was issued, somewhere after the terrible line 'Go, die alone!' he switches into English:

> 'Good-bye my love, I'm going away.
> But please remember to be true,
> My love!
> I'll think of you, day after day . . .'

and then he lapses into Bemba:

> 'You'll drive me to distraction.'

Later, when I knew enough Bemba to follow, I took this up with Nkhata. 'Well,' he said, 'it wasn't my idea. But anyway, it doesn't matter. We Africans often have verses that have nothing to do with each other in the same song.'

My favourite among Nkhata's songs was one with a haunting melody like that of a gipsy violin, so sweet and full of suffering.

It was a deeply allegorical song that he had adapted, but when the allegory was unravelled for me, it turned out to mean: 'Wait till I get that woman into bed. Man, the things I'm going to do to her. . . .' I never did understand the African musical conventions!

Nkhata's records gave him quite a good additional income, but that had its disadvantages. His large family came to look upon him for support. Unlike Zulu, he did not have the heart to brush them off. Their demands increased his need for cash. He contrived one scheme after the other for making money quickly. He bought a car to take his quartet on concert tours, then changed his mind and exchanged it for a vanette and spent his long leave trying to organize a fish trade between an unexploited swamp area and Lusaka.

'I can make a lot of money in four months' leave,' he said confidently.

After his leave he came back with the vanette nearly a write-off, having lost most of his capital.

'All I got was mosquite-bites,' he admitted ruefully.

'How can you expect to make money without studying business management?' said Zulu.

'Why don't you stick to what you do well, singing and composing?" I suggested.

'Ah well, stubborn fly followed the coffin into the grave,' grumbled Mlongoti.

But Nkhata was not discouraged. He made his wife start a trading-store.

'Concentrate on selling records,' we advised him, 'you know about these.'

But he did not think there was enough money in that. Instead, he tried to fill the long wooden shelves of the store with a few dozen cartons of cigarettes, some tins of jam, a few packets of candles and matches and one or two boxes of gramophone records. The store was badly understocked and dragged along dismally. I suspect most of Nkhata's salary and his record royalties went into paying the debts that it ran up.

'It is the same old problem,' said Zulu, 'his wife cannot refuse credit. They are all too soft.'

But Nkhata's confidence in the future never seemed to falter:

'I think I'll go to Europe on my next leave and sing in night clubs. That'll give me enough money to stock up that store properly.'

By contrast, as an official he functioned efficiently. He went on long tours to record music in remote districts, keeping to pre-arranged time-tables and bringing back many excellent records. At Lusaka he handled most musical auditions and recordings. Everyone who asked could be assured of a patient hearing and helpful criticism. Some came from hundreds of miles away to see Nkhata. At his sessions there might be a choir of school children, a group of old women with rattles, some smart young townsmen with guitars, saxophones and drums, and occasionally one of the almost extinct breed of blind minstrels. Nkhata sorted out those worth recording. He also handled the complicated arrangements for variety shows, making sure that all the artists were properly rehearsed and present on time for recording. This was no mean feat. It sometimes necessitated giving an artist an escort for the day who had to steer him away from beer-halls and hospitable friends. Nkhata always seemed to sense when this was required. If only he could have handled his personal affairs as ably! But these he managed with lackadaisical abandon. I only hope that one day he will turn his business misadventures into songs. They will be priceless.

Apart from money, a thing that always worried Nkhata was the poverty of Southern Rhodesian music. Our liaison unit there used to send up two types only, religious ditties after the manner of Sankey and Moody, and imitation jive seldom of any merit One day, when one of our Southern Rhodesian continuity-announcers was going back South for leave, Nkhata suggested that he try and trace some traditional singers in his home district and persuade them to rehearse. We agreed to try and get a recording van to him when he had got a sufficient number of items practised. But from his home our announcer wrote us sad little notes: 'Nobody remembers the old songs any more.' I could not believe him and when he returned after his leave I questioned him:

'No beer-drinking songs?'

'People do not drink beer any more.'

'Go on! Beer-drinking is the chief recreation all over Africa!'

'Not in our district any more. We are near a Seventh Day Adventist Mission.'

'So, don't they have any social life at all?'

'Oh yes. The mothers' union give a tea-party twice a week and they sing hymns.'

A social anthropologist had told me similar tales. I could not understand it, it was so unlike the places I knew where the religious and social life revolved around riotous booze-ups.

I took a closer look at the Southern Rhodesians on our staff. They were sent up by our Salisbury liaison organization, sometimes only for a few months each. When they came up they were certainly different from our own men. They seldom joined in the staff discussions unless asked a question, then they answered cheerfully, modestly and intelligently. They were obviously far more accustomed to European ways than our Northern men and they sometimes looked down upon the Northerners as 'uncivilized'. They were for example, far less likely to believe fantastic rumours, and they thought in economic terms as a matter of course. They did not need Zulu's inner struggle nor Nkhata's expensive experiments to find the way. They were very money-minded, indeed some invested their savings in a lorry and traded successfully as a sideline. Yet they seemed quite resigned to their subservient role in society. I had the impression of crushed, de-individualized people. But if this were true, they at any rate, seemed to be quite unaware of their plight.

Then I noticed that after some months of the atmosphere of Lusaka a change came over them. They became more lively, more aggressive, often less easy to get on with. Several of them all of a sudden launched into bitter tirades against their Southern employers, against their home governments and against the racial situation. Often this happened when there was some talk of their being transferred back to the South. It was as if a bottle had been unstoppered suddenly.

'Here in the North if I go to the district commissioner he gives me a chair and says "How can I help you?" but in Southern Rhodesia the native commissioner makes you squat on the floor and address him as *mambo* just as if he was a chief. And he hasn't even got a university degree like the DCs here.'

In Africa it is not 'done' to discuss a European behind his back with an African. This is a convention I always found it necessary to ignore. It was part of my duties that I should get to

know my African fellow men. I could not refuse to discuss matters
about which they felt strongly, like their treatment at the hands
of our Southern colleagues:

'He treats us like dogs,' said one Southern Rhodesian of a
European member of our liasion staff. 'We work until late in the
evenings, until after the last bus. Do you think he has ever offered
us a lift home? I have to walk for almost two hours while he is in
his comfortable home. But I'm just a kaffir.'

After this outburst he shrugged his shoulders and laughed with
apparent unconcern. The complaint itself was unremarkable. One
can hear the like any day in most parts of Africa. What I found
remarkable was that it had been suppressed for so long.

At the time there was much talk among Southern Rhodesian
Europeans and in their papers about the mistakes of Colonial
Office policy in Northern Rhodesia and Nyasaland. They were
saying 'The Colonial Office just makes the native discontented,
always strikes and riots and things. The native wants a strong
guiding hand. Look at us. We haven't had to turn guns on our
natives for over fifty years. We have no trouble at all and they're
very happy.'

On the surface it seemed true and it sometimes caused me some
secret worry. Were we on the wrong track in the North? I wondered whether it had to do with the different histories of the territories. Southern Rhodesia had been conquered by European
arms, but most of Northern Rhodesia had come under the Europeans by protectorate treaties. Could it be that the Southerners
were so docile because it was their tradition that vanquished foes
were enslaved? If so, they might consider themselves quite lucky.
They were much better off than slaves.

One day I asked one of our Southern staff how he explained
that there was so little 'noise' politically, in the South. He replied:

'Their sufferings are too deep for words.'

That was a few years ago. Today it is no longer so. The words
are starting to come. It causes the Southern Rhodesian Europeans
much worry. They are wrong. They should regard it as a good sign.

Some months later I was on an afternoon's duty with another
of our Southern Rhodesian announcers who shall also remain
unnamed. I noticed that he seemed very moved by a beautiful
Ndebele chant, one of the few traditional songs from Southern

Rhodesia that we had in our record-library. I gestured to him through the double window and he came out.

'It is very beautiful,' I said. 'What does it mean?'

'It is about Lobengula, our last king,' he said, 'and about the herds of cattle we used to have that we loved more than our lives.'

'What about them?'

He translated:

'Where are our fathers?
Where are our cattle?
You, oh great Lover-of-Cattle,
Where are they now?
Where are our fathers?
Where are our cattle?
That world has been overthrown!'

. . . a vast swelling melody, like the sea, that rose above the slow heavy, stamping rhythm, perhaps like the lament of the Israelites by the waters of Babylon. I noticed that for once their musical idiom and mine seemed to overlap.

We talked about Lobengula's last campaign and his mysterious death. I suggested that we should try to do a programme about how he really died. There were sure to be men still alive who had fought by his side.

'Oh yes,' he replied, 'my grandfather was among them.'

'Is he still alive?'

'Yes. He's about eighty.'

'Couldn't we get him to record?'

'He would be afraid to speak.'

'Surely not . . . not if you, his grandson, came with a portable recording-machine?'

He shook his head doubtfully: 'It wouldn't make a good recording. When I was a little boy I used to ask him about it. He would start to tell me and get all excited. Then he would falter and stop . . . and cry. He just cried and cried and refused to say another word.'

The next time I heard Southern Rhodesian Europeans say 'But our natives are so happy', I knew just what to think of it.

A certain event in 1952 united all my colleagues, however different their outlook.

One Monday morning Kateka rushed in, every trace of humour wiped off his fat face: 'Mlongoti is dying.'

Because of his diabetes, Mlongoti had been ordered to eat at regular intervals, to keep a strict diet and never to drink alcohol. He said: 'I am not a chicken on a European's poultry-farm' and ignored his doctor. That week-end he had attended a church synod of which he was a lay member. It had been a long session and he had missed his lunch. He went for a glass or two of beer instead. A short time after he collapsed. They tried to revive him with barley water, but he would not come round. He was taken to hospital and there he lay in a coma.

Sapper went down to the hospital and reported that three generations of Mlongoti's family were sitting around the bed, wailing. Mlongoti did not recognise his visitors. The doctors were battling for his life. On the fourth day he died without having regained consciousness. We were dumbfounded.

Kittermaster got up from his sick-bed with a high temperature and broadcast a tribute. He broke down in the middle and collapsed when he came out of the studio.

Next day we went to Mlongoti's funeral. I had great difficulty in getting anywhere near the church. All the approaches were crowded with his audience, so that I neither saw nor heard the service. After it we Europeans were bundled into a number of cars and followed the hearse and the taxi that carried his wife and children. I would rather have walked with the thousands of African mourners, but that is another one of those things not 'done' in Rhodesia and I had not yet learnt to do it. We drove at less than walking pace and through the windows of our car I saw faces appear briefly and then pass on, an African MP, normally bloated with self-importance, now walking with a bowed head, a wailing woman-relative wearing only a petticoat and a mourning-belt tied around her waist, Northern Rhodesia's first African novelist, wheeling his bicycle, weeping quietly, a choirboy holding aloft a cross and singing, a peasant woman in blue wrap, balancing a basket on her head and a baby tied to her back, a drunken old man in tatters yelling a pagan funeral chant. And looking through the front and back windows, I could see a mile-long column in front and behind us.

It was the largest funeral ever seen in Lusaka. I found it an overwhelming experience, this mass grief of thousands who had never seen the dead man. I too, found myself moved to tears.

In the weeks that followed, strange tributes were paid to him. Almost every day Kittermaster received letters from all over Central Africa containing shillings and half-crowns and even ten-shilling notes, 'To compensate you for your grief!'

One afternoon when I was on duty, one of the uninvited eaves-droppers at the open door quietly handed me a shilling. 'Because of Mlongoti,' he said.

In the Legislative Council, a European settlers' representative whom Africans had never considered their friend, said of Mlongoti:

'I learnt many things from him, patience and understanding. In his presence we knew we were in the company of a gentleman.'

Some three or four years later I was talking to a group of village teachers. They complained of some of our new announcers:

'They do not talk well . . . they are not like Mlongoti.'

'What was there different about him?' I asked.

The speaker thought for a moment, then replied:

'Mlongoti, he was not proud.'

4. PEOPLE POSE PROBLEMS

As THE MONTHS wore on I got to know all the regular contributors to our programmes, both the Europeans and the Africans. Some of them brought with them a breath of the wider world outside. They posed and discussed problems of which at the time, I was not aware. One of those was Father Ritter. He was a stocky, close-cropped Swabian Catholic who looked like a genial publican. He came to Lusaka once or twice a year from his remote mission-station at Ilondola. Each time he was a little stouter. Over the years that I knew him his belly grew to truly monastic proportions. He wore the long white gown and black boots of the White Fathers and one could find him perched on a little stool in our engineering workshops discussing the screening of microphone leads and the life of condensers in subtropical climates. Father Ritter was a recording enthusiast. He used a tape-machine that well-wishers had presented to his mission, to record for our library African traditional music and the exciting new church music based on African melodies which was sung at his mission.

The Father's interests were however not confined to recording. He was most useful to us as an acute observer of the reactions of rural listeners. He would come and sit in the little office that Kittermaster, Sapper and I shared and would watch the comings and goings, the questions and telephone calls and whenever there was a lull, he would give us his advice:

'Couldn't you include a bit more rural material? You're in danger of getting too slick, too townee. Couldn't you send your van out more often for events like the installation of new chiefs?'

Father Ritter was one of the few people who saw the enormous potential influence of broadcasting in Africa:

'You can hold up the good life by example, by bringing people worth imitating to the microphone. You can influence the minds of people enormously.'

We knew this, but did not like to face up to the full implications. We thought of propaganda and of social engineering with some feelings of guilt. Our background did not equip us for the job of high-pressure salesmen of ways of life. Our attitude was somewhat confused; certainly we wanted to sell ideas, but we hoped to limit our influence to health and agriculture and such fields. Yet, since a change in agricultural technique may shake the whole traditional structure of a society, the limitations we imposed upon ourselves were not strictly logical. We were aware of this, but, on the other hand, we did not have the heart to sit down and plan coldly to tamper with the souls of men.

The Church however, frankly wishes to convert and to change men, so Father Ritter looked upon social engineering without any of our British embarrassment. In his diocese the Church had a militant lay movement and conducted vigorous propaganda. Many of the continental Catholic missionaries I met, were certain that Africans had a great need for authority, for certainty, for emphatic guidance. Father Ritter never said as much, but I often suspected that he found us government people a little too easy-going and tolerant. I had these feelings confirmed over the Lenshina affair.

Lenshina, the name is a corruption of Regina, was a woman convert of the Church of Scotland mission at Lubwa, not many miles from Father Ritter's mission-station. One day, after a long illness, she appeared at Lubwa and demanded to see the parson in charge. She informed him that she had died and had gone to heaven, but that God had sent her back to earth with a third testament, mainly about the casting out of witches. The parson refused to acknowledge her visions. She came several times but failed to convince him. In the end she stayed away and started to preach on her own. She claimed that the parson had stolen a book she had brought back from heaven. Her movement spread rapidly and Lubwa lost most of its old-established congregation. She also won over some of the flock of the near-by Catholic mission. She collected a large hoard of witchcraft instruments and a mountain of pennies brought by her supporters. It became a movement of protest against the European-controlled churches and attracted many of the local leaders of the African National Congress. Several of them became dignitaries in her church. Nevertheless, she prevented the movement from becoming openly political and anti-European.

I saw this cult as a symptom of the unhealthy state of Central Africa, but was interested to observe that she did not preach that Jesus had been black or that only Africans would be admitted to heaven. This is in contrast to many underground sects in the

Belgian Congo and to numerous Bantu separatist churches in the Union of South Africa.

I used to wonder about this. A friend of mine, John Sharman and I debated frequently and at length how it came about that her movement did not conform to the separatist pattern elsewhere. We concluded that it was probably the result of the tolerant policy of the administration. They had preserved complete detachment. Touring government officials paid courtesy-calls on Lenshina, just as they might on any missionary. There was no repression.

But Father Ritter considered such toleration as going too far:

'She's a hoax, a fraud. She claims that God speaks to her from heaven. She makes her congregation close their eyes and then they hear strange, whistling noises. But it's her! She takes a leaf off a tree and puts it in her mouth. I know! We've sent over spies and they peeped. It's one big racket. How can Government stand by and do nothing?'

Among his next batch of recordings Father Ritter sent us a long talk from a local chief who was a staunch Roman Catholic. In the course of it the prophetess was denounced as a fraud and an impostor. We consulted some secretariat officials and they confirmed our view that this should not be broadcast. They said: 'Government does not take sides.'

When Father Ritter next came to Lusaka he seemed a little exasperated by our pro-consular detachment. I could not blame him, for his life's work was at stake. However, he continued to talk of his difficulties with humour:

'Of course,' he said, 'she does take a few converts away from us, but not very many. We have a pretty strong organization. But the Church of Scotland, they have hardly any congregation left at all. They're down to about a dozen. I've been over to Lubwa myself to see,' and his eyes twinkled, 'and to express my condolences.'

We laughed, and the Father's big belly shook with mirth.

Even straightforward health propaganda, uncomplicated by doubt, could pose wider problems.

Our chief broadcaster on health matters was 'Pop' Adams. He had a genius for simplicity of presentation, but this carried with it unexpected dangers. Adams was a former health inspector, now the tutor at a school for African male nurses and dispensary assistants.

Listening family: 'With a Saucepan Special radio I have all the world in my hut.'

Michael Kittermaster at Victoria Falls

He had had little formal education, but was full of intellectual curiosity. He excavated historical sites and collected books of Africana, studied the witchcraft beliefs of his pupils and wrote poetry of doubtful merit. He spent his home leaves in the libraries and cemeteries of Britain, seeking out the stories of obscure early missionaries and of health heroes. Their selfless lives moved him deeply. On the hundredth anniversary of the discovery of the Victoria Falls he tried to organize a party to march in the footsteps of his hero, Dr Livingstone. This came to nothing, but he commemorated the event by publishing, at his own expense, an anthology about the Falls which included some of his own curious poetry.

Some of the doctors he worked with sneered at his health broadcasts claiming they were naïve, but the shoe was on the other foot. 'Pop' understood our audience, whereas they did not. He knew how to approach them and his very naivety was his strength. It made it possible for him to say things that the doctors would have avoided for fear of becoming the laughing-stock of the European cocktail parties.

I must admit that I too, sometimes had difficulty in remaining quite serious when he was broadcasting. I hope he will forgive me. Some of his words still ring in my ears. He was lecturing about the common housefly. He explained that a fly eats human excrement and may then transfer its attentions to our food, vomiting out some of its previous nourishment. He grew excited:

'This dis-disgusting habit . . .' he stammered with indignation. 'This disgusting habit! Just think of it. Such filth is carried to *your* food. When you have your meal this evening, are you sure . . . can you be quite sure that no flies have been near it?'

I may have smiled at the time, but I have never felt quite the same about flies since, and neither have many of our audience. At one school the pupils went so far as to organize a fly-extermination club!

Adams's technique was worth studying. He concentrated on one idea each broadcast, developed it at a snail's pace, repeated and rephrased it until he was sure it had sunk in. He hammered many a point that the doctors probably thought obvious, yet to a large section of our audience they were novel and sometimes incredible. For example, he emphasized that the medicines given by European

E

doctors to African patients were the same as those given to European patients. He had his ears close to the ground, and knew that rumour had it that all the really strong medicines were reserved for Europeans. His superiors probably had no idea that this was widely believed.

Adams pleaded with the more ignorant villagers not to run off into the bush as soon as a smallpox vaccination team approached, but he studiously avoided mention of the virus that would be inoculated into them. Instead he asked, 'You admit that Europeans are clever at making aeroplanes and trains and sewing-machines? Well, why not trust them to make a good medicine?'

On another occasion he preached: 'Educated people defecate in latrines. Don't you defecate in the bush. That's the way hookworm is spread.'

Now in later years, as a section of our listeners became more sophisticated, some complained that he regarded them as inferiors, that he was talking down to them. In my own view Adams was much too good and simple a person to harbour any such thoughts. But that did not save him from unpopularity. As relations between Europeans and Africans all around us became more strained, the better-educated Africans grew increasingly suspicious of patronage. In editing scripts we learnt to bend over backwards to avoid it. We also learnt that the didactic tone acceptable to the masses could easily set up violent resistance among the more sophisticated.

Another regular contributor who helped my growing awareness of Central African affairs was John Sharman, the man with whom I discussed the Lenshina affair. John was a bearded and sandalled man in his early thirties and had eccentricities that stamped him as coming from one of the old English universities. After studying languages and linguistics he spent a year in a hut in the Northern Rhodesian bush, studying the Bemba language. Then he abandoned the scholar's career and joined the Publications Bureau, a new government department set up to encourage authors in African vernaculars, to publish books and to promote sales. John was almost one of 'us' by marriage. His wife Margaret was our record librarian. It was to him that Kittermaster turned when he wanted to broadcast a series of English lessons for adult listeners.

Kittermaster felt very strongly about the African Babel. The seven million people who were our potential audience spoke some seven or eight different languages as distinct from each other as say, English and German. They in turn were divided among some eighty-five different dialects. This is not as surprising as it may appear, since the area we covered was larger than Italy, Austria, Yugoslavia, Hungary, Rumania, Bulgaria, Albania and Greece together. Kittermaster thought that broadcasting ought to help with the linguistic unification of the country. He believed that broadcasting might do for the vernaculars what Luther's Bible had done for the German language. He also believed that we had a duty to spread one lingua franca, English. He asked various schoolteachers for suggestions, but they only proposed broadcasting adapted classroom lessons. Then he asked John Sharman to have a try. Sharman shelved a thesis on the Bemba language that he was working on and threw himself into the new task with characteristic enthusiasm.

First all of us got down to interminable consultations and experiments until we had clarified our ideas. We considered teaching English from scratch, but that would have meant multiplying courses, English-Nyanja, English-Bemba, English-Tonga and so on. This would have been difficult, but even more serious was the problem that we were sure it would need textbooks and helpers in the field and we had neither the men nor the money. Beginners' lessons without such aids would have required very much more effort from our audience than we thought they would be willing to make. We therefore concluded that we would have to restrict ourselves to improving the English of those who already had a basic knowledge of it. They were anyway the most zealous and progressive of our listeners. For them, multiplication of courses was unnecessary as the teaching medium could be English itself.

We held discussions with many such listeners and confirmed our impression that there was widespread interest in English as really spoken, in idioms, proverbs and colloquialisms as distinct from textbook English. We therefore decided to concentrate on a series of short daily broadcasts of 'English Words and Phrases', each one of which would be complete in itself. It was not the ideal way of teaching a language, but it seemed the best use of the predisposition of our audience and of the radio medium.

John Sharman set to work, writing two-minute introductions explaining the use of one or two phrases. These were then followed by two-minute conversations between 'Charles' and 'Mary' who made use of the phrases. The lesson ended with a short summing-up by Sharman. We all tried our hand at writing the illustrative conversations, but in the end we left the task to John's wife, Margaret. Seven were required each week, and we found it very difficult to keep the conversations to subjects familiar to Africans and yet to make them sound natural in the mouths of European characters. There was so little overlap between the experiences of the two groups. The conversations inevitably became strange caricatures of European life in the colonies, full of games of golf and motor-cars, visitors from out-stations and drinks-parties. They sounded even stranger because of the repetitive use of phrases like 'to be about', 'man-about-town', 'careless about', 'know about', 'run about', 'push about' and so on.

Over these lessons I got to know the Sharmans better and we became firm friends. John and I spent many an evening over a bottle of whisky, arguing. They were diffuse and discursive arguments, drifting from one point to another. We often disagreed, but his objections provoked me into formulating my own ideas more clearly.

'How can we have better race-relations,' he said labouring over his sentences a little pedantically, 'how can we have better . . . eh . . . what they call race-relations, if we can't communicate, if we don't know each other's language? It's all a problem of communications.'

'All?' I replied. 'Surely it's more than just a question of words.'

'I'm talking of language in its wider sense. In a language, if you have mastered it thoroughly, you see the soul of a people.'

'You mean some people see it. A poet might.'

'No. Understanding obtrudes itself. Now look at this: *Nshiku-ya-Mulungu*, the Bemba for Sunday.'

'Day of God?'

'Well, that's what they tried to say, our early missionaries. But they didn't. There are at least three errors in that group of words, three grammatical errors.' And he proceeded with a thorough and methodical analysis.

'Okay,' I interposed, 'it shows that the missionaries didn't know very much Bemba, but how does that help to understand anybody's soul? You think they should have been able to speak in tongues?'

'Nonsense. Don't you see? Four hundred thousand Africans all

knew that it was atrocious Bemba, but the word stuck. It's come
into common usage. Now doesn't that tell you something about
them? Don't you see? The Africans were so overawed by the white
man's superior culture and power, that nobody could be found to
say "But it's incorrect Bemba!" And the missionaries, so brash
and insensitive were they and so arrogant, that they never seriously
inquired.'

I had to admit that he had a point. I remembered Nkhata's song,
'Good-bye, my love . . . Go die alone!'

Sharman continued: 'The whole of our black-white relationship
is symbolized by this sort of thing. Don't say it's just words.'

Our conversation drifted off at a tangent, then gradually came
back to words and how the same word could have such very different associations to people of different cultures.

'Take Stephen Mpashi,' said Sharman. 'He's the nearest thing
this country has produced to an African poet. Well no, correction,
there's a lot of folk-poetry. Let's say he's the nearest thing to a
vernacular writer of merit. In his last book he's got a scene in a
hospital in which he keeps using a Bembaization of the English
word "stethoscope" in an odd sort of way, so I asked him what
associations he had with this thing. He said "Stethoscope? Cold,
cold and metallic and prying . . . brrr! . . . unfriendly, impersonal,
like European machines, inhuman . . . white coats and bright, hard
lights and iron bedsteads. I hate those little things." Well now,
Peter, are those the associations you have with a stethoscope? No?
Well, you see it's not just words I'm talking about.'

Our conversation drifted to hospitals and why so many Africans
still feared them and how a better understanding of their resistance
would ease the task of the medical men. Eventually we came back
to language.

I admitted that an understanding of each other's language was
important. 'But it isn't everything,' I insisted. 'Racial tensions
won't disappear that way. Look at me: I'm a German Jew. German
is my mother-language and has been the mother-language of my
people for centuries. They spoke it sufficiently well to have produced one of the greatest lyric poets in the language. Yet most of
our community was massacred.'

'You were something of a group apart with your own sub-
culture which the Germans didn't understand.'

'You're equating perfect communication with perfect love, but there are other and much more basic factors involved: aggression and submission, love and hate, all sorts of things.'

'But look at the Rhodesian set-up. You've lived among settlers long enough to know how much of the friction is due to misunderstanding. The settlers don't speak any vernacular. If they speak anything, it's Kitchenkaffir and that's a poor and insensitive jargon unfit for adults.'

'Granted, but even Kitchenkaffir makes it a bit easier to get across than it is for the new immigrants who speak only English, and yet you know who are normally better-disposed towards Africans. . . .'

And so our conversation dragged on, becoming more confused as the night drew on and the bottle became emptier.

At the Sharmans' house I frequently met John's colleague and friend Stephen Mpashi, the author who detested stethoscopes. He was a strange, complicated, moody man of about the same age as John. I found the Bemba of his short novels too difficult to follow properly, but could get just enough to see that John was right, Mpashi was the nearest thing to a real author that Central Africa had so far produced. He was also a fine musician. He became one of the most frequent African contributors to our programmes, for he appeared as a speaker, script-writer and as the leader of a small choir. To this choir he taught village songs of great poetic power. One was a lament of the young women whose husbands had joined the army and who received only the hard coins of the family allotment in place of love:

'The war in Libya oh my friends,
   the soldiers are stabbing each other,
   there, in Libya.
   I have known death before, oh my friends,
   I have seen death,
   how it struck those who bore my mother.
   We women sleep lonely together,
   we sleep together alone.
   What shall we do with cold coins in our womb?
   Only the aged are counting beads.'[1]

[1] Bemba women wear a string of beads around their waist, under their clothes.

Then a male voice sings:

> 'I shall come back, my love.
> The day I come back
> my stamping boots will call from afar:
> "Open the door, I have come."'

Another song reflected the lonely tortured soul of Mpashi himself in the no-man's-land between cultures and peoples,

> 'Oh, the restless wanderer!
> He has forgotten his tribe and his family.
> He picks up with any woman of the city.
> He sucks the sweets of Ndola-town.
> He has forgotten the taste of the wild fruit of the bush.'

And the choir repeated,

> 'Oh, the restless wanderer!
> Oh, the restless wanderer!'

On his good days Mpashi had a bright sense of humour, but he was changeable and moody. On his off-days he became gloomy, difficult to talk to, aggressive.

He had come very much under the influence of Sharman. John gave him books to read, advised him on his writing, discussed personal problems with him. Together they explored the subtleties of the Bemba language. At first Mpashi was pleased to find a European with such an interest in and respect for things African. For hours they discussed the precise meaning of the Bemba concept of *mucinshi*, respect, politeness, homage, decency. They analysed court cases to discover what miscarriages of justice occurred due to inadequate court translation. Sharman, in turn, was delighted to find an informant of such sensitivity, one who might yet come to be regarded as the Chaucer of his tribe. Unconsciously he started to shield him against the harsh world of race hatred, as all of us who disapproved of the system tended to do for Africans we liked. Mpashi came to depend upon him and to visit him frequently. As a result Sharman suffered much disapproval in the petty European suburb in which he lived, but he continued to associate with Mpashi and other Africans. If he was aware of the patronage relationship that was developing, no doubt he felt it justified because Mpashi was an artist and he a publishing man. But as their relationship became closer, Mpashi became restive. He felt he was being reduced to tutelage because he was an African. After all, Sharman was no older than he. He felt his individuality threatened. He was being dominated. His writing was no longer his own, nor even his private affairs, for in a moment of weakness he had consulted Sharman about his marital complications. He grew prickly, took refuge in more drink than usual and became aggressive. Then Sharman would drop a polite and gentle hint about European ideas of correct behaviour. On the next occasion Mpashi got far drunker and proceeded to rail against all 'bloody do-gooder Europeans'.

His artistic insight showed him John's weak spots. He saw that even liberal Europeans were not without the sexual fears common among a white minority surrounded by a black mass. One evening he brought a party of maudlin Africans to the Sharmans', just as John was going out to visit me. Mpashi immediately sensed and enjoyed John's predicament, whether to leave his wife to entertain three tipsy Africans or whether to stay and protect her. Or again, could all these uninvited visitors be taken along to some one else's house? Sharman did not know who else might be there. Afterwards he protested that it was simply an awkward social situation not peculiar to Africa, it might have happened anywhere in the world. But Mpashi thought differently. No doubt he came to the usual conclusion: deep down Europeans are all the same. None of them trust us. Look out for the liberal ones in particular. They lie more.

Despite all this Mpashi craved the affection of Europeans, whose culture he was coming to appreciate. He read English literature with increasing wonder and enthusiasm. Nevertheless he became ever more provocative, like a child that continually wishes to put its mother's love to the test.

For several years his employers had tried to get him a scholarship to go to England to do a course in literature. It was finally awarded at the time when he was at his most neurotic. We all hoped that a boost for his ego and a year away from Rhodesia would do him good. The greatest ambition of most Africans is a trip to Europe or America. They expect to absorb great wisdom at the older centres of learning. Most do not, but if they realize it, they certainly do not admit it upon their return. Mpashi, however, admitted it before he even started.

'I hope you'll find it a profitable year,' someone said to him.

'I don't think so,' he said, 'I don't suppose I'll learn much.'

'Then why are you going?'

'Because to be anybody at all in Rhodesia these days you must have drunk of the waters of the river Thames.'

Even if his imagery was strange, his understanding was good.

A few evenings before his departure he became very drunk at Northern Rhodesia's only inter-racial club. He abused his mentor and other Europeans with unfortunate insight. Sharman was deeply hurt, after all he had done for Mpashi. He must have had the word ingratitude on the tip of his tongue, but he did not use it, for he had tried a thousand times to prove to uncomprehending European housewives that Africans have different attitudes to giving and taking, generosity and gratitude. Instead, he turned away and went to find me and we discussed the latest happenings on the Copperbelt, where there had been some ugly scenes when European trade unionists helped to break a strike of African workers. He only mentioned Mpashi once, when he said briefly, 'I'm glad he lives in this civil servants' town. The Copperbelt would drive him to suicide.'

Mpashi, I was told, became morose in his corner of the bar and shrivelled up and shuddered, 'I'll be among a million strange faces, and they'll all be white.' Then he brightened up a little as he remembered that he would soon be seeing the only European who, he said, had ever really loved Africans, a young woman who had been run out of the country for her kind heart, or so he claimed, quite incorrectly.

A few weeks later he went to her flat in London for dinner. He seemed happy and was obviously learning far more than he had expected. Several English people who had lived in Rhodesia were present and inevitably the conversation turned to Central Africa's racial problems. At once Mpashi's mood changed and he interrupted:

'A solution? There's no such thing. Black and white are quite different. Diametrically opposed. You'll never understand our culture, nor we yours. We can only destroy each other. A few years from now we'll be cutting each other's throats.'

Then he poured himself a strong drink and lapsed into silence as the rest of the party tried to piece together the remnants of the conversation.

5. COPPER TOWNS

DURING THE dry season we took our recording vans into the remotest villages of the Rhodesias and Nyasaland. The towns, which are accessible all the year round, we usually saved for the rainy season, when many country roads become impassible. So it was during the rains that my duties often took me to the turbulent towns of the Copperbelt. I remember in particular one afternoon when Sylvester Masiye and I flew up to Ndola. Masiye had recently joined our staff with glowing reports from the Army Educational Corps at Nairobi. He had been running vernacular broadcasts for Northern Rhodesian troops stationed in East Africa. The army had sent him to England for advanced training and there, too, his ability and integrity had been recognized.

We arrived at Ndola airport at dusk. A small airways bus was waiting to take us to our respective hotels. Apart from Masiye and myself three other people climbed into the bus, two young ones and one older man, all European. I recall the two young men well. One was a clean, sturdy-looking lad with short, blond hair and a blazer. He spoke in the hard, unmusical Southern Rhodesian way. The other was red-faced and pimply and had an English north-country accent. While the African driver was loading our suitcases, they talked about seeking their fortunes on the copper mines, the Englishman as a clerk, the Rhodesian as a fitter and turner.

Just before one reaches the European quarter of Ndola, there is the Ndola 'location'. Masiye was to stay there in the African guest-house. Our driver turned off the tarred main-road to take him there. It is a detour of a few hundred yards. The young Rhodesian noticed the dirt-track and asked the driver: 'Is this the way to town?'

'Just now, sir,' replied the driver non-committally.

Some cheering African children ran with our bus.

'Kaffir location,' said the Rhodesian.

All my years in Africa had sensitized me to these situations. 'Oh God,' I thought, 'any moment now we're in for a scene.'

The bus drew up at the guest-house. Masiye and the driver got out to take his bags out of the boot. Only we four Europeans were left in the bus.

'What's this building?' asked the young Rhodesian.

'African hotel, just newly built,' said the elderly European. He seemed to have an Italian accent.

'What!!!' The young man was aghast; 'we go to the compound to drop a kaffir first?'

'Hotel à la Bantu,' sniggered the north-country youth.

Masiye came to my window to say good-bye. I hoped they would make no offensive remarks.

'Well, I don't know what this country is coming to . . .' grumbled the Rhodesian.

We drove off.

'I'm a Rhodesian, born and bred in Umtali,' he continued, 'and I think it's all wrong. It's those fellows in England . . .'

The young Englishman hastened to ingratiate himself: 'Yeah, they don't know what things are like here. I came out to Southern Rhodesia three years ago and I can tell you, when I first got out I also thought "Treat them like human beings" but now . . . well, now I know them. Baboons, straight off the trees. D'you think this could have happened in the South?'

Should I make a scene? Was there any point in it?

'Hey driver,' called the Rhodesian aggressively, 'do you always drop the boys at the compound before the bosses?'

This is where I would have to intervene, but the old Italian got in before me:

'It was on the way, wasn't it?' he said simply.

Sensing opposition, unexpected, white opposition, the Rhodesian subsided a little and grumbled:

'Well, all I can say is, this wouldn't have happened a few years ago. They're getting too bloody cheeky. . . .'

I had argued the point pointlessly a thousand times, ever since my schooldays, and I was sick to death of it all. I shut up. And yet I felt a coward for it.

That evening I sat on the veranda of the government hostel, alone and miserable. There were distant rumbles of thunder and lightning flashed irregularly on the horizon. The atmosphere was heavy with the expectation of a storm.

Here was an African with twice their intelligence, I thought, and yet these louts felt something very like righteous indignation when he was treated as a normal being. They couldn't see what effect their behaviour would have on an African, especially on a sensitive one. What bitterness it was producing! They couldn't see how one day this bitterness would erupt over the country in which they hoped to raise their children . . . in which I hoped to raise mine.

I could not settle down to my reading.

What could I have done? I formulated several possible things I might have said, sarcastic, reproachful or indignant. But even if I had turned on them with prophetic wrath, would they have changed? Still, if I and those who felt like me spoke up every time these things happened, we might create an atmosphere in which such incidents became less likely. No . . . they just wouldn't see it. They'd write me off as a crank or as a renegade. They'd say 'He probably sleeps with kaffir-girls' and imagine they had answered my argument.

I thought of getting up there and then and walking the mile or two to the location to visit Masiye in his segregated hostel, to discuss the matter with him. But a storm might break at any moment, and he was probably asleep by now. He had only heard the very beginnings of the incident, maybe not even enough for it to make any impression. Maybe he'd think his superior officer had gone mad.

I decided to raise it casually the next morning. But I never did. I was ashamed.

We drove over to Kitwe in a car borrowed from the African Education Department. It was a good road, but a dull drive. I thought about the teacher training college on the outskirts of Kitwe which was my destination. I had paid a first visit there a fortnight earlier and had recorded several hours of staff-room discussion among the teachers. They were a lively group with a wide range of experience. The European and the African teachers mixed freely and as equals. Among the Africans, several were graduates and one had taught in England. Most of the staff lived in bungalows in the school grounds. They made another one of those islands in which the Africans were cushioned against contempt and rudeness.

They were long, rambling preliminary discussions I had recorded, about activity methods and their special value among the

rather passive African pupils. I had then taken the recordings back
to Lusaka and had arranged to have verbatim transcripts made.
These I had edited down to a series of short, simple and precise
scripts, keeping as close as possible to the original, but eliminating
difficult words and concepts, cutting out all side-tracks and ham-
mering one point at a time. I was now going back to Kitwe to make
the original speakers record their own edited words. I knew that it
would be difficult to recapture the liveliness of the original unscripted discussion, especially since I would have to make them
read slowly and distinctly. However, I was sure that the advantages
of clarity and simplicity of presentation outweighed the loss of
spontaneity. We had to remember that many of the village teachers
seldom heard English spoken. They had been forgetting it steadily
since their schooldays. Some I had met in remote areas presented a
frightening picture of deterioration, dull, slow, lethargic, almost
illiterate. I was glad we could help the African Education Department by providing a little stimulation for their men.

The road took us along a broad clearing hacked out of the bush.
Pylons ran alongside the road, then branched off on a cleared strip
of their own. Thirty years ago there had only been a handful of
mud and thatch villages in this area. But today the roads and pylons
connect large mining settlements: slag-heaps and hoists and grids
of tarred road and long rows of identical houses. These settlements
were built with energy, but without love. They are painfully ugly
and charmless. Usually the streets and avenues are numbered.
Nobody could be bothered to think of two dozen names.

The European living areas comprise monotonous rows of
bungalows erected by some unimaginative engineer in the thirties,
high, red-brick boxes with corrugated iron roofs and gauzed-in
verandas. But they are widely spaced and have lush gardens around
them. The mines supply free water to their European employees,
so their wives and the 'garden-boys' have planted symmetrical
beds of flowers around neat little lawns, usually with a palm right
in the centre. Some have grown creepers over their houses, which
mercifully hide part of the structures. But the creepers attract
insects and make the rooms dark, so the practice is not as widespread as one might wish.

The green gardens are in stark contrast to the harsh colours of
the African quarters. From the teacher training college I could see

the bare barracks in the valley below. On Saturday afternoon I walked down to have a look around this 'compound'.

They are called 'compounds' as in South Africa. But they are different in that they are not fenced about and much of the accommodation is designed for families. Miners are encouraged to bring their wives with them. This ensures greater labour stability.

I walked along row upon row of windowless boxes built of concrete blocks painted white. The only contrast was provided by the occasional 'ablution-blocks'. The roofs were of corrugated asbestos or iron. There was hardly a blade of grass, only concrete storm-water drains. Trees had been bulldozed away. It was a most depressing eyesore and yet these solid boxes were hygienic and a vast improvement on the mouldy insect-ridden huts in which most of the miners had grown up. This heartless clearing had, after all, conquered the malaria-mosquito. I noticed a few young mango-trees rising to replace the trees bulldozed away. Their irregular branches made them look comic and incongruous, like some slap-stick comedians on parade with the Brigade of Guards.

But these drab and identical houses do not produce drab and identical people. Far from it! The place was pulsating with noise and vitality.

A crowd of eager children conducted me to the office of the African Assistant Welfare Officer. He offered to introduce me to some radio-listeners. There were aerials rising from hundreds of huts. We called on a man who was sitting in his open door, reading. I glanced at his book: 'How to write good letters'. We were introduced. A big smile lit up his face:

'Ha, Peter Fraenkel! But it is good that you come to see us.' (Not Mister, nor *Bwana*, just my name. I could always tell the listeners by that habit, because that was the way we were intro-duced over the air.) He continued, 'You people at Lusaka do a wonderful job. Man, you play us very sweet music. When I hear it I forget all my troubles. That song "Icupo", it is very educative.'

I knew the song he was referring to, but would not have des-cribed it as exactly educative myself. It was one of Nkhata's. In the song a village girl complains:

'What a world!
I was surprised when a young man married me,

and after only six days
he said he did not want me any more
because I'd shamed him
in the presence of people.
Then I begged:
No, no, my love.
I'm new to married life.
Give me a chance to remain with you
only another six months.
No! said the man.
I asked you to make tea
but—surprise!—you cooked the leaves like vegetables
and poured on ground-nut gravy.'

I quoted one or two of the verses in Bemba. He roared with laughter, whether at the song or at my pronunciation I did not know. He insisted on shaking hands again effusively. Encouraged, I continued:

'I did not know village women were so ignorant.
You must go back to your home.
Here, take this ticket. It is ready.
Thatcher's bus is waiting for you, there.'

By then we were surrounded by quite a crowd, mainly of children. One of them set up a shout: '*Zimene Mwatifunsa*' and the others cheered and joined him '*Zimene Mwatifunsa*,' 'that which you have asked for', the title of our request-programmes. The words were Nyanja but they had gone into Bemba town-jargon to mean 'super, wizard, very good'.

'Tell me sir,' asked the man in the door, 'do you think this Geneva meeting will give us real peace?'

I expressed my doubts.

'I'm very worried about war. I fear the fighting may spread to Rhodesia, as in World War I. My father was a carrier in that war, on the Tanganyika border. He went through untold suffering. Tell me, these Russians, they must be very strong. They're always seeking quarrels, just like Hitler.'

'That's what I'm like when I smoke *dagga*' (marijuana) 'just like Hitler,' quipped a young man at the edge of the crowd in a loud-check shirt and a cowboy hat.

'And what programmes do you like best?' I called to him.

'Jus' gimme jive!' he said, and holding his silver-studded belt with his thumbs he elbowed his way through the children. 'I'm the best jiver on the whole Copperbelt.' Suddenly he flung out his arms and did a lithe and liquid dance-step and chanted a Southern Rhodesian tune:

> 'Wa, wa, baby.
> Oh, baby.
> I wanna jive.
> I wanna jive.
> I wanna jive
> day and night
> with you.'

'Don't listen to these children,' said a man near by. 'Jive is nonsense. And this Nkhata, too. He is spoiling our good Bemba music. His words are Bemba but his tunes are English. You tell him to sing proper songs.'

'Proper songs, like what?'

'Like Thomas Mwewa's. He teaches us about town-women, but properly.'

I made a note to look up Mwewa's songs. When I did, I found that his best-known was a drinking-song in the traditional idiom in which a fisherman sings:

> 'Let me tell you about town wives.
> Even though I give mine plenty of fish,
> even though there is a bagful of salt,
> enough to sit in,
> yet she'll complain: "There is no meat."
> All day long she is never satisfied.
> She threatens: "I'll not stay with you."
> Yet, she remains, for I satisfy her at night.
> At night I fondle her.
> Her body becomes our playground.'

While we were talking the children suddenly disappeared. A few moments later they came back, dragging an embarrassed little boy and yelling with glee.

'Hey! Hey! Hey!' called the welfare officer. 'What's going on here?'

Ha-hi-ha' Mlongoti—
he was not proud

Nkhata's Quartet:
'Good-bye, my love.
Go, die alone.'

Conducting a play-rehearsal: *Mfumfumfu* Kateka, he from whom words pour
unceasingly like a river down a waterfall

Unscripted play on the air

They said something I could not catch. He turned to me with an apologetic smile:

'They want you to see this little boy. His name is *Wayaleshi*, wireless. Actually we try to discourage such names.'

I burst out laughing and the children joined in exultantly.

We called on a few more listeners and eventually came upon an open piece of ground which was being used as a dancing arena. A crowd of about a hundred people was watching the dancers.

'They are the famous Kalikiti group,' said my guide.

We stood on our toes to watch. A group of musicians was squatting, one beat a small drum lightly, another knocked together two hoe-blades. Three dancers sang loudly and hoarsely:

'This is how they do it in the hospital. This is how they do it in the hospital.'

There were two men and a boy. They shuffled up and down with a short dance-step and enacted how a man drags himself to the hospital with a stomach-ache. Suddenly they did an 'about turn' and changed their demeanour. They impersonated the business-like doctor and their dance-steps became long and purposeful. They examined their invisible patient methodically. Then they stood back, scratched their heads, disinfected an imaginary arm and slowly, oh so slowly, filled an hypodermic syringe.

'About turn' and we saw the apprehensive patient trying to edge away, but the doctor caught him, held him with a strong arm and jabbed him deeply and sadistically. The patient shrieked and then hobbled away holding his belly with one hand and rubbing the point of injection with the other. The audience cheered and cat-called. I thought it surprising that they did not have separate roles. First all three acted the doctor, then they all became the patient.

Next they started to sing: 'This is how the DC lives. This is how the DC lives.' They mimed for us a stern district commissioner studying files in his office. Every now and then he picked up a pencil to make a note. Then he called for his clerk imperiously and gave him some typing to do. I wished that some DCs I knew could have seen the deliberate and pompous gestures of their impersonators! Next we saw the clerk typing. This provoked such laughter that the scene had to be repeated several times. The dance-steps became quite small as the dancers balanced their bodies, squatting as if on a chair. They typed slowly and carefully

F

with only one or two fingers. At the end of each line they made the sound of a bell and pushed back the carriage. All was performed in triplicate! Next the DC was brought his tea and it was good to see the relaxed pleasure that came over his three faces as he imbibed the life-giving liquid.

After that a collection was taken. Members of the crowd handed up their threepences or sixpences. The oldest of the dancers announced that next they would do 'Nsenga woman'. The women of that tribe have a reputation for both beauty and lasciviousness. I wondered what was coming next.

The musicians started their tune and the dancers sang: 'This is what the Nsenga women are like. This is what the Nsenga women are like.'

But it was not a woman they were miming. It appeared to be a tired miner coming home from work. Suddenly his face lit up as he beheld some lush piece of work. He made frank approaches to her, but she, that is the three dancers, now acting all coy, rejected them. But not quite, a provocative come-hither look lingered. The miner renewed his suit, time after time, offering his money, his watch, his shoes. In the end the girl giggled and melted. The male set to work fondling her. Slowly, she proceeded to take off her clothes. The crowd shouted bawdy encouragements. At last the affair was consummated. Even the welfare officer forgot his mission-training and laughed uproariously. Seeing myself unobserved, I did so too.

We continued our walk around, seeing a Watchtower choir practise in one corner, hearing the noise of revelry come from the beer garden. At a water-tap two women were yelling at each other. Elsewhere some men were sitting in a shelter chatting sedately. Maybe they were elders judging some minor dispute.

I could feel all around me that immense, resilient mass, humorous and vigorous, boastful yet also frightened and insecure, generous to a fault, yet also cruel ... changing all the time, learning in a thousand ways to adapt themselves to the new surroundings of the town.

As we strolled back to the welfare hall I caught sight of one of the new leaders. A vanette passed us at speed. At the wheel was one of the trade union bosses. 'Our new paramount chief!' said my guide jocularly. 'The old one used to distribute wives and cattle after a war; the new one gets us wage-increases after a strike!'

.   .   .   .   .

The 'paramount' was an old acquaintance of mine. I was reminded of one of my first visits to the Copperbelt some years before. I had come to arrange some radio discussions on trade-unionism. I had approached a number of Europeans and Africans to find suitable speakers. The mine management decided not to participate, but introduced me to some Africans I wanted to try out. The 'new paramount chief' had been among them.

But the first African leader I met had been Godwin Mbikusita Lewanika,[1] the son by a minor wife, of Lewanika, the great paramount chief of Barotseland. He was then already organizing the African Staff Association, a body of African senior personnel which was later to come into sharp conflict with the trade union. I had heard a lot about him.

'A responsible African leader of high calibre,' said the European press.

'A stooge,' said almost every African I ever came across.

I observed him suavely trying to get out of taking part in so public a debate, yet without giving offence. I could see he had learnt his political discretion early. As a young man he had been exiled from Barotseland for some years for conspiring against the paramount chief. It was obvious that he would be anything but forthright in a radio debate and would not strike sparks off the more extreme leaders, as I had hoped. We agreed that he would take part in a debate 'at some later date, when he was not so busy'. I did not see him again until I met him in Barotseland.

The other African leaders were of a different type. One of them was a nervous youth full of vituperation, who saw conspiracies all around him. He has since been exiled to his remote home-village under new emergency regulations which allow the Government to do this to all who become a little too troublesome. I decided he would contribute nothing but abuse to our broadcast and did not use him. One whom I did use was a former teacher and sociological research-worker, a pleasant, smiling young man who is now serving a prison-sentence for embezzling trade-union funds.

Another, Ezekiel S., was of a different sort, he is now a member of the African Representative Council and speaks more to the point than most. He is honest and conscientious and urbane. Not

[1] Now one of the 'African' Federal MPs, elected predominantly by Europeans.

so long ago he was going to stand for a still higher office, but I was surprised to hear that he withdrew his candidature after friends warned him that, being a young man, he did not know the charms and medicines to protect himself against the jealousy and witch-craft that a man in such a position might provoke.

Finally, there was the 'paramount chief', a tall, virile man who seemed to be a born leader. He had been an underground miner and then a clerk. He spoke commandingly, rolling his rather empty mass-orator's phrases. A few months later a British industrial disputes arbitrator described him privately as 'a very capable negotiator . . . superior to the Europeans put up by the Chamber of Mines'. I was surprised at this and suppose that around the conference-table he must have dropped his militant phrases and become shrewder and more flexible.

There was one thing remarkable about all these leaders, about all except the vituperative one who is now in exile. They did not hate Europeans. They did not suspect my motives when I, an official, offered them a chance to broadcast.

It is sad that this should be remarkable, but it is. The reason why they bore no hatred, was probably because the very existence of the unions they ran was evidence of the goodwill of *some* Europeans. They had been started by advisers sent out by the British government after 1945 and they had had European support ever since. They had received advice, co-operation and friendly visits from parallel British unions. Several of the leaders had been to Britain and had personal memories of fraternal pub-evenings there. They spoke enthusiastically about solidarity among workers of all nations and they had been persuaded that their struggle was one of labour versus capital rather than of black versus white. They were pained at the absence of fraternal feeling among the Copperbelt European Mineworkers' Union, but confident that it was they, the Africans, who had the sympathy of trade-unionists overseas. Once or twice during strikes, British unions had sent them gifts of money. This had aroused the Rhodesian whites to apoplectic fury. They should have been grateful. It meant that these Africans never generalized about all Europeans being the enemies of their movement. Whether the Africans still feel this way today, after the mass-arrests and exiling of union leaders during the 1956 emergency, I do not know. In 1952 they did.

In our radio-forum we discussed the special functions of trade unions in Africa. As debaters the African leaders made a poor show. They spoke only in vague phrases. They did not seem to see that trade unions in Africa might be called upon to solve problems different from those of Birmingham or Stockport, and even about the trade unionism of Britain they knew little more than its slogans. They had certainly never theorized about the special conditions of Africa.

After the rather fruitless discussion had been recorded, I offered to drive several of the speakers back to their homes. The 'paramount chief' asked to be dropped at the beer-hall. On the way there I asked him:

'Will you be able to hear yourself? Have you got a radio?'

'We're getting a very fine new one,' he said, 'the British Mineworkers' Federation has presented a big new set to our Union. It should be here any day now.'

'And have you got some club-room or social centre to set it up in?'

'Oh no,' he grinned, 'I'm taking it to my own house.' Ah well, anyway, I knew he kept an open house for all his Union. I suppose it could have been called a social centre.

I remembered this incident of a few years before when one evening, I settled down in the lounge of my Kitwe hotel, a tasteless pile of the thirties with some heavy club chairs in tubular steel frames and round tables with black glass tops. I was paging through the script of a discussion on geography teaching by activity methods that we were going to record the next day, when the receptionist trouped in with three young European men.

'Hi!' said one. 'I'm Ian Mason. This is Willie de Graaf and that's Titch Davidson. We heard about you from Don Lightfoot.'

Lightfoot was our energetic sports broadcaster. He had asked me to record a few items for his 'Sports Review' which was part of the short programme for European listeners which we broadcast every Sunday morning.

'He phoned from Lusaka?'

'Yep, about an hour ago, so I got the boys together and we came over to see you.'

'Well, sit down and have a drink.'

The one asked for beer, the others for coca-cola, 'We're in training, you know.'

It turned out that Willie de Graaf and I had been to school together in Southern Rhodesia. He was my junior by one or two years. I remembered him vaguely as a nice lad, who excelled at rugby rather than at schoolwork. I think he also swam.

He and his pals were proposing to record three short talks, one about baseball prospects, then a review of the season's hockey and finally plans for the coming rugby season.

'Have you prepared scripts?' I asked.

'No.'

'I can't interview you, you know. I'm not very well up in sporting matters.'

'That's okay, Pete. We'll just waffle.'

We adjourned to the quiet of Titch's office at the switchgear station. Titch was six foot three and an electrical engineer. Willie was an underground pipe-fitter and Ian a miner. These two treated the tall engineer with jocular respect, often addressing him as *bwana*. Quickly and efficiently they helped me to rig up my recording machine and then delivered their pieces. I was surprised how confidently and fluently all three spoke. I cannot remember exactly what they said because I did not understand it all, but I do remember that after the recording I asked them whether it was true that baseball was replacing cricket on the Copperbelt. Titch replied, 'I don't know about replacing, but there's too much damn' snobbery about cricket. There are some that think you can't bowl an off-spinner if you don't talk lah-di-dah.'

Then they said, 'You know Pete, we really oughtn't to have done that piece about hockey without George. You see, Ian here is only the rep for hockey on the USFC, but it's George who is the hockey-king. He's the chairman of the KHC. We tried to bring him but his missus said he'd gone to a church-meeting. He's a bit of a bible-puncher you know, but a real white man nevertheless. If you don't mind, we'll go to his house and get his okay. He should be back now.'

We piled into Titch's large American car and drove at speed through the suburb.

'So you work for Lusaka broadcasting, Pete?' said Willie.

'Yes.'

'Christ man, how do you stand all that kaffir music?'

'I don't mind it. In fact, I like it. It's an acquired taste.'

'Well, I dunno. Couldn't you get a job with Salisbury broadcasting?'

'Man, that's the last thing I'd want. They do what almost every broadcasting station in the world does, only not so well. But in Lusaka we're always trying new things, and trying them on a new audience.'

'Well, I suppose you must know.' And then, to excuse my eccentricities, Willie explained, 'Pete always used to be full of ideas at school. You remember the time you tapped the public address system and gave us phoney announcements?'

We laughed. 'That was after speech-day, when all the teachers were having a booze-up.'

At the corner we had to break sharply to avoid an African cyclist who was swerving across the road nonchalantly.

'No bloody sense,' swore Titch who was driving.

'Hey, hey, hey,' quipped Ian, 'mustn't kill them these days. Royal game, you know.'

'Road sense takes some time to develop. He's probably only come to town recently,' I lectured.

'That's right. Only just down from the trees. Hasn't had a knot put in his tail yet. But what really gets my goat is some of those bastards who cycle all over the road with their arms akimbo and whistling. Christ, these fellows need their hides tanned. But they don't allow it these days. Mustn't touch the governor's little black darlings.'

I felt I had an unpaid debt from a few days before. With unwonted vehemence I said:

'I'm bloody sure you did the same thing with your first bicycle. Only you got one when you were a kid, because you were white.'

There was a surprised silence. Willie felt that as my old schoolmate he had to soften my uncalled-for remarks:

'You were always a bit of a Bolshie at school, hey Pete? Man, to hear him argue with the masters, I'm telling you, between them they used to bullshit the hindlegs off a donkey.'

'No, you've got something,' said Ian, 'the raw kaffir underground, he's a damn' fine fellow. It's the educated ones, they're the

bad eggs. *Mister* Minamusungu! *Mister!* Man, the other day I had
to laugh. There was one of those clerk-boys in a suit and spectacles.
He was holding a meeting talking to some of our underground
munts, and talking in English! And there was a second boy there
who put it into munt-language.'

They laughed.

'You should have heard him. He was using such jaw-breakers,
I didn't know half of them myself. "Constitutional rights" he said,
and "Atlantic Charter".'

And they laughed heartily.

They knew Africans only as menials. To see one in this, to them,
incongruous position provoked just the sort of amazed laughter
that the chimpanzee's tea-party arouses in the zoo.

I kept quiet and Willie sensed that another explosion was
coming. He changed the subject:

'Do you ever see "Putt" Jackson these days? Gee, that man
used to have it in for me. One day he returns my geog notebook
with an essay I'd cribbed somewhere and he says: "This is rubbish, de Graaf, utter rubbish!" "Yes, sir!" And then he's off on
his usual moan: "You chaps don't seem to realize . . ." he always
started like that, "You chaps don't seem to realize that if you don't
pull up your socks you'll lose your privileged", or some such word,
"your privileged position. What makes you so sure you'll always
be the bosses in this land? There are thousands of natives around
who *want* to learn . . . *want* to learn. Twenty-one of them for every
one of you, and keen as mustard. They'll have overtaken you in no
time at all. You can't rely on your white skins protecting you for
ever. Now look at de Graaf here. You know what you'd be in
Europe?" Hell, man, that fellow used to have it in for me in a big
way. But I got my own back on him. I tripped him up on the
hockey-field.'

We laughed. I remembered 'Putt' well.

'Maybe "Putt" was right,' I said jocularly, 'maybe *Mister*
Minamusungu is already overtaking us. He seems to know some
pretty big words.'

We arrived at George's. It was one of the typical red-brick
boxes, but a little larger than most. He was apparently a senior
man. He was still away, bible-punching. In his living-room there
was a heavy three-piece suite upholstered in a green material with

large brown flowers. A ball and claw foot centre-table gleamed
with furniture-polish. Mrs. George was a cheerful, simple woman
who made us feel at home. She opened the top of the large radio-
gram to reveal a cocktail cabinet with a mirror-back and concealed
lighting.

'Help yourselves,' she said, 'I don't know anything about
drinks. There's beer in the frig.'

Two more young blazered men came in and decided to wait for
George. Some of the others went off to play table-tennis on the
large gauzed-in veranda.

'Any good shooting around Lusaka?' asked one of the new
arrivals.

I did not have the vaguest idea, but searched my memory:
'Lots in the new Namwala game reserve, but they won't let you
get at it.'

'Why are you staying in that damn' hotel. Lot of dronkies. I hear
there was another fight last night.'

I confirmed that I had indeed watched a fight between a Pole
and an Afrikaner the evening before. I described them standing on
the terrace, panting at each other, their faces taut and white like
their knuckles. My audience shook their heads in distaste.

'Come and stay with me,' said one, 'I have a spare bed. That
bug-house is expensive, too.'

'It is, but the NRG are paying.'

'Of course,' they chaffed, 'our civil servants. That's what we
pay taxes for, so that they can stay in posh hotels and drink tea all
day long in their offices.'

I replied in kind: 'You make me weep. Look at your copper-
bonus. You need a lorry to carry away your pay-packets these days.
What do you chaps earn?'

One was getting £160 a month, the others a little less. They
spoke of one underground miner whose pay cheque had been £230
the previous month.

'What are you going to do with all that money?'

They became serious.

'I'm saving up to go over to Scotland for my leave,' said Titch.
'I want to see where my grandpa came from.'

'And you, Ian?'

'I don't really know. Maybe I'll buy a new Jaguar every year

and hit the bottle with what's left over—like some of the others.'
He laughed.

'That'll take care of the Jag before it gets too old,' I suggested.

'I know what I want,' said Willie. 'I'm saving up for a farm.'

Of course! Willie de Graaf, the name was Afrikaans. He was
thoroughly Rhodesianized and spoke English better than Afrikaans,
but the old Boer love of the land was undiminished.

'Do you know anyone driving over to Mufulira tomorrow by
any chance?' I asked. 'I need a lift.'

One of the lads who had come in a short while before said:
'Want to borrow my car?'

Another came forward: 'I've got a day off tomorrow. I'll drive
you over.'

They were like that.

I watched the table-tennis players on the veranda. They were
playing cleanly and precisely. What strange people they were!
They were generous, friendly, informal. They had not a trace of
snobbery, but plenty of self-confidence and guts. No anxiety or
meanness. Uriah Heeps just did not grow in the open air of
Rhodesia. What fine qualities they displayed, if you were white.
They reminded me of '1066 and All That': 'Magna Carta guaranteed free speech for everybody, except the common people'. They
were open and generous and kind to everybody, except the black
majority around them. Could only a privileged caste produce such
virtues as theirs, and only within such narrow confines? Were
people too small to have virtues large enough to embrace all men?
And how did they develop this dual personality? Could it be that
as infants they had learnt to project all the hostility felt for their
parents upon the black nanny, whom it was safe to hate without
fear of parental disapproval?

But what about the many adult immigrants who became almost
indistinguishable after a few years? What about the north-
country youth in the airways bus at Ndola? It was all very strange.
Maybe an adult projects that part of himself which he hates upon
an easily identified out-group? Certainly I had observed that the
more self-hating and unbalanced a European was, the more virulent
was his hatred of Africans.

Or was it group-pressure alone that made the new ones toe the
line? Certainly the pressure was strong and hard to withstand.

The group looked upon the non-conformist, like myself, as immoral, unhealthy, much as schoolboys look upon the adolescent who still wets his bed. And the worst about it was that we, the minority, came to reflect this. In their company we started to feel somehow guilty, as if we *had* wetted our beds. It took an effort for me to say to myself: 'I am right. They are wrong. For all their open smiles and firm hand-shakes, they are most deeply corrupt.'

At long last George arrived. He was in his early forties and had once been a great rugby player, but now served as a selector and sat on numerous sports-committees. He and his wife kept an open house for the sporting bachelors. I played back our recordings to him. It turned out that he had been expecting me and had actually prepared a script about hockey-prospects, but he generously waved aside Ian's protestations that he should record it in place of the other.

'Nonsense, Ian. Your talk sounds much better. I'm not much of a talker and you've said everything I meant to say.'

They discussed the activities of organizations with mysterious initials and of people I did not know.

'How's Hughie?' asked George. 'I hear he's in hospital.'

'Yes, he is.'

'What's the matter with him?'

An awkward silence. 'Don't know.'

'I hope he'll be fit for the rugby season?'

A short time later Mrs George left to make some milk-shakes for the lads in training who refused alcohol. We heard her electric gadget humming in the kitchen.

One of the young men lowered his voice, 'About Hughie. I couldn't tell you in front of your missus. He's ruptured himself, you know where.'

They nodded sympathetically. I thought with amusement of the Kalikiti dancers, half a mile and one world away.

George chased us home at half past ten.

'You've got to get a lot of sleep if you want to get fit for the coming season,' he said.

6. LION MANE AND SPECTACLES

THE RAINS neared their end, swelling rivers and flooding roads. A small plane took us to Barotseland, probably the most backward part of Central Africa, or the most unspoilt, depending on your point of view. For three bumpy hours we flew over deserted grasslands pockmarked by trees. Then the scraggy monotonous savannah below us changed to a richer green. We were approaching the Zambezi valley. My African colleague, Edward Lubinda, became more impatient. We flew over lakes and swamplands and drainage canals. Suddenly he indicated a cluster of huts somewhere among a long ribbon of villages along the water's edge. 'My home,' he said.

We came down on the bumpy runway of Mongu airport. The pilot turned around and apologized: 'It's made of two layers of brick held together with tar. That's the most economical method on these deep sands.'

Mongu is the headquarters of the Resident Commissioner. It lies on a tongue of high ground stretching out into the broad Zambezi valley. From the RC's flagstaff we look out over the flat shallow plain below us. Most of it is under water and it looks almost like a lake. It is quite treeless except for occasional clusters of eucalyptus that indicate the sites of villages. Smoke is rising from some of them, which shows that the Lozi have not yet moved. We have come on time, but the day is near for the Kuomboka ceremony, the annual exodus from the valley.

These last few weeks the Zambezi has been rising steadily, bringing down waters from Angola and the Congo border. First they covered the grazing-lands and the fields, but now they have reached the higher parts of the valley, the mounds on which the villages of the Lozi people stand. These mounds have become islands, shrinking day by day. The waters drive before them, and into the little villages, the fierce red serowe ants, the mice, the rats and the snakes of the plain.

The Lozi are impatient. They want to leave for the escarpment where they have their winter homes, but they may not move until their Paramount Chief, Mwanawina III, starts the exodus from Lealui, his capital.

We make a noctural barge outing to Lealui, a village of thatched huts now surrounded by water. Already pools are appearing in the council hall, but the chief's residence is still dry. In the quiet, palisaded enclosures they are singing in the archaic court-language of Luyana. A scraggy old man beats a harsh, metallic-sounding xylophone and chants a plaint such as I imagine, the lone man in the moon may sing among his deserted craters. A dignitary of the Barotse Native Government squats beside me in the dark and whispers a translation:

'Come out, thou many-coloured stick.
Come out, oh big snake.
Show thyself to the people.
Why dost thou hide from the nation?
Leave us not to drown.
Come out, many-coloured stick.
Come, lead us up from the plains.'

The people wait for the chief, but the chief waits for the new moon. Until it appears the Lozi must endure the vermin and the mosquitoes and the damp rising up in their huts.

A few days later the time comes and at night the great war-drums are beaten. I hear them, miles away at Mongu, deep resonant drums calling out over the waters. They are calling the nation to the capital, calling the men whom the Paramount Chief wishes to honour to be his paddlers this year, calling the keepers of the royal graves, who must all be there on the day of the Kuomboka ceremony.

Dawn comes. The villages in the valley seem to be floating on a sea of mist, but the hot sun disperses it and we see they are all islands in a shallow lake.

A swarm of canoes and barges converges on Lealui. We are among them, sixteen sturdy paddlers take us there. We pass canoes laden with household goods whose occupants wave greetings to us. The excitement and the shouting is enormous.

At Lealui, the charming Administrative Secretary of the tribal government meets us. 'We start at ten,' he explains. He is wearing a loin-cloth and a head-gear of crane feathers. Ten o'clock comes, then eleven. But this is Africa: at twelve we are still waiting. I wade around aimlessly, trousers rolled up, my shoes around my neck.

They are loading up the state barges, the Nalikwanda and the
Notila and the other barges, each with its own name and rank.
They are strange vessels. A basketwork shelter divides them into
two. This shelter stretches across the entire width, making the
movement of paddlers from the front to the back impossible.

Some time after twelve, when the heat has become intense,
there is a stir in the crowd. They are bringing the Maoma drums.
They are wading through the water and lift them on to the
Nalikwanda. First the big drum, the male one, then the slightly
smaller one, the female, finally the small one, the child. Then the
exodus begins.

The royal procession emerges from the palisaded enclosure.
First come a file of carriers bringing the royal spears, then the
rifles. After that come the musicians. And now, splendid in grey
top-hat and Edwardian morning-coat comes Mwanawina III,
Paramount Chief of Barotseland. With slow, measured tread he is
walking towards the landing-stage. Women let out ear-piercing
ululations. An old man steps out of the crowd to shout praises.

I join the procession. Proudly, like a mace, I carry my microphone. I try to look as if I always wore my shoes around my neck
and the bottoms of my trousers rolled, as if it were normal ceremonial dress for a broadcaster.

We pick our way among little pools of water and go through
some shallow ones. Suddenly the procession comes to a halt. We
have come to a stretch of water we cannot pass and there is con-
sternation. Should the Paramount Chief take off his shoes and
socks and wade? Or be carried pick-a-back? There is shouting and
arguing, then some men rush forward carrying a long canoe. They
throw it over the water as a temporary bridge and the crisis is
averted.

We board the Nalikwanda. I am the only European there. The
Administrative Secretary finds me a place in the back half, near the
Mwenduko drums. 'We will call you when the Maoma drums start
up in front.'

Seventy paddlers strain to free the Nalikwanda from the land,
but fail. It is a new barge this year, bigger than ever. Men wade into
the water to help push us off. Eventually we get under way. A
xylophonist and two drummers strike up a song. Seventy half-
naked bodies bend in rhythm to the music.

'Bend!' sing the musicians in the ancient tongue of their fore-fathers. 'Bend, like Situmo, like Inambao . . .' They chant of the exploits of great paddlers of the past.

The lion's mane head-dresses bend. The painted paddles move in unison. The antelope skin loin-cloths shake. It is hard work, moving this great barge, and this is the hottest time of the day, and those who have been chosen to do it are not youngsters but men in their fifties and sixties. Some seem older.

Hundreds of canoes follow us. Others are waiting *en route*, shout their greeting, then fall in behind us. The small European community of Mongu is there too.

A canoe is making fast against our side. I crane my neck to see what is happening. A paddler says something to me in Lozi which I cannot understand. He gestures to me and two or three others join in. The canoe is for me. They help me over the side and hand me my recording gear. With a few swift strokes we pull up against the front part of the barge. A dozen naked arms stretch to lift me out. I salute the Paramount Chief with my raised microphone and am about to make some polite conversation when I notice the hushed silence and make haste to set my tapes running.

A powerfully built man steps up to the great Maoma. The paddlers pause. He lifts two great drum-sticks and beats them down on the drum a few times, rapidly. A deep-chested sigh, as of relief, comes from the expectant paddlers. Then he lurches at the drum and beats a rapid and powerful rhythm. A second drummer jumps forward to beat the 'female' Maoma, then a third. They beat a complicated pattern of cross-rhythms, like some dance on Olympus. I have never heard such drums before, so deep and powerful and resonant.

Pleasure comes to the faces of the old paddlers. They take up their work with a will, straining to keep up with the beat. An old man, over seventy, not content with the backbreaking paddling, skips up and down between strokes. He yells a blood-curdling war-cry and stabs at the waters with his paddle. Another, four or five feet farther away from me, shouts with all the energy he can command. I can see the veins sticking out on his neck, but I cannot hear him. He might as well be whispering in a thunder-storm. The drums drown everything.

The chief sits beneath the egg-shaped canopy. His fingers follow the rhythm of the drums and his unmoving, intelligent face watches the paddlers. They are not as disciplined as paddlers in the days of his father. They no longer keep perfect time.

The *induna* in charge of the barge sees it too. There are some not pulling their weight. He gives a signal and someone rapidly sticks a paddle between the offender's legs, gives a jerk and pitches him overboard. There is a yell of delight from the remaining paddlers. One of them explains to me in English: 'In my father's youth, such a man would be left to the crocodiles, or to drown.'

Today a canoe comes quickly to the rescue.

I doubt his story. There do not seem to be any crocodiles about and the floods are too shallow for any man to drown. But the Lozi enjoy these stories of their gruesome past. The same man tells me that in the old days they used to entomb live babies in the drums, to make them cry aloud. Who knows? Maybe they did.

The paddlers are still laughing and imitating how Muyunda spat. This will be the joke of the year. Even Mwanawina smiles. Then he turns around to watch the swarm of canoes and the forest of paddles that follow us.

The pounding of the drums sets my very insides shaking. It surges through me. I stand with difficulty upon my *bwana*'s dignity. If they beat it much longer, I too shall skip up and down and yell.

A new paddler jumps forward to take over the drum-sticks and sound the Maoma. I recognize him. He is the same Godwin Mbikusita Lewanika I have met on the Copperbelt. In his London-tailored lounge suit he has addressed parliamentarians in England and Moral Rearmament followers in Switzerland. But today he is here in his loin-cloth and lion's mane head-dress, pouring with perspiration, biting his lower lip, his powerful frame jerking ecstatically, drumming. Only his spectacles look a little incongruous.

A small boy, son of a vassal chief, joins the drummers. Then an old man. He is the *Natamoyo*, the giver of life, third in rank to the chief. His was the prerogative of mercy, in the days before the Europeans came with their impersonal justice. Any man threatened with death who reached his house or touched his person was saved. The old custom has gone, but the great drums remain, beating, pulsating.

A snake slithers out of a half-submerged bush as we pass. A swarm of red-breasted bishop-birds rises and chatters in protest against this noisy intrusion. A formation of pelican fly off. And no doubt, the evil spirits, too, flee as we approach.

The barge of the Resident Commissioner draws up alongside. The RC comes aboard, every inch the pukkah sahib. He and the Paramount Chief are served lunch that has been cooked over an open fire in the Nalikwanda. I sit around hungrily and a little embarrassed, pretending to concentrate on my recording machine. While they are having coffee, a retainer approaches me and invites me to lunch. I enter the canopied shelter, where a little table is laid and an excellent stew is served. I compliment the chief on his cook. He smiles: 'He used to work at the Victoria Falls Hotel.'

While I sip my coffee, a canoe is dispatched to invite the Agricultural Officer for lunch. He comes and he, too, is served a solitary lunch. After him, the Veterinary Officer. My twinge of annoyance disappears. At any rate I was served before them!

At last the long journey to Limulunga, the winter-capital, is almost over. We are approaching the escarpment and can now see the Paramount Chief's European-style residence on the top of the hill. But our progress becomes slower. The waters are too shallow for our barge and we have to keep to one of the canals dug in the last century which is now silting up for lack of slave-labour. Repeatedly we get stuck and paddlers have to jump overboard to push us off. It was a point they overlooked when they built this year's bigger-than-ever royal barge. The hill in front of us is alive with people. Some have waded out on the plain to welcome their ruler. Curtains are pulled across his shelter to hide him from the gaze of the masses. We approach the landing-place. The enormous crowds surge forward and the first ranks are pushed into the water by the pressure from behind. Some men start to fight for a vantage point. A woman throws herself headlong into the water and splashes her face as a sign of obeisance. The royal guards use their whips to clear a path, but again and again dancing groups crowd into it, the guards lash out ferociously. Our barge is now made fast and the drums beat a finale with renewed fury. Then the curtains are pulled aside. A roar goes up and, like one man, the crowd goes down on its knees. Mwanawina emerges. Servants help him ashore. The musicians strike up xylophones and we form a procession. Slowly Mwanawina climbs the hill, he seems oblivious of the people. Once he whisks his antelope-tail fly-swatter to chase an insect, but he does not seem to see the crowds. Behind him they rise to their feet, row after row of them, like a field of wheat in the wind. They close up the path behind us and dance up in our wake. A cloud of dust engulfs the entire scene.

Mwanawina settles down in a small pavilion outside his residence and the festivities begin. For three long days now they will celebrate, three days and three nights.

The *indunas*, elders and office-bearers come to pay their respects. They crawl into the royal presence, squat down and let out a long-drawn 'Yo-sho, yo-sho.' They throw some sand over their heads and clap their hands.

Missionaries and administrators come to exchange pleasantries with the chief. They share his pavilion and watch the dancing. School-children, neat little boys and girls in European dress, march on and sit down behind their banners. They are waiting impatiently to show off their physical jerks.

How haughty little girls can look! They and their teachers can scarcely hide their contempt for the barbaric antics of the three masked Makishi dancers who hold the arena.

The dancers advance with vigorous little jerks, shaking the rattles on their arms. They stamp heavily. The first one, covered from shoulder to knees with long chicken-feathers, mimics the death-agony of a fowl. Then comes a sort of clown, wearing a grotesque mask, three or four times the size of a human face. He throws himself on the ground before the chief and beats his face on the floor. Then he dances to the drum and rattle music, exaggerating every movement in a clumsy, comic way. He pretends to stalk an animal with an axe, rushes in for the kill, lurches at it and topples over.

Now the third one steps forward. He is clothed in a kind of fur made of bark-cloth and sports a long phallus made of hide. A sort of magnified shiver goes down his body. He arches back and his loins jerk forward rhythmically. He is dancing out the sex-act. He goes around in a circle, his arms spread out. He shakes the rattles on his wrists. The drummers shout encouragement to him. A toothless woman at the edge of the crowd dances a female counterpart. His mask is cruel, dark, with small slit eyes. From these eyes come two streams of painted tears. They cut up the hard face with white lines. The face is turned towards the heavens in some unvoiced, dumb suffering. The dance mounts to a crescendo. There is vigour in it, joy and suffering, procreation and weeping. He pulls himself to his full height, balances for a moment, then collapses on the ground.

The royal guards rush in to clear the arena. A drummer protests. They lash their whips at him. The masked dancers scatter.

From the opposite side, a crocodile of little African girls marches into the square, barefoot in neat red gym-tunics.

They form up and start to sing with shy little voices. Then they take each others' hands half-heartedly and slowly gyrate in little circles.

The missionary who is sitting with the chief turns to his lady-colleague and says:

'Look! Look! How charming. They are dancing the minuet.'

My next assignment in Barotseland was more prosaic, Namushakende, the government development centre. The name is derived from Namusiya-wa-Kende, a legendary figure in Lozi history who is said to have taught her nomadic tribe settled methods of agriculture. It seemed a good name since one of the chief aims of the centre is to raise agricultural productivity.

The place is sixteen miles from Mongu over a track that skirts the flooded valley. Edward Lubinda and I spent an uncomfortable hour in a bumpy Land Rover. We passed through village after village, primitive and derelict. I had never seen such dense settlement in Africa, but it is only ribbon-development on the fertile alluvial soil just above the flood-line. We passed old women sitting under luxuriant mango-trees. They grabbed toddlers out of our path and waved cheerfully. Men took off their hats or knelt as we passed, chickens scurried over the track. The driver had to brake sharply, so I asked him to slow down. We were hugging fragile portable recording machines in our laps.

How tenderly we hung on to these little battery-operated machines, no bigger than a woman's shopping-bag. Before they came on the market, our recording-tours away from electricity mains needed two trucks full of equipment. Flying was out of question. Large parts of Central Africa were virtually inaccessible with so much equipment. And I wonder how many speakers and singers became inaccessible, intimidated by the lengthy preparations and the white technicians.

But now we could really get close to people. We could climb to mountain villages, could board royal barges, could visit ordinary people in their huts, chat informally around the little machine, switch it on if something interesting was said, let it rest if there was nothing. There were no impatient technicians stamping up and down while we spent an hour in exploratory small-talk to sound some old man's memory. The real *vox populi* was starting to come over the air.

We passed Sefula, the oldest mission-station in Northern Rhodesia dating from 1887, then a cluster of bungalows overlooking the valley, Namushakende. This is the base for community development teams travelling in the villages. It is also an adult education centre. Longish courses are held to train craftsmen, short ones to improve the work of court-clerks and hygiene-assistants, chiefs and traders. There is also a farm, used partly for demonstration, partly for experiments. From here extension workers go out to preach drainage in order to reclaim the fertile edges of the flood-plain. They also try to introduce new crops, mainly rice. Barotseland can no longer feed its population, a population increasing rapidly as a result of European medicine and *pax Britannica*. But the Lozi do not take easily to novelties. It is characteristic that the African agricultural assistants, AAA's as they are called locally, find it wise to keep emphasizing that drainage, at any rate, is no innovation, but a return to the methods of the forefathers. But today the healthy young men go away to the towns, and the gangs of slaves that the forefathers kept are no longer available. The old Barotseland is doomed.

We walk over the experimental farm and record the gongs of the little boys who are driving the birds from the paddy-fields, and the rhythmic song of the rice-thrashers. As I start recording, their leader improvises a new verse:

> 'We thrash the rice,
> but we get little pay.
> Who will eat the rice?
> Not us. Not us.'

An old man who has been following us at a distance marvels at our machine: 'It would be wonderful for making witchcraft.'

'How is that, grandfather?'

'If a man and a woman have an argument in their hut and they bring it to court, sometimes the elders do not know who is telling the truth. But if a diviner has such a box, it would tell him what really happened.'

Neither he nor the thrashers had ever seen a recording machine before.

One evening I walked down to the little club-room attached to the education centre. There were about twenty young men around, listening to the wireless. Two or three of them introduced themselves in English, a clerk, a carpentry instructor, a dispensary assistant. They were the local intelligentsia. The others sat quietly and modestly. They were recent arrivals from the villages, men in their twenties, training to be carpenters or tanners or shoemakers. Most had had no schooling and were only just learning to read and write as part of their vocational courses. They spoke Lozi only and the clerk translated for me.

The clerk stood up to sing the praises of the CABS. It sounded not unlike the archaic eulogies at the court of the Paramount Chief. I did not have the heart to cut him short. At the end I thanked him with due formality, but I'm afraid my phrases rolled less impressively than his. Then I tried to get down to business:

'If you tell me that everything we do is so good, there will be no improvements. You must tell me where we go wrong. You must tell me which type of programme you would like more of and which you want us to stop.'

Some embarrassed laughter. Then silence.

'It is our job to try and please you. We get paid for it. You pay taxes, don't you? Well, I get paid out of your taxes. You have a right to make suggestions.'

It was not strictly true. The British tax-payer paid half, the company tax collected from the copper-mines most of the rest.

Silence.

I told them some stories about musicians whom they knew. Thaw set in. They started to argue about the respective merits of

town and country music and I egged them on. Then the first
complaints came out:

'Why do you broadcast more in Nyanja than in our language?'

'Why does it take so long between our writing to your request
programme and our request being played?'

They were standard complaints all over the country and I gave
the standard answers. Then I asked about news. Oh, yes, they
loved to hear news, they wanted more news, it taught them about
their country and the world. I concentrated on the 'raw' trainees.
What news could they remember hearing?

A cobbler recalled the appointment of a new district commissioner in the neighbouring district. A carpenter said how sad he
had been to hear that his sub-area chief had died.

'What else?'

'No more, sir.'

I turned to the three 'educated' men.

They remembered the death of King George VI, the coronation
of Queen Elizabeth which the Paramount Chief had attended.
Then, after some coaxing:

'There is trouble in Korea. They are quarrelling in a tent.'

The date was June 1953. The Panmunjon negotiations were in
progress.

I noticed a whispered conversation among the trainees.

'Now, what's your problem?'

They were nudging one of them.

'Go on. I'm going out with the Community Development Team
tomorrow. Then it will be too late to ask.'

In the end the man spoke up:

'Please, sir. About the war against the Germans. Who is
winning? We don't hear of it any more.'

The date was June 1953.

The clerk walked back with me to the house of Lewis, the District
Officer, where I was staying. He carried a hurricane-lamp to light
my way. He said: 'The whole of Mwanawina's court, they are
backward fools. A few of them used to be okay, but then they had
their mouths closed with big jobs and now they are just like the
uneducated ones.'

I was flattered by his risky confidences and wanted to hear more, but was afraid of overplaying my hand. But he continued without prodding:

'They make us crawl up to the chief on hands and knees. Have you ever seen the *showelela*, the royal salute?'

'I have.'

'It's shaming. Europeans don't do such foolishness. And if a man is a teacher or a clerk they make him *showelela* for five minutes before they return his greeting.'

I knew he was right. I had seen it myself. Nevertheless I told him about curtseys and bows at European courts. He did not think they were the same sort of thing.

'And they don't do anything to develop education. They don't advance progressive young men, only men who are related to the royal family. And industries. They don't do anything to encourage industries. No wonder we are poor.'

'But industries would bring Europeans into Barotseland. At present you only have a few administrators and missionaries and a handful of traders, but industries would bring large numbers. Are you prepared to have them?'

'Oh no. They must be nationalized industries, like they have in England.'

'You'll need skilled men.'

'We'll train them.'

'What about capital?'

'Capital? Lealui is our capital.'

'I mean cash. Money to buy machines.'

'People in England will give us.'

'Mmm. But are there any minerals in Barotseland?'

'They will be found.'

'Is it true that the Barotse Native Government don't allow prospectors into the protectorate?'

'That's because they are stupid.'

'But the prospectors would be white!'

An awkward silence. For a moment I enjoyed his discomfort, then relented:

'Are there many people who are so dissatisfied with the tribal government?'

'Many, very many. But they are afraid to speak. One man on the line-of-rail who started a progressive group . . . he was fined two hundred and fifty pounds when he came back. Fortunately the district commissioner interfered and they had to reduce his fine.'

'How many people feel like you here, at Namushakende?'

'There are six of us, maybe seven.'

'Among how many hundred?'

'But we are the educated people.'

'How many educated people are there in the Luandui valley, where I'm going tomorrow?'

'None at all. That's only bush.'

We had reached the district officer's house. I thanked him for lighting my way.

'It was a pleasure,' he said, 'one doesn't often get a chance to talk rationally. Educated gentlemen are rare here, except of course, the DO.'

The darkness hid my smile. He was loyal! But I could not imagine him chatting freely and indiscreetly to the cold and austere Lewis.

Later I was to see how wrong I was.

In the shade of a tree a crowd of Africans was chanting. There were withered old men wearing the traditional Lozi kilt, a few younger men in shabby European clothing and then—at a proper distance behind them—women of every age, some with babies tied to their backs. They were not chanting any tribal legends. They were repeating after their teacher:

'Ta . . . ta . . . tata . . . ba . . . ba . . . baba.'

They were taking part in a mass-literacy course which Lewis's Community Development Team was conducting in the remote Luandui valley. It was one of several courses conducted simultaneously, each under its own shady tree.

In all, the team consisted of six African men and two women instructors. And then there was Lewis, but he kept in the background.

The team stays a few weeks in each village, then moves to a new site. That is not enough to make a man literate, but the primers are designed for home-study and another teacher follows up a few weeks later.

I strolled over to another group. They were women, knitting needles stuck in their curly hair, listening to a talk about baby-care.

After the lecture they were given pamphlets on 'cooking for babies' which they carried away proudly, although they could not read them yet.

There was also a short course in simple village carpentry. Elsewhere in the territory there are training-schools turning out tolerably skilled carpenters, but hardly any of these trained men settle down in the remote areas, such as the Luandui valley. They make for the fleshpots of the Copperbelt or Livingstone. For this reason the Community Development Team gives rudimentary training in carpentry to peasants who will stay in the villages to make simple furniture with native tools.

I liked the carpentry instructor. He had very little book-learning, but great histrionic talents. I saw him trying to recruit trainees among the assembled villagers:

'Is it good to sleep on the floor and be bitten by the vermin?'

He demonstrated the violent itch of a flea-bite.

'Is it good to eat off the earth like a dog? I can teach you to make tables and chairs and beds. . . .' and other such unheard-of luxuries.

There were three or four volunteers for his course. I was surprised that the remainder of his audience could resist his salesmanship.

Apart from the courses there were a number of simple propaganda points that the 'public relations unit' of the team preached in speeches, improvized plays, by slides, films, posters and in songs:

'Spray your huts against insects.'
'Drain your valley-soils and grow more food.'
'Move your villages to healthy, dry sites.'
'Send your daughters to school. Even girls need education these days.'

One of the songs that the team sings, accompanied by the hygiene-instructor on the guitar, asserts that the team's bugle, which they blow every morning to call the villagers to the courses, 'heralds the dawn of a better age', but the extremely conservative peasants of the Luandui valley look upon all these new and unsettling ideas with much suspicion. Yet, one morning, *before* the bugle called, Lewis and I did surprise an old man, ugly enough to have escaped from the imagination of some misanthropic cartoonist, who was sitting under a tree, using a piece of wood as stylus, scratching letters on his black forearm. As we came nearer we heard him mumbling:

'Ta . . . ta . . . tata.'

The evening was cool and clear and the tall trees stood out against the sky. We sat outside our tent, Lewis and I. The last of the servants had departed. The chirping of the crickets and the occasional sound of drumming from across the valley floated over to us. Tomorrow some of the pupils on the courses would look grey and bleary-eyed!

I watched Lewis refill his glass and mine and thought to myself: 'Lord, let me never judge a man rashly and uncharitably again.'

He sat back in his canvas chair and continued:

'The vital thing is to encourage, not to bully. A subtle distinction, sometimes. It calls for sensitivity, but it's very necessary. Too seldom have our Africans any sense of participation in the actions of their rulers. We'll never make a real impression on this territory until we can give them this sense of participation.'

I asked: 'How?'

'By encouraging a flow of ideas upwards. I try to do it by keeping my courses very flexible. No two are alike. When we do a preliminary survey of an area, I always ask: 'What do you want to learn?' Some of the suggestions may seem a little pointless to me, but I try to fall in with them. Here in Chief Yusokwakuonga's area, for example, they didn't want a first-aid course. They said there was a dispensary seven miles away, so they didn't need it. Well, if they feel that way about it . . . On the other hand they insisted on more knitting lessons. It's a new and useful skill and the women love it. They love it so much that in one area the husbands came and complained to me that they don't do any more cooking! Knowing this spot here, I would have thought it would be more useful if they learnt more about baby-care. The mortality-rate is very high. But we tried to fall in with their wishes—up to a point. They get a lot of knitting-lessons, but I've suggested to the instructresses: Wait until one of the babies starts crying. Then ask what it is being fed on. . . .'

Lewis had a gaunt, finely chiselled face, which showed unusual animation that evening.

'Mass-literacy?' he continued. 'In isolation it is of little use. Most of the mass-literacy campaigns in the territory have folded up because the pupils lapsed into illiteracy again in a few months. What incentive is there for villagers in these parts to read? We try and give them some good reason for wanting to stay literate and some useful literature. That's why we spread pamphlets and duplicated articles around in such profusion, even among the illiterates. I'm going to send them follow-up literature too, and a little duplicated magazine full of local news. You know, it's quite a thing to receive a pamphlet of your own for the first time in your life. It makes you want to know what's in it. We also try to sell novels and other books. The Publications Bureau at Lusaka is starting to bring out some good Lozi stuff. . . .

'I never take the team into any area unless the chiefs and headmen have asked for it. Now I've invited the chiefs and headmen from the neighbouring areas over here for the film-show next week. We'll give them hospitality for the night and they'll probably take the opportunity to chat to the locals. That should produce a few more applications for the services of the team. If it doesn't, I'd rather employ the team back at Namushakende than force them on a village.

'Our way is slower than the Russian way. Old Stalin breaks down resistance by terror and hopes that sooner or later his subjects, or their children, will see that he's right. Our British way is slower, especially in the beginning, but I'm not sure that it's less efficient in the long run. The human costs are less. Anyway, we don't have a choice. Our temperament and our traditions don't equip us for the Stalin way. Nor our legal system. I can't say I regret it. . . .'

I inquired: 'Did you meet with any real resistance?'

'We had some difficulty over land to start with. At our first camp we stretched bunting around to make it look gay. Then they said: "No previous district officer has done this. They are pegging land for European settlers." You know their ever-present fear. I called a meeting and told them that if they did not want us to hold classes we would go immediately. That did it. They asked us to stay.'

I asked: 'How did you choose your team? They seem a pretty lively crowd.'

'Some are civil servants, some native government employees and a few were retired men. I chose them mainly for their ability as showmen, not for their great knowledge of the subjects they teach. I gave them a few weeks' course. Well, it was really one long conference. At first my presence inhibited discussion. But after a few days the sparks started to fly. It was really quite stimulating, and they produced a few good ideas and phrases and slogans that we've been using in the campaign. You can't govern people properly without this upward flow of comment and ideas. I'm afraid the indirect rule system produces a lot of bottle-necks. We started by talking about the purposes of development. We talked for days, arguing about the obvious, going off at tangents. There was an amazing number of misconceptions they had to work out of their systems: suspicions of our motives, doubts about the advantages of any development at all, doubts whether anything could be done without changing fundamentally the Barotse Native Government. You'd be surprised if you knew what a great undercurrent of discontent with the BNG there is among the so-called intelligentsia. . . .'

I nodded. Lewis continued: 'Now I think they know what they are doing and why. It tells in the way they put things across. Their plays and speeches, they're full of lively imagery and ideas. They're all their own. Sometimes minor technical inaccuracies creep in, but I don't think it matters. It's better than an accurate dry-as-dust lecture written by an expert.

'Results? They're very difficult to measure at this stage. It must be the same with your radio propaganda campaigns. We find that the enthusiasm of the villagers wanes somewhat when the team moves on. When we check up a few months later, we find that a lot is remembered, but that not very much of it is applied. Few get down to it immediately and use what we have taught them to improve their lives. But progress is bound to be slow. They're like the district commissioner who had his pending tray labelled "too difficult". But I know that if we keep at it, more and more of them will transfer their knowledge into the "for action" tray.'

Lewis lapsed into silence. He had not spoken so much in the fortnight I had known him. How I had misjudged the man! When I had stayed with him and his family at Namushakende I had thought them frighteningly typical of the colonial service, reserved, dull but honest. The only contact he seemed to have with Africans were the curt orders he gave them and the excuses they made when they had not carried them out. His conversation over sundowners had consisted of the usual regrets about too much bumf, the bad weather they had had on their last leave in UK, the charming cottage they had rented, and had I read this or that war-escape story?

But that was not all there was to Lewis. I imagine that at his public school, when he read a book of poetry, he hid it in the covers of a volume of cricket-averages. Under the open sky, in the area of Chief Yusokwakuonga, and after a few whiskies, Lewis blossomed.

During one of our consultations at Lusaka we had decided that since the Lozi did not take easily to novelties like the wireless but lived in the past, the natural bridge could perhaps be provided by historical programmes. The most ancient written records of Barotseland, Livingstone's *Missionary Travels*, are only a hundred years old. We had dramatized this and Coillard's books repeatedly. To bring new life to our historical programmes we would have to track down old men who remembered.

At Sefula, the oldest mission-station in Northern Rhodesia, I visited the grave of Francois Coillard. It was sixty-eight years since he had founded the place, almost fifty since he had died. I had written several historical plays based on his diaries. It was like visiting an old friend.

He had been one of the Paris Evangelical Society, a small band of French and Swiss Protestants who, finding the French colonies virtually closed to them, had concentrated their missionary efforts on Basutoland in South Africa, a territory which soon after came under British influence. Coillard and his Scottish wife spent most of their adult life in Basutoland, but as a middle-aged man he abandoned their cottage and the fruit-trees, just about to bear for the first time, and pushed into the unknown interior. A handful of Basuto evangelists accompanied him. They had decided to found a mission-station in what is now Southern Rhodesia. But there they were almost murdered by hostile chiefs, then captured and held by the Ndebele. Frustrated in their design, they had bypassed the hostile Ndebele, crossed the Kalahari desert and

then, in the green lands beyond the Zambezi, had come upon the
Lozi. Through an accident of history these Lozi spoke a language
almost identical to the one Coillard had learnt in Basutoland, a
thousand miles away. His evangelists were welcomed as chiefs.
They had leapfrogged over hostile tribes and strange languages and
had come upon a nation of friends.

Coillard won the confidence of King Lewanika and established
schools and churches. But converts were slow in coming. Mono-
gamy was the main stumbling-block.

The King managed to preserve his own, highly individual,
balance between Coillard's teaching and the tribal traditions. He
led a cattle-raid against the Ila, despite the fearless remonstrances
of Coillard, but decreed that raiding should cease on Sundays
because it was the Lord's day.

Coillard preached 'Thou shalt not shed blood'. King Lewanika
seemed impressed and gave orders that in future those who
incurred his displeasure should be throttled to death.

Lewanika was never converted, but he did come to accept
Coillard's advice in many things. Eventually he stopped the annual
raids on neighbouring tribes. He brought to an end the almost
daily executions of plotters against his reign. He invited Queen
Victoria to extend a protectorate over his country, and over large
regions to which he had no claim. In the end he became quite a
tolerant and enlightened ruler.

Towards the end of his life, Coillard started to make proselytes.
One of the first of these is still surviving. I met him at Sefula, and
it was he who really made the yellow pages of the Coillard diaries
come to life for me.

He was William Kwalela, a man of over seventy, and he told
us how Coillard first asked his congregation to cover their faces
with their hands, close their eyes, and join him in prayer. Kwalela
said:

'I didn't close my eyes. I peeped through my spread-out fingers
in case the white man tried to murder me or bewitch me. One could
not be too sure in those days.'

And Kwalela chuckled. Within the lifetime of this one man, it
had become a joke.

Both Lewis and the missionaries had given me the same advice:

'Take a canoe to Nalolo and see the *Ishe Kwandu*. He knows more about the history of Barotseland than any man alive.'

It turned out to be a six hours trip in the broiling sun in a hollowed-out tree trunk. I had tried to travel light and had a short-sleeved bush shirt and shorts only. As a result I got myself the worst sunburn I have ever had.

Hour after hour we balanced precariously on the camp-chairs that had been placed in our canoe. Our approach disturbed large swarms of birds. Sometimes we pushed through tall grass that grew out of the water, sometimes through delicately coloured water-lilies, pink and yellow and mauve. At other times we made fast progress over open stretches of water. Our canoe filled with fat little spiders and with beetles that were clinging to the grass. We passed deserted villages on mounds. Near one we saw four or five snakes hanging in a half-submerged bush. Before I could protest, one of our canoe-men beat them with his paddle. Fortunately they were too tired to move.

When I had looked my fill I picked up the book I was then reading, the autobiography of a British ex-Communist, disillusioned, purposeless, full of unfocussed anger. How far away that world seemed from these silent, flooded plains and my swift, purposeful canoe. How could they complain of emptiness, of aimlessness, when there was this continent of Africa crying out for teachers, engineers, agricultural officers?

I put away the book and turned to Lubinda to find out more about the man we were seeking. He explained that the Paramount Chief's court has an elaborate system of constitutional checks and balances, but balanced against the whole court at Lealui there is a second court at Nalolo. Here a woman reigns, the *Mulena Mukwae*. She is a kind of viceroy over the southern part of the country, a niece or aunt of the Paramount Chief, and usually at loggerheads with him. Her husband has a fairly humble position at her court, a prince consort. His title is *Ishe Kwandu*. This was the man we were hoping to see.

Lewis had advised me to ask for accommodation at the Paris Evangelical Mission on a mound about a mile from Nalolo. We crossed the Zambezi and called there, but found that the missionaries had left for the escarpment a few days before. There was only an old African caretaker. He was most hospitable and promised to arrange one of the houses as best he could, but there were no sheets and blankets left. They were dark, dank houses with sagging ceilings and broken mosquito-gauze around the verandas. They certainly did not live in luxury, these missionaries!

We sent a messenger across the plain to Nalolo. He returned a short while later to invite us over. We canoed across in the late afternoon sun and were met by an excited crowd. We made our way to the chieftainess's residence, were ushered through a series of palisaded courtyards like those at Lealui and eventually came to a large barn-like structure with wide double-doors.

An old man stood in front, tapping his way towards us with a stick. He had a warm, handsome face, but was blind. This was the *Ishe Kwandu.*

He led the way into the large and high audience-chamber-cum-living-room. It had heavy wooden rafters which reminded me of a baronial hall. On a large, faded European settee sat the *Mulena Mukwae.* Her bandaged legs were propped up on an easy-chair. She apologized for not coming to meet us, but her legs were swollen and she was in pain.

Chairs were brought for Lubinda and myself. He glanced at me briefly. I knew what he meant. At the court of Lealui he had only been allowed to squat on the floor while a few curt royal questions were addressed to him, then he had been dismissed. Here he was treated as a welcome visitor and as my equal.

Visitors seldom come to the inaccessible second capital. Most find enough of 'colourful Africa' at the rival establishment at Lealui. The court at Nalolo feel neglected and forgotten. Hence their pleasure at seeing us, and the list of complaints I was asked to take back to the governor at Lusaka.

I tried to explain my very limited influence and the purpose of our visit. The *Ishe Kwandu* agreed to record for us both ancient Lozi history which he had heard from his grandfather, and some episodes he had witnessed himself. But there was the problem of his blindness. He could not see where the microphone was and kept directing his voice 'off-mike'. I asked the two or three councillors present to keep silent, placed the mike between the *Ishe Kwandu* and our announcer, then instructed the latter to punctuate the old man's account suitably with the traditional Lozi hand-clapping of respect. After that the *Ishe Kwandu* addressed his remarks only in the direction of his polite listener, and our microphone. The clapping on the recording added atmosphere.

The *Ishe Kwandu* started by recapitulating the complicated negotiations between Rhodes's BSA Company and King Lewanika which led to the protectorate-treaty. He summarized the speeches of the anti-treaty *indunas*, then the pro-treaty orators, what the prime minister had asked, what Coillard had advised. His voice reflected the anger, the suspicion, the cajoling, the oratory. He seemed to capture the tone of them all.

Then he described how as a young man he himself had been a steward to Lewanika and had accompanied him to England for the coronation of King Edward VII. He re-enacted the gracious waving of the king, the cheering crowds leaning from the windows, the clatter of the horses' hooves. I had never come across such a 'natural' before.

It was getting dark. Someone brought a hissing pressure-lamp, but I waved it away. The noise was interfering with the recording. We continued by the light of a few candles.

By then I felt I was running a temperature because of my sunburn. Perhaps that is why the scene assumed a weird, dreamlike appearance. The flickering candles and the moving shadows only hinted at the expanse of the hall. The resonant voice of the blind old man lost itself among the rafters. I knew only a few words of Lozi, yet I seemed to understand everything that he said, so great was his dramatic ability. Once I took my eyes away from him and was surprised to see that the hall was filling . . . was almost full of quiet, barefooted children who were creeping in and sitting down on the mud-floor to listen to the tale. A little later the throng was crowding the open doors and windows too, their large eyes reflecting the candles.

A small child, perhaps a great-grandson, crept up against the old man's chair and he fondled it as he spoke. He must have sensed the hundred eyes upon him in the dark. His voice rose. Resonant phrases rolled off his lips. He chanted the archaic praises of some long-dead chief. Then he brought his great and precise story-telling talent to bear upon the turbulent history of the Barotse civil war of 1885.

He surprised me with a tale of a European who had fought at the side of Akufuna, the pretender, in that war. He was a great shot and

H

did much slaughter among Lewanika's men. There is no reference to such a character in any of the records but the *Ishe Kwandu* is a reliable witness. Perhaps it was a Portuguese hunter or trader, we shall probably never know.

The *Ishe Kwandu* described the attempted assassination of the chief, battles in the swamps, flights, pillages, massacres. He imitated the sharp report of the rifles and the groans of the men stabbed in battle. He made us see the courageous man who jumped into an enemy canoe and did great slaughter.

It was late at night when we departed. The *Mulena Mukwae* lent us some hurricane lamps to light our way. It was only a mile to the mission, but we lost our way and floated over the waters in the dark. I did not care very much. The cool air was pleasant on my burning skin. The paddlers, too, remained cheerful. They could not stop praising the liberal hospitality that had been accorded them in the outer courtyard. At Lealui, they grumbled, they had not even been admitted to the enclosure.

At length we saw the lights that the old caretaker had lit in the mission-house and found our way to the island. There was a galvanized iron tub of hot water waiting for me. I washed and ate some of the eggs the caretaker had brought, then lay down on a bed without blankets or mosquito-nets and slept fitfully.

I dreamt I stood in the ranks of black warriors calmly firing a gun at the ranks of the enemy. But a moment later I was alone, wading over the flooded plains, pursued by swift war-canoes with enormous drums beating. I woke up in the middle of the night, still burning all over, and got up to search for some water. I stumbled about the dark unfamiliar house without matches or a torch, but could not find any. In the end I climbed back on my bed, thirsty and shivering, and lay listening to the whine of the mosquitoes in my room and the croaking of the bull-frogs outside. It seemed an age till dawn.

Early in the morning a messenger arrived from Nalolo to bid us a good morning, to say the *Mulena Mukwae* hoped we had slept well and wished us a safe return-journey. What old-worldly graces these people had!

The caretaker came with a present of a chicken and explained that the river was choppy and that it would not be safe to cross by canoe. He would escort us across in his large barge. Once on the other side, on the floodplain, we should be safe. The water there was not deep. 'But keep away from the river,' he said, 'so that you don't meet any hippos.'

So we crossed the wind-swept river in his barge. The paddlers brought up our canoe, keeping close to us for protection. On the other side I turned to the old man and was about to give him the usual tip. Something made me hold back:

'I thank you for your advice and for taking us across. Also for the many gifts you have given us. I am afraid I have not brought any suitable presents. Will you let me give you a small gift of money?'

I'm glad I asked.

'Sir,' he said, 'when the missionaries are away, I am in charge here. This is my place. You have been my guest. It is right to feed a guest and to honour him. You would insult me if you gave me anything in return.'

I shook my head in wonder. Elsewhere in the territory clamorous mendicants demand payment for every little service. But here, in this backwater . . .

As I settled down in our narrow canoe for the uncomfortable journey up-river, for a brief moment I felt at one with the old-time administrators who kept bemoaning the passing of the old order. These Sanderses-of-the-River, some now at the very top of the administration, they had never come to terms with the turbulent towns they had to administer, with the masses in miners' helmets and overalls, full of vitality and extravagance, with the uncertain, brash, arrogant, promiscuous youths who were struggling, experimenting to adapt themselves to the new.

I knew they were wrong. But for a few minutes, as I watched the old man skilfully piloting his barge down the river, I too was overcome with regret for the passing of the old ways, when there was certainty in human relations and respect of man for man.

Then the sun came through the clouds briefly and, carrying no adequate clothes, I put my pyjamas over my khakis to protect my blistering arms and legs. If only I could get some sleep!

But the wind whistled in the half-submerged bushes. Our canoe shipped a little water and one of the paddlers started bailing with a rusty tin. Thunder-clouds were mounting. A drenching—that was all we were short of! Why did I always have to be clamouring to leave the comforts of our office at Lusaka? Heavy drops started to fall lazily. I put the tapes into my shirt to keep them dry. The feel of them cheered me, for I knew for certain that they would create a response such as no Lozi broadcast before had ever done.

7. MEN BETWEEN

WHEN WE returned to our tiny studio-building at Lusaka, our colleagues crowded around us and questioned us about our tour. To most of the non-Lozi the ceremonies and customs we described were almost as strange as they are to Europeans or Americans. They studied the photographs I had taken with great interest. One of these produced a reaction I had not expected. This was the photograph of Godwin Lewanika, the Copperbelt politician, in tribal dress, reproduced opposite page 144. It caused a sort of crystallization of different attitudes. The office-orderlies passed it by with such remarks as,

'What is it he wears on his head?'

'He is a strong man, isn't he? Was he a good drummer?'

But the broadcasters and clerks were staggered:

'This . . . this is an educated man? A man who has been to England?' They shook their heads then burst out laughing:

'He can't afford a suit, hey?'

'And he went barefoot?'

'Man, man, man, what a sight!'

'It is uncivilized. It is shameful.'

Only one, 'Pepe' Zulu, thought differently:

'It is good,' he said. 'Here is a man proud of his traditions.' Zulu, the most westernized of them all! I wondered how deep his conviction went. It was only a few months since I had heard him say, 'Our past has nothing to teach us. Nothing.'

What an astonishing range of contrasts in attitude there was among this small group—some looking nostalgically back towards the tribal past, others striving towards further integration with the society of the dominant Europeans and rejecting the past, and some trying to do both at once.

The times we were living through were times of struggle and mental anguish and confusion. Sometimes Africans were grasping at new ideas overhastily, then they suffered reactions and tried to revert to older ideas, but these had by then lost their attractiveness.

Industrialization and urbanization were bringing great changes and demanding profound adjustments. My travels in Barotseland

and on the Copperbelt had convinced me that it was not the
teachers and missionaries and their ideas that produced upheaval.
Barotseland had had missionaries and schools longer than almost
any other part of Central Africa, but it was still one of the most
'intact' traditional societies. The Copperbelt, on the other hand,
was only thirty years old, but there new ideas and organizations
were sprouting and proliferating.

The older Africans and the old-time administrators saw in all
the changes brought by industrialization nothing but disintegra-
tion. Things were getting worse all the time. One listener, praising
a broadcast about old ways and customs wrote:

> 'Behaviour in nowadays is disgraceful, most of us are always
> saying I don't mind with (care about) anybody else, because
> I have got too much money which can even build up a store,
> which is not good saying at all.'

The same thing was being said by many administrators, in
their own particular style of English. They all saw only

> '. . . the restless wanderer.
> He has forgotten his tribe and his family.
> He picks up with any woman of the town.'

But isn't the wanderer also a seeker? Is he not finding something bigger than family or tribe and better suited to the times?

The older Africans complain that the traditional mutual aid
arrangements are being neglected. But these are the tools of a
society which had no means of exchanging goods and services
except by customary obligations, 'You help to lift the roof on to
my new hut. That is your duty as my nephew. I will provide
cattle when you get married. That is my duty as your uncle.'
Was 'Pepe' Zulu not right when he believed that in a money
economy such obligations were no longer efficient? Now it is
possible to hire a builder and to earn cash for marriage payments.

The new individualism often does run riot and there is disloca-
tion, destruction before reconstruction and a painful time-lag
between. The traditional obligations of the family to provide for
the aged are going, but there are not yet any old-age pensions and
family allowances instead. The Belgians in the Congo are alone
in Africa in facing up to this. In all other African territories there

is still this time-lag, but new organizations and obligations will come eventually.

The preponderance of male workers in the new towns attracts the good-time girls, the *kapenta*, a word derived from the English 'to paint'. The older Africans and many of the administrators consider them a great social evil, these lipsticked, wideawake young girls in their bright cotton dresses smiling provocatively in the beer gardens. They regard them as merely prostitutes, but are they? Only very few of them are regular street-walkers. Most of them are short-term wives. They come and live with a man until they tire of him or he no longer gives them enough presents. After a few years of this promiscuity they do seem to settle down to domesticity and a more stable liaison, not much the worse for their experience, and maybe more alert than their staid and respectable sisters.

These *kapenta* come from a society in which women are allowed very little independence. All, excepting a few princesses of Barotse-land have a status very much subordinate to the men. Occupational opportunities for them are few. They cannot even become domestic servants in European households because the men regard this as their prerogative. They have no trading tradition or experience such as the women of West Africa have. One of the few ways of asserting their financial independence and revolting against an outmoded social system is by selling their favours. Is it surprising that many of the brighter and better-educated choose that way?

They flourish largely because of the disproportion between the sexes which is maintained by tribal and municipal regulations which hinder the flow of unattached women into the towns. But one day the chiefs and municipal councillors will wake up to the fact that their restrictions on women coming to towns do the opposite of what they set out to do. When they relax them and the disproportion no longer exists, maybe then a sounder relationship between men and women will emerge, based on the equality and independence that the *kapentas* now claim.

The backward, docile, traditionalist women of Africa are among the most serious drags on African advancement. They cannot teach their children anything of the new world. They cannot live up to their husband's aspirations, they shame their husbands by cooking tea-leaves like vegetables—as Alick Nkhata sang. Educated

Africans trying to live in what they consider the civilized manner are always being shamed by their illiterate wives.

At a garden-party given at Government House, Lusaka, to the visiting Archibishop of Canterbury, a number of prominent African layworkers of the church were invited with their families. During the playing of the national anthem one African baby, terrified by the drums and cymbals of the police-band, started to yell. The mother shifted the baby from her back to her side, pulled her breast out from under her blouse and suckled it in full view of the public. The embarrassment on the faces of the European ladies in their picture-hats and pastel-coloured cocktail dresses had to be seen to be enjoyed. But the African father did not find it at all amusing.

The old Africans complain that marriage-ties are becoming looser, that adultery is much more frequent than before. No wonder: the old moral code rests on taboos which are being disproved. In the past, if a woman died in child-birth, this was attributed to the infidelity of her husband and her kin would see to it that he was heavily punished by a tribal court. Similarly if a husband away at war or working in the mines had an accident or received injury, a case of adultery lay against the wife. But nowadays these beliefs are being discredited. This causes disruption, but is it not an unavoidable one? Is it our intention that mineworkers should make their wives wear chastity-belts rather than that they should don safety-helmets themselves?

Disruption exists because the tools and externals of European technology are accepted first, but the 'internals'—the philosophy and the ethics—take much longer to establish themselves. European theories of natural causation are only being accepted very slowly. It is far easier to switch on a wireless than to understand the scientific theories that made such an invention possible. Similarly it is easier to accept DDT spraying, than European scientific theories.

Most Africans still believe firmly that accidents and illness are caused by broken taboos and witchcraft. They are constantly afraid of malevolent opponents bewitching them. This is hardly surprising if we remember how short and how superficial European contact has been. No more than a few hundred Central Africans now in their fifties had ever even heard their traditional beliefs challenged until they were past the impressionable age and it is

hard to unlearn childhood experience. Very few Northern Rhodesian Africans even pretend not to believe in witchcraft. When
Pop Adams questioned trainee dispensary assistants who already
had an average of two years' medical training he found that seventy
per cent readily admitted that they believed that magic caused
disease and that witches could kill at a distance. They admitted to
having seen germs under the microscope, but who or what caused
germs to attack one person rather than another?

Witchcraft beliefs are a closed system which evidence like
seeing germs does not disrupt. After one of our broadcasts about
witchcraft a listener wrote in:

> 'Listen to me about witchcraft. I went to bed on June 10th
> and untied my shoes. When I woke up next morning I
> found that my two shoes were missing. I found them outside
> having been gnawed by a rat. I believe that rat was sent by
> a sorcerer.'

Europeans express surprise at the apparent contradiction; the
physical cause, the rat, is known, and yet it is attributed to witchcraft. But why should that cause such surprise? Is a Christian's
recognition of the physical causes of disease in both humans and
birds in conflict with the belief that 'not a sparrow shall fall on
the ground without your father'? To the Bantu, not a rat shall
gnaw without a sorcerer.

African witchcraft beliefs have not been shaken seriously. Since
it is no longer legal to lay a charge against a supposed witch and
to subject him or her to a poison-ordeal, many Africans feel very
much less protected. If anything, there is more witchcraft now than
there was before; the old cannot participate in the new advances,
so they try to reaffirm their authority with this weapon which is
their exclusive preserve and which no young man can master.
As a result young men are afraid to experiment with new agricultural methods lest success and pride make them targets for
witchcraft. A choir of young men expressed this in a song they
recorded for us.

> '"Why don't you build better houses? Speak"
> "It's because we are afraid,
>   afraid of jealousy and witchcraft."

Witchcraft and jealousy, people are afraid of them.
These are the things that hold us back.
They fear to build better houses.
They fear to make big fields.
They fear!
You who spread tales of witchcraft,
hold your tongues!
Stop spreading fear.
Stop discouraging people.
You are hindering our progress.'

But it is not only the old men; schoolboys have been known to
use witchcraft to try and pass exams. Ezekiel S. the labour-leader,
feared to stand for high office in case his rivals used it against him.
After the death of *Ha-hi-ha* Mlongoti there were accusations
that the broadcaster next in seniority had bewitched him in order
to step into his shoes.

Witchcraft is being adjusted to new situations, to the tensions
and anxieties of modern living. It is one of the symptoms of the
difficulties of adjustment that Africans are having to make.

But it is not Africans alone who are suffering from difficulties
of adjustment. The rapid changes of the last twenty years have
made the Europeans too, lag behind with ideas and philosophies
that are no longer valid. The European administrators, for
example, find it extremely difficult to think of Africans as per-
manent town-dwellers, and to change their own role gradually
from that of trustees of naïve savages to that of public servants
of free citizens.

It is not an easy adjustment, but it is complicated increasingly
by the fact that most of the senior officials have had no real contact
with Africans since the 'bush-bashing' days of their youth. And
even among those officials who are touring the villages today,
there are few who make any more attempt to understand the people
they rule than the Turtons and Burtons and Callendars in E. M.
Forster's *Passage to India*. No doubt it is hard to combine the
duties of the ruler with those of the confidante of the ruled, but
politicians do it all the time. Should it be so difficult for civil servants? Very few of the detached, just, cold masters-of-men are at

all sensitive to the problems and feelings of their subjects. Very few of them are self-effacing enough to draw out and to take in opinions contrary to their own. Men like Lewis of Namushakende were a great rarity. This is bad enough in a static society, but it is much more serious in a rapidly changing one.

When the Mau Mau rising in Kenya caught the administration there altogether unprepared, this caused even the senior men in the Lusaka Secretariat to sit up. They instructed their district officers to do more touring in the villages. But the centre of political gravity had shifted to the towns decades before! In the villages the district officers maintain contact mainly with the chiefs and councillors, all of whom are dependent on the government for their livelihood. They avoid the 'bolshies' of the African Congress who represent the new Africa, and their chief informants remain sycophantic boma-messengers, the factotums of the DCs.

It was no wonder that the only Europeans who knew what Africans were thinking and saying were some of the missionaries who made regular house to house visits or heard confession, and the sociologists and social anthropologists whose job it was to study the situation.

Some of the latter incurred the surveillance of the Special Branch of the police for being too friendly with African politicians and trade-union leaders. A pity that such searching attention could not have been given to the administrators who neglected to keep in touch with their public.

Not only did the administrators not keep in touch themselves, they were not even prepared to use the information made available to them by the social scientists. In fact, they seemed to resent it; because it so often exposed the half-truths and vague generalizations they had built up over a lifetime. They understood the *indaba* far better than the public opinion poll.

A certain official, one of the most important in the land, seeking an answer to the drift to the towns that he could not control, and the alleged degeneration of Africans in the towns said, 'It is the bright lights of the cities that draw them We have to reproduce these bright lights in the rural areas, more mobile cinema-vans, more dance-bands.'

If he had ever come out of his residence in the evenings and walked through the unlit compounds, silent after the nine p.m. curfew, or attended the once-weekly showing of cowboy films or the occasional dance held in the light of a few paraffin-lamps, he would never have said this.

The day after his remarks had been reported in the local press I happened to go to the Rhodes-Livingstone Institute for Social and Economic Research to use their library. There I came across one of their senior researchmen, 'Hallo,' I said, 'have you started to measure the candle-power of city-lights yet?'

I had obviously started something, 'Have you seen it?' he shouted, 'Have you seen it? Fellows like that shouldn't be allowed to live. Do you know that years of research have been done into this sort of problem, at the cost of thousands of pounds to the government? And now he comes out with this balderdash. The calorie-intake of an African here at Lusaka is over twice as much as that of a Bemba villager. Over twice as much, though God knows even here they don't always get a square meal towards the end of the month. The main reason for leaving the villages is that there just isn't enough to eat. Starvation, plain and simple starvation. Bright lights, my foot! If only those bloody fools in the Secretariat would read the stuff they wouldn't talk such bullshit.'

'You can't tell me that he really hasn't read it,' I interposed.

'I know he hasn't. He never does. When he got one of our recent publications—and a damn' good paper it was too, reviewers all over the world said so—he gave it to one of his juniors and said, "Condense it. Not more than two sentences, please." Can you beat it? And such people rule the country . . .'

I had never seen this particular social scientist so devoid of academic detachment, but I could sympathize with him.

Some of the Africans who flock into the towns in search of higher standards of living do live vicariously the adventures of the heroes of Westerns. Others drug themselves against the buffetings of a difficult and unfamiliar world, with beer. But a large number seek a bright light in their vision of the World to Come.

One of these was Amon Chapusha. He was born in the Lenje tribal area, not very far from Lusaka. He had only two years of primary schooling in a mud-and-thatch school-room in a village, four or five miles from his own. He learnt to read Lenje and to write barely legible letters in it, but his parents did not see much point in any further schooling. As a handsome little boy of ten he started to work for a poor Afrikaans farmer, some thirty miles from his home village, as a nurse-boy for the baby. 'I wanted to earn money. In some seasons there was very little food in our village, and I wanted to have proper clothes.' One day the farmer, his family and the nurse-boy set out to drive to town in their old jalopy. On their way they had a puncture. The farmer accepted a lift into town for himself and his family, but left young Amon to guard the vegetables and pigs in the back of the car. The boy had long watched his master driving. Nobody had explained the controls of a car to him, but he had invented his own names for them, the clutch for instance became 'I-kick-you-Go-faster'. Left to himself for most of the day, Amon started to experiment.

When the master returned in the evening he found the car several miles from where he had abandoned it. The punctured tyre was probably ruined. Amon was taken and beaten severely and promised further beatings the following day. That night he ran away to an English farmer near by, a retired civil servant, who was known to have a hearty contempt for the poor-white Afrikaner. The Englishman was shocked by the condition of the boy and drove him to the police-station in town to lay a charge. Amon's master was fined ten pounds. The Englishman then took on Amon as 'kitchen-boy', to peel potatoes and to chop firewood. He was a kindly old man and Amon stayed with him for several years. He got advancement from 'kitchen-boy' to 'house-boy', cleaning rooms and serving at table. Then he decided to seek his fortune in town. 'Money was very little on these farms. I got fifteen shillings and food per month. Also, I was bored.' He came to Lusaka and got employment with my parents, first as a 'house-boy', then as a cook.

He was a variable employee. If there was anything new and interesting to do, like preparing a dish he had never tried before or repairing the plumbing, he was enthusiastic and enterprising. Routine work he found boring and did indifferently. His efficiency as a worker was low. It took two full-time servants to look after our two bedroom house. A third one came in occasionally to help with the garden. This is in keeping with a Central African tradition which is only dying slowly. Larger households have as many as five servants.

Amon married, but his wife soon gave him grounds for suspicion. He tried to divorce her, but this was difficult because she was the daughter of a minor chief. I suspect his own marital record was not as clean as he claimed. His life made him listless and discontented. He did not know what to do with his spare time, there were no channels for his talents. He had no ambition to excel at tribal dancing or beer-drinking because they were 'uncivilized'. He spent his afternoons gossiping aimlessly in his compound. Most of the time he was in financial difficulties, settling old debts by means of new loans. Once he bought an English primer and tried to learn English. During my vacations from boarding-school I helped him, during my absences he lost interest. But he had a restless, inquiring mind and started to ask awkward questions:

'If we were all created in God's image, why are some of us black and some white? What colour is God? If God really loved the world why did He create some to enjoy life and some to suffer?' One day he surprised me, 'This story about Adam and Eve and the snake and the apple, I think the Bible is speaking in riddles, like our old people. What it really means is that Adam had discovered how sweet women were. What do you think?'

These questions, I soon discovered, were the fruit of lengthy theological speculation and controversy that he was overhearing in his compound. The lay-preachers of the 'society' on their house to house visits were causing a great ferment of odd theological ideas. I asked what this society was,

'*The* society. There is only one, the Watchtower and Bible Society, or Jehovah's Witnesses,' he explained.

This is a movement of American origin, pacifist and fundamentalist, who predict that the end of the world is near, and consider it their duty to limit very strictly the regard that is due to Caesar. In Central Africa during the war, they were persecuted as pacifists and for some years virtually deprived of white guidance. Thus they alone of all the Christian sects were not tainted by identification with the white 'establishment' and they grew to enormous proportions, drawing on the latent organizing ability of humble, simple Africans, until they had become the biggest single denomination in Northern Rhodesia.

Their message appealed to Amon. They had all the certainty of belief that his ancestors must have had before the coming of the disruptive Europeans. Amon bought a Nyanja Bible and started to read that language. Almost all his spare time he pored over it, in the kitchen, in the garden under the bananas, in his little round mud-hut in his lower-class compound. Soon he accompanied the lay-preachers on their afternoon rounds. He and one of his friends, Blackwell, started to work on me, too. In self-defence I had to read my Bible carefully, but once I had accepted the Bible as our premise, they usually got the better of me. In the end I had to deny belief in the Divine dictation of every single biblical phrase. This brought the prophetic wrath of both Amon and Blackwell upon my head. It was no wonder, they said, that my Israelite ancestors had been cursed by God if they were all as stiff-necked as I.

Blackwell had a prodigious memory. Although he too was barely literate, he knew his Bible so well that he could answer questions like 'Matthew two, verse twelve, what does it say?' 'Judges three, verse eight?' Alas, not many months after I had met him, Blackwell was purged for deviationism. He had persuaded another member of the society that the Bible demanded that he share his wife, 'We must love one another and share each other's worldly possessions. . . .'

Amon, however, remained true to the society and became a lay preacher and a member of its excellent choir. There was no priestly hierarchy to hinder the progress of a humble, uneducated man. His former listless gossiping had been transformed into preaching with an urgent purpose, to prepare all men for the impending Armageddon. It took up most of his spare time. His ability came to be recognized. He was happier than I had ever known him.

One evening some African policemen arrested him for being out a few minutes after nine p.m. without a 'night-pass'. They bullied him and made him sit up all night. When I fetched him from the charge-office next morning, he looked grey and humiliated but only said 'God sees it all'.

He was quite absorbed in his religious activity, recapturing some of the fervour of the early Christians. But he found the irregular hours of a domestic servant interfered with his preaching and he had ambitions. He asked to be transferred to my family's dry-cleaning business. There he immediately made himself useful by repairing the electrical equipment and delivery-bicycles that had previously been sent out for repairs. He was soon a sort of foreman.

Some years later my father disposed of the business. Amon had by then been with us twelve years. We arranged a new job for him, but he turned it down to start a dry-cleaning business of his own. Working from the little round hut in his lower-class compound he developed a flourishing business among Africans and some Europeans. He expanded and employed several younger relatives. They worked on tables in the open and there was some talk of the municipality building a proper workshop for him. Occasionally he called on my father to consult him about the purchase of chemicals. On these occasions he would always some-how contrive to search his pockets for a pencil or a notebook and in doing so would manage to pull out a thick wad of five-pound notes, symbols of his success.

Sometimes he came to see me at Broadcasting House. He was vaguely amused that his little *bwana* Peter should now be a civil servant and have several smartly-dressed 'clerks' to do his bidding, but it did not intimidate him at all.

'You do very wrong in the sight of God, *bwana* Peter, by broadcasting church-services.'

'Why?'

'It is written "Thou shalt give praises to the Lord".'

'Well?'

'It does not say "Thou shalt listen to someone else giving praises". It does not say "Thou shalt let the wireless do the praising for you". No, we must lift up our own voices. You do very wrong to do it for us.'

On another occasion he came up with a choir of Watchtowermen to record for us. Hymns, not complete services. A phalanx of young cyclists, many of them on gadget-studded bicycles, rode up to our converted tin-hut studio.

'Society!' called one, like a military command, and they all braked suddenly. 'Dismount!' called another. 'Best choir in Africa!' called a third. Then they laughed and trooped into our studio. Amon kept a little apart. They were rather younger and more boisterous than he. They sang a number of beautiful hymns, some of them composed by members of the choir. Afterwards I chatted to Amon.

'How's business these days?'

'I have been flying,' he replied.

I did not catch on, 'Flying?'

'Yes, last week I flew to Kariba in a Viking aeroplane.'

'Have you opened a branch there?'

'No, just to see. I've never flown before so I wanted to try it.'

Then I understood. 'My, my, my!' I said loudly, so that the onlookers should hear it. 'You must have masses of money.'

He smiled happily.

Some months later I wanted to ask his advice about an idea I had for some broadcasts. He was a useful contact, so different from my sophisticated African colleagues. He had moved from his one-room *rondavel* to a larger hut. They gave me the number. I left my car and walked for some time along unmade roads amidst concrete-block houses with corrugated asbestos roofs. In the end I found his. It was one of the larger type, with four or five little rooms. Outside it was a sign-board he had probably painted himself which showed up his mere two years of education:

'AMON CHAPUSHA. SAME-DAY LANDULE & DRY CLEANERS.'

The last few letters had been squeezed in clumsily. Amon was not there, nor were his employees, his wife nor his children. A neighbour came up,

'He has gone. He has lost all his money.'

'Good Lord, how?' I asked, but I might have predicted it.

'One of his employees, his nephew, ran off with all the clothes for cleaning and Mr Chapusha had to pay up. He didn't have enough money to pay everybody so he ran away. I think he is fed-up and has gone back to his village.'

I walked back to my car sadly. The new African entrepreneur! Why the hell does he have to employ relatives? But . . . he will be back. Next time he will know better.

I remember he once said to me, 'After Adam had eaten of the apple he saw that he was naked. And after you Europeans came to teach us new things we also came to see that we were naked. And now we're ashamed we were so ignorant before.'

I

He has eaten a little of the Fruit of the Tree of the Knowledge of Good and Evil. How much longer will his questions be confined entirely to the World to Come? How long until he starts to question the nine p.m. curfew?

Others of the 'New Africans' feel that they have tried Christianity and found it wanting. One such is Kenneth Kaunda, the secretary of the African National Congress, a man who has a reputation for fanaticism and, a much rarer one, for financial honesty. He had been at school at Lubwa mission, where the prophetess Lenshina later arose. There he had been an intensely religious youth. Once when he was reading the lesson and came to a particularly beautiful Bible passage he was so moved that he started to cry and to shake all over and could not continue.

Today all his fervour goes into the cause of African nationalism.

I met Kaunda one evening at the Kabulonga Club. This club was started by Harry Franklin, the former Director of Information, the man behind the Saucepan Special Radio, to provide a place where people of different races could meet. It was the first of its sort in that part of Africa. I had looked forward to meeting Kaunda. I had hoped to get his views on the prophetess Lenshina, especially since I had heard that his brother was one of her lieutenants. I wondered why Lubwa mission had produced so many dissidents. However, when I put this to Kaunda he was uncommunicative. It was not easy to make conversation with him. He was a taciturn, embittered young man, one of those who 'see nothing save their own unlovely woes'. He shrugged off Lenshina.

'You went to Lubwa mission yourself, didn't you?'

'Yes,' he replied, 'my father was a preacher there.'

'But Kaunda is a Nyasaland name?'

'Yes.'

'How did your family get to Bemba country?' I pressed.

'My father came from the north of Nyasaland with the Scottish mission.'

I kept at it, 'Long ago?'

'He helped to start the mission.'

'And you went to school there?'

'Yes. I was a very troublesome youth.'

'I'm sure you were!'

'I would insist on asking awkward questions.'

'Questions like what?'

'Like why the European missionaries had padded seats in church, but my father who had been working for the mission for longer than most of them had to sit on a wooden bench like the rest of the African congregation. I demanded to know whether it would be the same in their heaven!'

Kaunda laughed briefly and relapsed into silence.

Yet generations of kindly missionaries have retired from Lubwa and gone back to Scotland convinced that they have sacrificed a lifetime's labour and lived in poverty to convert and raise up the heathen. They have forgotten about the padded seats.

Partial acceptance is not enough.

'We must create an African middle-class,' say some of the Europeans, mainly among the industrialists and businessmen of Southern Rhodesia, 'a middle-class who will have property and a stake in the country and will avoid dangerous experiments because they will have something to lose.'

This is a very much more valid suggestion than that of those hidebound administrators in the North who dream of preserving noble rustic savages unspoilt by the brightly-lit Babylons. To create a middle-class does seem a way of fusing Africans with Western civilization in a gradual and orderly manner. But it seems to me to depend on those padded seats, on whether the African property-owners will be absorbed into the European middle-class as complete equals—equal in political participation and social status—or whether they are to be bought off with some economic advance only. At present very few of the exponents of the middle-class theory are prepared to go as far as the Romans did and to give full participation. Their constitutional devices are always designed to give only strictly limited political participation to 'respectable middle-class Africans' and they deny them social equality. Everywhere there are escape-clauses; even if all Africans were to become respectable, well-educated, propertied people, they must never dominate us. For example, the Southern Rhodesian Minister of Internal Affairs and Justice, explaining the Federal constitution when it was discussed in 1953, said that it clearly contemplated that there would be a European majority in the House, and that it seemed it could be altered as circumstances required to ensure that the position was not reached where Africans had a majority in the House at any time. Such constitutions do not seem to me the ideal way to produce a contented and conservative stratum, on the contrary. In other lands and times middle-classes have never been satisfied with property alone. They have seldom hesitated to risk their property to gain political and social power. Economic gains, clothes and cars and houses, are not enough. The African Congress have a song about it composed by none other than Kenneth Kaunda.

> 'Others cry out for smart berets,
> we cry for our country.
> Others cry out for suits.
> We cry for the iron in our soil.
> Our wealth has been taken from us.
> Alas, our iron.
> Mothers, cease your weeping.
> Fathers, do not cry.
> I ask, "what are you going to do about it?"'

In the nineteen-fifties in Northern Rhodesia, Africans with university degrees equivalent to those of Europeans started to come on to the labour market. Had they been given the same salaries and titles as their European colleagues it would have given them authority over some junior Europeans. This would have demanded some unwelcome adjustment of attitude from the Europeans. To avoid unpleasantness, the government created special titles and slightly lower salaries for the Africans. In the Education Department they became 'assistant masters' though their duties were the same as those of 'masters'.

It did not make for conservative, moderate men. They seethed with impotent, anarchic fury. How often the powers-that-be spoiled the ship of state for a ha'porth of tar. There are some who cry out for suits, but others cry for self-respect and real status in the land of their fathers.

Even if white Rhodesians were to succeed in selling their brand of partial acceptance to middle-class Africans, even if they could supply genuine padded seats for those who make the grade, it would still not satisfy those who have not made the grade and would get no seats at all. In present-day Central Africa they are the great majority.

Those who extol the 'Roman solution' forget that it was never very adequate in its time, the Romans had plenty of trouble with their subject peoples. The spurned and rejected have a need for self-assertion as powerful as that of their 'betters'. At the moment much of the suppressed emotional energy of the rejected still goes into religious movements. The Amons feel that in heaven all will have padded seats, for God will accept them, even if Europeans do not.

I decided that if one day Amon's need for acceptance and status drove him to search for solutions other than those provided by the Watchtower, he would probably sooner or later turn up at my house and ply me with questions and discuss the matter with me. But I had to make a disconcerting admission to myself; hardly any of the acquaintanceships I had made as an adult with better-educated and more intelligent Africans had this intimacy and frankness. Few of my newer African friends could ever quite forget that I was a civil servant. Only rarely, when they were drunk, would they speak really freely. There was much, I felt, that they would not normally tell me. And there was so much in their behaviour that I could not understand, whereas I might have if they had been Europeans. I felt that my usefulness as a broadcaster was limited by the shallowness of my understanding. If I did not look out, I too would become as remote from the problems of the day as the men in the Secretariat. One day I would wake up, like Rip van Winkle, and find myself in a strange land whose ways I could not understand.

Some of my European friends tried to console me, 'Seeing the danger is half the answer,' they would say. An American sociologist working on the Copperbelt said: 'Do you realize that thousands of Africans up here feel that the Europeans with whom they have most contact, the ones they know and trust best, are the four or five of you who broadcast regularly from Lusaka?' It did not console, it worried me all the more. Was the gulf between Europeans and Africans so great that we who talked to Africans from hundreds of miles away seemed closer to them than all the Europeans they saw in the flesh? This lack of contact between Europeans and Africans, between myself and my audience, was

becoming something of an obsession with me. I knew that change
in Central Africa comes so rapidly that it takes very little time to
be entirely out of date.

A mere year after my African colleagues were in fits of laughter
over Godwin Lewanika's tribal dress, Congress-secretary Kenneth
Kaunda led a demonstration in Lusaka dressed only in a loin-cloth
and carrying an old man's staff, and nobody even smiled!

I could not help thinking of Jomo Kenyatta in his leopard-skin
and spear, and of the Mau Mau. How long would it be until the
despised and rejected of Central Africa also tried to escape from
what they thought an intolerable present and tried to revive the
past? How long until they turned back to the witchdoctors and
human sacrifices? How much time did we have to save our land
from such affliction?

Kaunda's garb did not catch on. His chief, Congress-president
Harry Nkumbula, continued to wear the blazer of the London
School of Economics, but the incident showed me once again how
quickly climates of opinion could change.

The Africans seemed to me to be hovering in the balance
between the loin-cloth and the LSE blazer. Which would they
choose?

There was danger in moving in too limited a circle. I had to
break out of my circle of friends and colleagues and regular contributors. I had to make a more conscious effort to keep in step.[1]

---

[1] From time to time individual abuses are reformed. While this book
was being written the 9 pm curfew was suspended and a few African
graduates promoted to 'European' posts. But such reforms only come
after long agitation which leaves its residue of bitterness.

8. KEEPING IN STEP

I PLUNGED into the problems of listener research.

Our organization had been expanding. When I arrived our programme-staff had consisted of three Europeans and twelve Africans. Three years later it had more than doubled in size. Our programme hours had trebled and our audience had expanded even more rapidly. In 1950 there had been no more than five thousand sets owned by Africans. By 1954 the figure was over six times as large. The manufacturers of the Saucepan Special were getting competition from four or five other firms, some of them the very firms who had originally refused to manufacture such a set. Wireless receivers were even being built in Southern Rhodesia. The Legislative Council voted us money for large new studios, and the architects and surveyors were busy measuring up the open ground behind our studios.

At this point Sapper, who had long been second-in-charge, left the CABS temporarily and I took over most of his duties. He had done some listener-research as a side-line, in between writing radio plays, leading a band, arranging advance programme schedules and announcing!

Listener research was a duty that I took over with the greatest of enthusiasm. It suited my need for wider contacts, for getting to grips with our audience. Kittermaster agreed that it needed to be expanded greatly. We were spending increasing amounts of money on programmes without knowing very much about their effects on our listeners. He lightened my other duties as much as our staff, still far too small, permitted and I set to work. My basic training was confined to a few weeks' course in statistics some years before, but fortunately the Rhodes-Livingstone Institute had a library and a staff who could be persuaded to help.

First I pored over our old files to learn from our previous experience. In the beginning, when Saucepan Special sets had first come on to the market, repeated appeals had been broadcast asking the new owners to send in their names and addresses. Almost all of them had done so, as we could check by comparing the wholesalers' figures with our own. In those days radio owners thought of themselves as an elite group, almost as an exclusive club. They considered it their right to have their names entered in the books of the broadcasting station and to have their greetings and messages to friends broadcast in the request programmes. It had been easy to keep in touch with them and to get answers of a sort to questionnaires sent out by post.

Some of the early questionnaires had yielded results which were instructive in more ways than one; an attempt was made for example, to determine the musical taste of listeners. Questionnaires were sent listing the names and performers of twenty-eight records of various types which were going to be played in a series of special programmes called 'Do you like these songs?' Listeners were asked to tick all the ones they had enjoyed. The selection ranged from European light classical via American cowboy and African jive to traditional African music. Among the records there had been one made by Sapper, who was an accomplished pianist and a former band-leader. It was a sophisticated piano-variation on some African themes.

When the results came in they tallied closely with what Kittermaster and Sapper had expected, except for one remarkable difference. Sapper's slick piece unexpectedly tied for top place with another. Alas, in the four or five years that had elapsed since that inquiry thousands of records had been asked for in our daily request-programmes, but that record of Sapper's was not among them . . . not once!

It was only too obvious that the questionnaires produced answers carefully calculated to 'please the *bwanas*'. Our files were full of evidence along these lines. M. G. Marwick, a social anthropologist working among the Chewa tribe, found much the same problem in a house-to-house poll of public opinion. He had to report failure:

'White-African relationships are essentially authoritarian, a condition that militates against effective public opinion polling by a white or white-sponsored interviewer. The informant tends to give an accommodating anything-to-please response whenever he can.'

The problem is not unique. Even in so poll-conscious a country as the USA it has been found that in certain situations interviewees tend to modify their response to accommodate inter-viewers associated with the upper class or race.

It seemed to me that we should drop investigations into tastes and opinions of listeners and concentrate on what they actually remembered of broadcasts and what they understood. Sapper had made some attempts to do this in postal questionnaires, but in each case far fewer forms than usual had been returned. It seemed that it could only be done if we interviewed our listeners face to face.

The problem of not getting true answers was not the only one apparent among the material on our files. A new one was arising rapidly. By 1954 radio ownership was no longer confined to the fairly homogeneous elite of clerks and teachers. Even our postal questionnaires were showing that over a third of those who had written in were artisans or labourers. Wireless ownership was spreading rapidly down the social pyramid. It coincided with the increasing industrialization of Central Africa and the rapid in-creases in African incomes. Radio was becoming a 'must', a coveted symbol of status among a wide range of people.

'Wireless is good,' said a domestic servant interviewed at Lusaka, 'it makes the house smart. When you have a wireless you are just like an educated man.'

People like this domestic servant were much less likely to write and report their purchases to us than better-educated owners. Illiterates and semi-literates probably made up a much larger proportion of our audience than the questionnaires showed.

Already in 1950 Kittermaster had made an attempt to overcome this by starting listeners' clubs whose duty it was to gather the comments of all strata of society and to report them to Lusaka. But the results sounded unreliable and it required far more time to encourage and organize the work of these clubs than could be spared. After some months he had allowed them to fade away.

But the problem had to be faced. There was a serious danger in tailoring our programmes exclusively to the tastes of the literate minority. The BBC transmit three simultaneous programmes designed to cope with the tastes of different strata of the people of Britain, yet how much more homogeneous their audience is, than ours. While I was going through our files, not ten miles away there were young men studying to be witchdoctors, learning spells

in archaic tongues and how to consult oracles and anoint amulets
with the blood of sacrificial chickens; and not so far from them
there were young Africans in blazers discussing Elizabethan
drama and making experiments in laboratories. We had to keep
step, not with a troop marching together, but with numerous
clusters of people moving at different paces and in different direc-
tions, who could not be expected to have the same tastes.

The stratification of musical tastes was neatly illustrated one
day by the experiences of Noah Matongo, the first African graduate on our staff. He observed how the young girl who announced
and compiled the Tonga request programme was working through
a pile of several hundred letters in front of her. Since she could
only play about a dozen requests, she rapidly selected a handful
of letters that were neatly written or typed and ignored those more
difficult to decipher.

'That's not right,' said Matongo. 'Look at these poor devils
who're barely literate. They're the ones you should give prefer-
ence to. They've made a real effort.'

From her pile he selected a handful of almost illegible letters
and together they deciphered the requests. That day the Tonga
request-programme had an entirely different character, so different that I, who was on monitoring duty, made inquiries the following day to find out what had happened. Instead of the usual
preponderance of 'town-music' and American hill-billy tunes, the
programme consisted entirely of tribal music. After that we reorganized the selection of requests.

I tried to keep in mind these problems when I started my own
investigations. I decided to tackle a problem that had long been
worrying us, whether the efforts we were expending on simple
English programmes were worthwhile, or whether the time would
be more usefully employed on vernacular broadcasts.

First I had to work out what would be a representative sample
of the population. If among those interviewed there had been,
for example, too many members of the Yao tribe, who are Muslim
and seldom go to Christian schools, our results might have shown
too low a proportion of listeners to English. Unfortunately there
was hardly any basic information available about the composition
of the population of Central Africa. Since there has never been a
complete census, nobody could tell me for example, how many

males between 16 and 21, speaking Tonga with Standard VI education there were in the country. The only information available was for some of the towns of Northern Rhodesia. This has been gathered by the research-workers of the Rhodes-Livingstone Institute. However, they had not touched the villages, nor Southern Rhodesia nor Nyasaland.

I decided to start with one town, keeping in mind that no generalizations for the whole of the Rhodesias and Nyasaland could be made from the results. Lusaka was the obvious one to start with, but I hoped that later we might get some money to recruit interviewers and send them to other towns.

Since we had no full-time interviewers it had to be done on the smallest scale possible. Fortunately investigations in the USA have shown that the use of even very small samples, provided they are carefully selected, can give surprisingly accurate results. Cantril and his associates have proved that with no more than two hundred interviews they could predict election-results for the State of New York or for the whole of Canada with errors averaging no more than five per cent.

Of course larger samples do give more reliable results, but beggars can't be choosers. I worked out a sample of two hundred, representative of the whole town with respect to education, age, tribal group, residential suburb and sex.

Noah Matongo volunteered to do the interviewing, so we took him off other duties for a few weeks. First he and I discussed the approach to interviewees. We knew that we would have to overcome fear and suspicion made worse by rumours, not unfounded, that a radio licence-fee would shortly be imposed in Northern Rhodesia. We therefore decided that interviews would have to be quite informal, as much like natural conversations as possible. Matongo would make no notes in the presence of the interviewees. Then we thought up a number of approaches to steer conversation around to the questions we wanted answered. Among these were whether the interviewee owned a wireless set, if not, whether he listened elsewhere and where, what his mother-language was and so on.

We bought a radio-battery and Matongo tried to sell it to selected interviewees.

'It's probably flat,' most of them said.

'Try it out,' replied Matongo, 'have you got a set?'

'No, I listen at my brother's.'

'Why not buy one? You can start with the battery. They broadcast programmes in just about every language. What's yours?'

This answered three of our questions and started a conversation that could normally be steered around to English broadcasts and what the interviewee remembered of them.

In other cases, when the interviewee looked as if he might be illiterate, which was one of the things we needed to know, Matongo handed him a slip of paper on which he had previously written an imaginary name and asked for help in finding this person as he, Matongo, unfortunately could not read. In almost every instance interviewees then wanted to know why Matongo wanted to see this person. He would reply:

'I hear he has a wireless for sale. Do you know anyone here who has? Have you?'

'No. Do you want it for yourself?'

'Yes, to learn English. Do you think it's possible? Do you listen to English broadcasts yourself?'

So long as an interviewer takes care not to influence his victim, this informal approach has a great advantage, very few refusals. Only once or twice did Matongo have to beat a hasty retreat after being accused of being a police-spy. A handful of people broke off the interview when they realized they were being questioned. One said, 'I have lived in town so long, I cannot be cheated by anyone!'

One of Matongo's toughest assignments was to get his quota of interviews in an area of speakeasies where there were regular police-raids and the brewers of illicit concoctions were ever on the look-out for detectives and informers. Matongo demanded an 'entertainment allowance'. When he turned up at the office next morning he looked as if he was really suffering in the cause of science!

The results of this survey showed, among other things that almost ninety per cent of the interviewees had occasional access to a wireless-set. Twenty five per cent could quote examples of the contents of English programmes and we were very satisfied with that.

To be really useful this pilot-investigation should then have been repeated in other towns and, in amended form, in villages, but there was no money, no personnel, no time. Matongo had to go back to programme production.

Instead, I concentrated on a number of small-scale investigations into the comprehensibility of broadcasts. For such investigations it did not seem so necessary to work with representative samples.

Some years before I had done a pilot-investigation into recall and comprehension. This had been with a self-selected group of listeners. Several welfare officers helped and on the selected evening they dropped in at the listening-rooms at their welfare-halls in various suburbs of Lusaka. As they often called in there, it aroused no suspicion. The crowd that had assembled to listen to dance music thinned out as a background to the news talk was announced. The talk dealt with the Mau Mau rising in Kenya, then at its height. After the talk was finished the welfare officers switched off the radios and asked for the collaboration of all those present. To the literates they handed questionnaires that I had prepared. The illiterates were interviewed by some helpers.

I had set a 'new-type' questionnaire, that is, one that only requires the ticking of 'Yes', 'No' or 'Doubtful'. When I analysed the replies I found that only a very small proportion of listeners had a proper grasp of what had been broadcast and that these few were all people with at least six years of schooling. Listeners with less education missed even the points that had been hammered repeatedly and put very simply. The distortions were interesting. For example, although the talk emphasized that most of the victims of Mau Mau attacks had been Africans, a number of listeners claimed to have heard that more Europeans than Africans had been killed. It seemed like wishful thinking!

We decided to strive for even greater simplicity.

Again, such distortions are not unique. In many parts of the world investigators testing the recall of election-speeches among supporters of different parties have shown that there was a strong tendency to forget the material that did not harmonize with the interviewee's own preconceived notions.

However, I was disturbed to find an unexpected fault in my

methods. When in doubt our listeners tended to tick—not 'Doubtful'—but 'Yes'. This is a common form of behaviour among
Africans. They teach their children to say 'Yes' to please and to
avoid trouble. The Yes-No-Doubtful questionnaires had to be
dropped. It was a pity: they were so easy to administer even with
almost untrained interviewers.

I now cast around for other techniques to find answers to the
questions Are we understood? What misunderstandings occur?
What are the items most difficult to assimilate? Why?

On the whole vast continent of Africa no one was doing any
research of this sort. Various governments and Colonial Offices
were now starting to pour tens of thousands of pounds into new
transmitters and studios, but nobody thought it worthwhile to
spend a penny finding out what was understood. The few pounds
that I was using had to be fiddled under 'Spares for Transmitters'
or 'Payments to Artists', so our methods had to be very economical.

I decided to adapt the brain-storming techniques used by
some advertising research workers. I invited selected groups of
Africans—never more than six—to the studios and asked them to
listen to a radio-feature or play. Then I arranged them around a
microphone of a tape-recorder and—over tea and cigarettes—asked
them to re-tell the story of the broadcast, one listener saying only
one or two sentences at a time. The next was then to continue
with one or two more sentences and so on, around the circle.

I tested certain programmes 'to breaking-point' to discover
below which standard of education listeners could no longer make
head or tail of them. My main interest, however, lay in the nature
of the misunderstandings and distortions that occurred.

I started on some English programmes designed for the 'intelligentsia', that is, for listeners with some eight or nine years of
schooling. They were part of a series of broadcasts I had written
after a request by the African Representative Council. This body
is composed of representatives of tribal councils and urban
advisory councils and then acted as an electoral college for African
MPs. The council had asked that the broadcasting station should
'do something to explain to us about different kinds of government, especially about communism, why it is bad.' We decided
to do a series of very simple radio-plays dealing with political
institutions. There was an African to ask questions and a narrator

who unravelled the mysteries of constitutional history by intro-
ducing a number of dramatized inserts. I started, not with the
Greek city states, but with African tribal councils at which every
adult may speak, moved on to the more centralized tyrannies of
the Zulu and the Ndebele, then switched to the Britain of the
Tudors and Stuarts and the way parliament came to be dominant,
and how the franchise was gradually extended as education
became more widespread. Several of the latter plays dealt with the
new tyrannies, the Fascists and Communists. I tried to show how
only an educated and wideawake electorate could preserve its
liberties and finally, how local and tribal government in Africa
was the training-ground for proper democracy.

One of the programmes I tested dealt with Communist col-
lectivization. It was a radio-play about a family of East German
farm labourers, the Bauers, who in the beginning are given a farm
as a result of Communist land reforms. A state-inspector, Mr
Bonze, then tries to persuade them to join a collective. When they
refuse they are subjected to pressure by compulsory state deliveries and low prices, but rather than join a collective they abandon
their homes, dodge border patrols and flee to West Germany.
The play was based on the experiences of people I had spoken
to when on vacation in West Berlin.

The rural background and perhaps, the pestering by government officials were familiar to my audience and the programme
was understood even among listeners who were educationally well
below the intended target standard. However, I continued to test
it on groups of still lower education to see the 'points of failure'.

I noticed how in every session the listeners got intense amusement out of a subterfuge of the Bauers. They sold their cattle on
the pretext of raising money to pay a fine imposed on them for not
fulfilling their state deliveries, then took the money and fled to the
West. This, rather than the flight and pursuit, appeared to many
listeners to be the highlight of the programme. Presumably we
were getting close to the pattern of so many Central African
legends whose hero Kalulu, the clever hare, is a master of successful deceit. Ulysses and Jacob had nothing on Kalulu.

There were some misunderstandings in connection with the
European convention of drinking to the health of people or institutions. In the programme the Bauers raised their glasses twice.

After the Communist land-reforms they drink 'to our Communist government which gives land to the poor', and after their flight to the West they drink 'to the democratic West and down with the Communists'.

This caused some confusion. In one session with a group of low education, well below that of the intended target audience, one listener associated the toasts and the altercations between government inspector and peasants over compulsory delivery of crops in the following way,

> 'The government was send inspector to see the farms because that people living on the farms cannot ploughing good, just going away to drink beer. No anything to plant in the garden (fields) just drinking beer.'

The listener's perception was apparently coloured by his previous knowledge of the problem which agricultural officers in Central Africa often have to face!

When I asked what had been the status of the Bauer family before the Communist land reforms (they had been farm-labourers) the same group were unable to reply until one member suggested, 'They were slaves.' This received the immediate assent of all the others. In Rhodesia in the old days only slaves had no land of their own. A landless freeman was unthinkable.

After each session I invited subjects to ask any questions they liked. One incredulous listener wanted me to confirm that Communist governments really did not permit people to own shops and tea-rooms of their own.

'What about if I pay tax?' (ie licence).

When I confirmed what the programme had said he demanded:

'I want to know why people are like that. Are they not educated?'

Education! Africa's cure-all!

During these free-for-alls the conversation repeatedly came around to Hungary where at that time, the Russians were crushing the revolution. I was surprised that even among groups with very little education everybody had followed the events in Hungary and expressed great sympathy with the people there.

A few years ago such Africans were still cut off from all contact with the outside world. Their sympathy would not have been

Godwin Mbikusita Lewanika
on the river Zambezi with
tribal drum . . .

By the river Thames with
Commonwealth parliamentarians

Knitting lesson in Barotseland: 'Encourage, never bully'

extended to anyone outside their own family or clan or, at the most, their tribe. Even now there were hundreds of thousands of villagers who will not listen to any music that does not come from within a few miles' radius of their homes. Beyond that all is 'rubbish—not fit for human beings'. But not these new townsmen; their range of identification could extend to the sufferings of people thousands of miles away whose country they had first heard of only a few short weeks before.

Truly, the turning of the dials was producing a revolution!

9. IMPACT

WE WERE making an impact and we ourselves were getting a much clearer idea of what the function of broadcasting in Africa should be, a bridge between the new and the old, the means of helping Africans to make an informed adjustment to the new society. An increasing number of our programmes came to be planned consciously to serve these ends.

How lucky we are, we kept saying to each other, that our audience make no resistance to being taught, so long as we did not talk down to them. We had no need for any 'do good by stealth' programmes such as those of European and American stations. Our audience considered it great praise when they called the radio the 'great teacher'. True, their protestations were often no more than passing lip-service to the tribal ideal of acquiring wisdom, but there was certainly no stigma attached to being taught. There was much that our audience demanded to learn and to know.

We ran numerous Brains Trusts and Questions and Answers programmes to deal with their questions, trying various shapes and forms to make them snappy and easy to listen to. The letters we received for those programmes give some insight into the gropings of the newly-literate for a Weltanschauung to replace that destroyed by the coming of the Europeans. I quote some below. In their original form these questions often had a vigour of phrasing which was, unfortunately, lost in editing them into the plainer English in which they were broadcast. The largest part of the questions was religious, followed by political and racial problems:

'Why in the beginning did God say "Let Us make a man" instead of "Let Me make a man"? Who was with Him?'

'Scientists tell us that man's origin is the ape. The Bible says his origin was Adam. Which is right?'

'If the missionaries had not come to teach us how to worship God, would none of the people of Africa have been able to enter the Kingdom of Heaven?'

'If God can do anything, why does He not broadcast so that we can hear His voice and know how He wants us to live?'

'Why are there so many religious denominations when there is only one God?'

'If a murderer is punished by a court of law is he then free from God's punishment?'

'Is there any proof at all to show that missionaries are not just as good businessmen as any storekeeper, and is not the present racial strife in Central Africa the fruit of their work?'

(Even the frugality of the life of missionaries seems like great wealth to most Africans. Many resent the missionaries as the advance-guard of the conquerors and settlers which unintentionally, they often were.)

'Why are some countries more civilized than others? Which was the first country to be civilized? In which continent is it?'

'Why are Africans not allowed to buy whisky and brandy? If they are bad, are they not equally bad for Europeans? Are our stomachs made differently?'

'Why is there a difference between Africans and Europeans in that Europeans are punctual at work whereas Africans are not? Is it because Europeans have a higher standard of education?'

'Why is an African who takes a European woman punished, yet there are Europeans who take African women?'

'How is it that horses can breed with donkeys?'

(This was one of those questions with a hidden implication which came into the open after discussion with our African colleagues. The offspring of such a union the mule, is imperfect in that it cannot procreate. This happens because horses and donkeys are of different species. However, a union between a European and an African produces offspring who are perfectly able to have children. Ergo, we are all of one species. Then why treat us differently and why not let us breed freely?)

'Why do European shop-girls call an African "boy" even if he is a grown-up and well-educated man?'

(There was seldom a week without this question.)

'Why is it that in some shops Africans are not allowed inside to see the goods but are served through a hatch? If we are dirty, is not our money also dirty?'

'Why are our African politicians not made ministers of the government?'

'Are chiefs necessary for African advancement nowadays?

Would we not advance more quickly if educated people took their place?'

'What is the difference between the Labour Party and the Conservative Party in England and which makes the better government?'

'What is meant by Industrial Revolution? Is it a good thing for human beings?'

'Why must the government collect taxes? Can't they just print more money?'

'Why do Europeans eat with their left hand?'

(Another question with a hidden implication. Central Africans are taught to use their right hand for eating, their left for the 'secret ablutions'. Is it not unclean, implies the questioner for Europeans to eat with both hands?)

'Are all Americans cowboys or are there some ordinary people like villagers and clerks?'

'Are the cowboys we see in the films employed people or do they look after their own cattle?'

(Like so many of the questioners this one probably knew the answer. He was getting a dig at the unemployed juvenile delinquents of the Copperbelt dressed in cowboy clothes and living a Wild West phantasy life.)

'Why does the government not give bursaries to people to learn such things as making bicycles?'

'Why is Lux Toilet Soap recommended above all others?'

'How can we know good advice from bad advice?'

How indeed! I never envied the people, a parson, a doctor, an African teacher and a European teacher, who took on the task of answering these questions. Sometimes they must indeed have wished that God would broadcast Himself 'so that we can hear His voice and know how He wants us to live.'

Considering that all these questions came from listeners literate in English, it seems at first sight surprising that they should have been so ignorant of European ways. But then, hardly any of the questioners had had the benefit of literate parents versed in the ways of the modern world. There had been no books in their homes. In fact, when they were children there had not been any books printed in their mother-languages except the Bible and some primers. Obviously six or seven years of schooling are not enough to overcome such handicaps. Further, they had had no opportunity of mixing socially with Europeans. I often found Central Africans with good matriculation certificates ignorant of facts that an average European child of six has already picked up from its parents.

Conversely, Europeans who have spent all their lives in Africa are often ignorant of matters that every child in an African village knows, how to build a snare, how to find one's way in the bush, and that decent people eat with their right hand only.

But the ignorance of the Africans mattered more because it was the industrial, European society which was dominant.

Our Salisbury branch started women's Radio Homecraft Clubs and recorded talks, competitions and songs at the meetings of these clubs. This stimulated the formation of more branches. They multiplied rapidly, possibly taking the place of some of the traditional social organizations that conquest and christianization had shattered.

In Lusaka, Edward Kateka persuaded shy, timid African women to discuss marriages and what could and did go wrong with them. Once he had got them going there was no stopping them. We even started to receive letters of comment from women. There was something stirring in the land when the voiceless women of Africa came to write their opinions to broadcasters who were not members of their family or clan, but total strangers.

In other programmes we held up individual effort and success as worth imitating. We tried to create the image of the energetic, self-reliant New Man, the Log-cabin to White House man in African terms. In one series called 'Going Forward' Alick Nkhata the guitarist, interviewed people about their successes as traders and transport operators, builders and farmers. Certain types of 'swanking' are not objectionable to Africans and they talked about themselves without false modesty. Most of their stories followed the same pattern, 'I used to work for a European or Indian, there I learnt my trade, now I'm independent and don't have to put up with a boss any more.' That seemed quite as desirable a prize as the higher income that usually came with independence.

They were repetitive, these success-stories, but then so are the lives of saints and the feats of stakhanovites.

·   ·   ·   ·   ·

Originally we had fondly imagined that as broadcasting became
less of a novelty, our listeners would become more sophisticated
and we could make greater demands on their intelligence. What we
had left out of account was the increase in the number of listeners.
As radio-ownership spread down the social pyramid, the average
standard of sophistication became lower. We had to simplify and
simplify still more.

I suggested that we try slogans, that we hammer home a few
simple lessons in repetitive little verses, cutting into musical programmes with them. Kittermaster had his doubts. He thought it
undignified, possibly unethical, altogether too much like commercial radio. I argued that there was nothing unethical about telling
people repetitively how to avoid traffic accidents. I was not proposing to sell them a dud deodorant. In the end he gave me my
head. He suggested that I start on the advantages of education for
girls and on the dangers of the common house-fly. They were
lessons that needed repeating.

I asked John Sharman and Stephen Mpashi of the Publications
Bureau and Pepe Zulu of our own staff for their help. Mpashi had
been working on a collection of Bemba proverbs. I explained that I
thought these might be useful. We might hook the new teaching-
matter on to the known traditional wisdom.

'And why not use the traditional form, too?' suggested Sharman. 'The chief or elder never says the entire proverb. He says one
half, the other is added by the man he is speaking to.'

'Like this,' demonstrated Mpashi, ' *Ubukula tabukula . . .*' then
he pointed at Sharman who thought for a moment, then replied
triumphantly,

'. . . *nga meno ya mu kanwa.*'

I tried to translate it, 'A garden does not grow like . . . like what?'

'A garden does not grow by itself, like teeth in the mouth. It
needs effort.'

Zulu joined in, 'When we were children we used to play such a
game in the evenings around the fire. One of the old men would
start it. He would call out "One white ant . . ." and one of us
would reply quickly "does not build an antheap." Then the one
who had given the answer was allowed to ask next, "Whosoever
feels diarrhoea . . ." and another would complete it, ". . . it is up
to him to open the door."'

'That sounds fine,' I said, 'we could have the slogan spoken by two voices. Yes, I like that idea. We'll be able to test what our listeners remember by saying one half of the slogan to them. Then we'll see whether they can complete it.'

'Why not have the second half spoken by a chorus,' suggested Sharman. 'These tonal African languages lend themselves to it.'

Before many minutes had elapsed everybody was enthusiastically scribbling away at possible proverb-slogan combinations. We wrote and debated and rephrased for many days. In the end we recorded a number of slogans in Bemba and another lot in Nyanja, among them the following. (The underlined words were spoken by a chorus of three.)

Young trees: they make the future forest.

Let us educate little girls: tomorrow they are the young mothers.

Though it's small: yet it's a heavy load.

The fly: though small, is dangerous.

It gives us disease: You, kill that fly!

Oh, it's nothing: may make your leg swell up.

A man may kill a fly. A fly may kill a village: You, man, kill that fly!

Oh, it's nothing: may make your leg swell up.

The last line is a proverb meaning 'Don't say, "Oh, it's nothing, only a small scratch." It may make your leg swell up. Big troubles have small beginnings.'

We broadcast these and similar slogans for several weeks, then tried to assess their effectiveness. I borrowed several of our staff for an afternoon and sent them out to interview listeners with a simple questionnaire. I also asked Father Ritter to make similar inquiries at his remote mission-station.

The results were startling. Almost everywhere the slogans were repeated word-perfect, but only very few listeners understood them. The literate townsfolk knew all about the need for female education and about the dangers of the house-fly.

'You are quite right. There are many reasons why women should be educated. They are like the front wheel of a bicycle and the one behind are the men. As a bicycle cannot run with one wheel so we men cannot raise the country lonely.'

'These are good words and useful. The fly likes filthy things and brings diseases which can make the living body into a dead one. We should not ignore it because of smallness.'

However, these townsmen were completely bewildered by the proverbs. First they ignored them, but when pressed they tried to interpret them literally, 'A fly, though small, may infect your leg through a small cut and may make it swell up.' Many of these townsmen had only learnt Bemba or Nyanja when they came to the Europeans' towns. They had never learnt the 'deep vernacular' of proverb and idiom. But even those whose mother-languages were Bemba or Nyanja had already become estranged from the wisdom of the fathers.

Father Ritter reported the opposite about the villagers near his mission. The proverbs were known and commented on at length but the villagers saw no connection between them and our new lessons. When pressed, a few of them appeared to know about flies and such things, but spoke of them as of an entirely different matter, in no way connected with the proverbs.

We had fallen squarely between two stools.

Yet all those interviewed had been fairly regular listeners. Since the target audience for these slogans was to include occasional listeners and the illiterate townsmen who might in future become listeners if incomes continued to rise, I decided to extend the scope of the inquiry.

We called in a gang of dull-eyed, ragged labourers. Kitter-master, Zulu and I spent an hour or two playing them the recorded slogans and questioning them. They were suspicious and uncommunicative and it seemed that they only had the vaguest idea what the slogans were getting at. Most of them refused to believe that a fly which does not bite can carry disease.

The following day Zulu met one of them in the street. The man said, 'We have been thinking about it, and I understand it all now. It is like this, though it's small, it's a heavy load. Though the Europeans are few, yet they are powerful. They'll get the better of us over this business of Federation. Though they are few, they are so powerful that we'll never be able to drive them out of our country.'

An equally fantastic reaction came from Senti, my illiterate old cook.

'You speak wisely,' he said. 'Though it is small, yet it's a heavy load. The fly is small, but it brings disease. One man can spoil the happiness of an entire village. He may be a witch. He brings fear and hatred and suspicion among the people. He may even give the chief an illness by his witchcraft. "Kill that fly" means we should send such a man out of the village. Nowadays Europeans will not let us kill them, but just one such man can spoil an entire village. Though it's small, yet it's a heavy load.'

First I took it all very seriously. It is fortunate, I thought, that these traditionalists who see deep allegorical meanings in everything are also the people who do not take to new-fangled ideas like the radio. Their system of ideas is still intact, they have no need and no place for new ideas, for radio . . . then Kittermaster laughed *Black Mischief!* and I too burst out laughing. It was so much like the experiences of Evelyn Waugh's hero, Seth, Emperor of Azania, Lord of Wanda and Tyrant of the Seas, Bachelor of Arts of Oxford University who has posters put up all over his African kingdom to advocate 'something very modern called Birth Control'. They illustrate the ideal one child home and contrast it with the poverty-stricken hovel of the parents of many. Inset between the two scenes is a detailed drawing of a contraceptive. The Azanians are impressed: 'There is rich man: smoke pipe like chief, but wife she no good, sit eat meat. Rich man no good, he only one son . . . There is poor man: not much to eat but wife she very good, work hard in field. Man he good too, eleven children, one very mad, very holy. And in the middle, Emperor's *juju*. Make you like that good man with eleven children.'

It took me some time to live down the slogan-episode! But Kittermaster said:

'You'd better cut out the proverbs and make the whole thing longer. This slickness and brevity is un-African.'

'You mean you want me to carry on with slogans, after all this?'

'Sure. There's no way we can learn but by trial and error.'

'Well, as a matter of fact, I was hoping we might try some short conversations between two characters with distinct names and voices, maybe about traffic-accidents. But I hardly dared suggest it.'

So in the end we succeeded in devising simple, repetitive little playlets to drive home selected teaching-points to our mass of new listeners. They were more effective and were used as interruptions in request-programmes and so far as I know, they still are.

We decided to try a family serial in Bemba for Copperbelt listeners, designed to let our audience identify itself with the hero who suffers the common experiences of town life and solves his problems in an intelligent, modern way. Experience had shown us that no European could write such plays and make them sound plausible, but neither did we want to leave them entirely to our African broadcasters. They had come to think of radio-plays as dramatized tribal legends or as light comedies with heavy morals. But this series was to be different. It would have to be a joint venture, Europeans and Africans working together, script-writing by committee. We did not imagine that this was the way to produce great radio drama, but then we were not broadcasting primarily for the sake of art. It would indeed be a fine thing if ever we did produce a real work of art, but that could not be our chief aim. At some radio stations in West Africa much more was being done to encourage the writing of poetry, but it seemed to us that in Central Africa there were more immediate tasks. I used to imagine myself in the midst of a great construction-project like that at Kariba, where sweating gangs of labourers were digging trenches and thundering cranes were pouring concrete and all were working against time before the rains brought down the floods. In such a place one could not stop to manicure one's finger-nails.

Our committee of five or six met every Tuesday morning for two and a half hours in my office. The first Tuesday, in between acting as receptionist, I told the team what I had in mind. Among them were the most sophisticated and the simplest members of our staff and again, both Mpashi and Sharman from the Publications Bureau.

'He must be independent and individualistic our hero, but not improbably good. Let's not have a Sunday School St. George. He's got to have troubles, like how to get on with an uneducated wife, and whether to send his little daughter to school or back to the village, and what to do about the unsuitable suitors that hang around his big daughter. As for the boy friend, maybe we could make him a real town-spiv and poke fun at him. The listeners mustn't identify themselves with the rogue.'

On this framework the team started to build. We argued and interrupted each other and all shouted at the same time while we constructed brief personal histories for each of our main characters. And so Shimwansa Kopolo was born and planted in the African suburb of Wusikili outside Kitwe, employed as a foreman in the mining-company's foodstore and blessed with a vixenish wife Namwansa, and three children Mwansa, Mateo and Mandalena.

Namwansa (Mother-of-Mwansa) we made a totally illiterate woman, but well-versed in proverbs and folk-lore. To allow us to provoke frequent arguments between her traditional outlook and her husband's more modern one, we made her a Crocodile, a member of the royal clan of the Bemba. Her husband was only a member of the River clan, which made it possible for her to take more liberties than an average woman would.

Their eldest daughter Mwansa, was a pleasure-seeking, rebellious girl just out of school, in danger of becoming a *kapenta*, one of the painted ones. Her latest boy friend we called Smart Jim. He was a spiv in a cowboy suit, with some education possibly from a reformatory and a seductive tongue. To him we attached an apprentice-spiv who called himself Bob Superman.

It seemed like a good morning's work, but I was worried that the serial would become weighed down by our joint didactic zeal, so I insisted on some light relief that could be brought in whenever necessary. None of the suggestions made sounded hopeful until Mpashi the novelist, proposed that as a neighbour and friend of the Kopolos we plant a member of the Ngoni tribe.

He had hit the nail on the head. In the last century the Ngoni, an invading tribe of Zulu origin, were often at war with the Bemba. They have since developed a 'joking-relationship'. Whenever they meet they pour out ribald mockery at each others' persons and customs without offence being meant or taken. This is a recognized institution, so much so that native courts dismiss cases of insulting behaviour when these two tribes are involved. And so Kangacepe joined our family. Throughout its long run he kept the groundlings amused with a comic commentary on the main events of our plot.

If there was nothing worth commenting on he trotted out the popular stereotypes,

'Like monkeys these Bemba, always climbing up trees to lop down branches. Is that the way to cultivate crops?'

He got back as good as he gave,

'Look who's talking! Ngoni, are they human, dancing without any clothes on?'

'We do not!'

'Oh, you don't? Now tell us, what is it that you must wear?'

(An evergreen, this reference to the Zulu penis-sheath.)

The Kopolo family had their full share of troubles. Their son Mateo misused school fees to buy a guitar, their daughter Mwansa refused to marry the villager recommended by her uncle who had come from his village to make the arrangements. I asked how she was to refuse.

'She says, "It is your wish? Do my parents wish that I marry this man?"'

'And what do they reply?'

'Nothing. They know that she refuses.'

'But I thought she was a brazen young thing?'

'Yes. So she is. She is very impudent.'

In a few weeks with the team I learnt more about the everyday life of Africans than I had in the fifteen years before. My suggestions were shot down and pulled to pieces and reshaped to make them plausible. How little I knew! I had lived in Africa most of my life, but how shut off from Africans by this colour bar. So much had passed by without my seeing it. To the Africans my questions must have seemed quite as naïve as those our listeners sent in had seemed to me.

Our plots had a second rehashing from the actors. As always, the actors did not work from a verbatim script. The producer assembled them under a tree behind our studio, read them our one or two-page story-outline and then let them improvise their lines. For safety we pre-recorded everything. During the rehearsals and the recording the actors then made minor amendments to the dialogue which brought the final version still closer to the expectations of our audience and thereby made it easier to understand.

The serial assumed a sort of life of its own. Sichanda, the village uncle who comes to arrange Mwansa's marriage, unexpectedly grew to be a major character, a pathetic old man trying to do his duty by his family in a strange world whose ways he cannot comprehend.

'What are all those people doing over there?' he asks. 'Is it a fight?'

'No Grandfather, it is a bus-queue.'

'Oh, oh, people everywhere, jostling, scrapping.'

'Grandfather, in town we queue for everything, doctor, *boma*, to buy meat, firewood, to collect wages.'

'You *buy* firewood? But why don't you send the children to cut some?'

They explain to him the ways of the Counters-of-Leaves, the Forest Guards, and the reasons for their work.

'Some Europeans,' they explain, 'even have to pay for their water.'

'It can't be! Do they charge people for air, for life?'

He demands to know why the Kopolos cannot build a few grass-huts on to their concrete house to accommodate their growing family. Young Mateo lectures to him about hygiene, but old Sichanda grumbles:

'Nonsense. Have I not lived to a ripe old age without knowing such things? And my father before me?'

He resents the intrusion of the DDT sprayers into the home. Everything is explained to him patiently, but he finds he cannot fit into this life, dictated by shrill factory-sirens instead of by the movement of the sun and the seasons.

'And who would bury you if you died in this fearful place?'

Least of all can he understand Smart Jim and his friend Bob Superman, 'Why is it that they do not respect their elders? And why do they have these European names?'

But when Mwansa explains to him about the Superman of the films, he smiles in recognition, 'It is an old legend, like that of Bwalya who flew on a drum.' In the end he gratefully returns to the quiet of his squalid, neglected village, though not without first cadging gifts to take back to the members of the family there.

For our actors, we tried to choose people as close to the characters as possible. For example, the actress who played Mwansa was a girl of marriageable age. This posed a problem because just as she was getting into her stride, her betrothed refused to let her continue. The producer went to try and reason with him. The young man explained that it wasn't so much that he objected to the love-talk on the air. He realized this was only play-acting. It was the company we expected her to keep. The producer saw his point and offered to have him written into the serial in a minor role so that he could keep an eye on the girl. This the fiancé agreed to. It brought him a good fee.

The bad company that the young man objected to was the actor we had cast as Smart Jim. He fitted the role to perfection. He was one of the most engaging spivs and vagabonds I have met. He called himself John Square. He was usually dressed in a blue boiler-suit, a silver-studded cowboy-belt, a four-gallon hat and occasionally, a bright red or yellow scarf. He was in his middle twenties and had a handsome face which somehow looked permanently startled. Usually it was disfigured by sticking-plaster and patches over the eye. One day his whole head was bandaged. He had got himself into a real rough-house that time. He had a very distinctive and deep voice and led a choir which sang cowboy songs about riding along on the range, my trusty horse beneath me.

He played the guitar quite well. One day our serial demanded a love-song. On the spot he composed one to Mwansa which was in every way more convincing and poetic than those I have heard in the Wild West films that John Square admired so much.

On another occasion we asked him to improvise some terms of endearment. He responded bravely in a mixture of English and Bemba. 'My sweet choc'lot! My nibbly little ear-lobe! My Hollywoody dolly!'

Eventually the villain of our serial had to come to a sticky end. Smart Jim takes on a job as a petrol-pump attendant and proceeds to fill up cars with the meter still registering the previous purchase. He boasts of his cleverness, is discovered and arrested.

John Square indignantly refused to act the part. 'I don't want to go to jail. It's not fair.'

I thought he was worried about being ragged by his listening friends, but no, he was thinking of the loss of actor's fees! By then he had become so famous that we readily agreed to let him make a come-back after escaping from prison a few weeks later. It would make a nice problem for our modern-citizen-hero, whether or not to collaborate with the police to help recapture the villain.

I got interested in our actor and asked about his background. He had not been born in a tribal area but on the line of rail, at Ndola. 'He has never even known his home,' people told me. After some years of schooling he had been entrusted with his father's grocery-store, but he only succeeded in having the old man declared bankrupt within a few months. After that he came to Lusaka and tried to live dangerously, like his cowboy heroes, until the courts put him under a probation-officer as a juvenile in need of care and protection. The probation-officer had him trained as a shoemaker. This trade gave Square an independence such as few African townsmen in the Rhodesias enjoy. He certainly enjoyed it, drinking, fighting and making love when he pleased, repairing shoes when there was no one to sponge on. While he drew our actor's fees he worked very little at his trade but maybe we were doing the public a service; on one occasion he was said to have sold a sackful of shoes entrusted to him for repair and to have financed a momentous party from the proceeds. When the irate owners came to demand compensation he challenged them all to fight. Perhaps that explained the mass of sticking-plaster.

I continued to see him occasionally even while he was not acting for us. One afternoon a friend and I met him at a football match in the 'compound'. He greeted us effusively:

'Ride 'em, Radio!' he called out to us, bowing like someone out of the 'Life of Johann Strauss.'

'Drinking again, Square?' said my friend jokingly.

'But definitely, sah,' he replied, 'all day long.'

A few days later he phoned to invite me to a performance that his concert-party were giving at a welfare hall. Unfortunately I had another engagement.

'You should have come,' said Alick Nkhata the guitarist, the following day. 'They sang quite well, but when the audience didn't clap enough Square stopped the singing, came to the front of the stage and threatened to beat everybody who didn't make enough applause. It was very unusual.'

A few weeks later Square rushed into my office panting,

'Sah, you must save my life. I shall be beaten to death. I shall be torn to pieces, tonight.' He stammered badly when excited.

I expected to be touched for money, not for the first time.

'Why?' I asked coldly.

'I have organized a beauty-competition and a music-competition, and I have guaranteed a European judge. They don't trust Africans. You must save me. . . .'

I agreed, but asked that I be given two African assessors to help with the judging. I did not wish to impose my tastes. He accepted my condition only too readily. That evening the assessors outvoted me every time and awarded the music prizes to Square's own group. The beauty-prize went to his latest mistress. I gnashed my teeth, but I had only myself to blame.

An informed adjustment to modern society . . . could it be that John Square had achieved it?

When we brought him back on the air again I happened to make out the first payment voucher.

'I am afraid you have misspelt my name,' he said.

I had made out many vouchers with the same spelling.

'It is Squire, sir. Not Square. S.Q.U.I.R.E., like the knights of long ago.'

I wondered what films he had been seeing lately.

Our Shimwansa Kopolo serial went from strength to strength. The identification between audience and modern citizen-hero that we had aimed at, succeeded beyond all expectations. An enterprising Copperbelt trader even called his new shop 'Shimwansa Kopolo's Groceries' and claimed to be the hero of our serial. Listeners wrote to ask for the Kopolo's hut-number, because they wanted to discuss their problems with them.

As for myself, by then my sympathies were entirely with the villain.

Luunda Chief Kazembe XV and Labour Chief Clem Attlee

Blind minstrel in Nyasaland

Author recording in Nyasaland—better than wrangling
in smoky committee-rooms

10. VULTURES HIGH AND LOW

DID I EVER believe that our broadcasting station would be able to continue indefinitely to work quietly and without interference, isolated from the ugly racial tensions of Central Africa? I certainly hoped so, against accumulating evidence. But as the campaign for the Federation of the two Rhodesias and Nyasaland grew in intensity, I was forced to see that this was not to be.

During the years I have written about, the future of Central Africa was being thrashed out, at Victoria Falls, in London, Salisbury, Lusaka and Zomba. Meetings and debates and white papers followed each other with increasing rapidity, voices became louder and angrier, the atmosphere more nervous and hysterical. I attended press-conferences and sittings of legislative councils and official briefings and then escaped back to my office to write my news bulletins and background talks and to instruct our translators. I tried to explain complicated issues simply and struggled to preserve detachment, as hatred rose like a flood threatening to drown us all.

I made something of a fetish of my civil servant's detachment. Whatever my personal sympathies, I would continue to do my duty without taking sides. I refused to admit to myself that there might be moral laws that had greater weight than General Orders and Colonial Regulations.

I was against the Federation proposals, but I could see that some of the arguments that the advocates used were valid.

The majority of the Europeans of the three territories clearly wanted Federation mainly to wrest control of Northern Rhodesia and Nyasaland away from the government in London whose 'pro-African' policies, they feared, would bring about native states. They wanted to join Southern Rhodesia because there the will of the settlers reigned supreme.

It was a point of view with which I had no sympathy. The settlers' fear of a black future seems to me the result of their own hostility towards Africans. I believed that if we gave Africans a chance to become fully accepted citizens we had no need to fear the future. I believed that it was still possible, but only just, to set

L

Northern Rhodesia and Nyasaland on a path that would lead to a society like that of Brazil or the West Indies, where considerations of race are of minor importance. I refused to believe that a black majority in parliament need mean the expulsion of all white men from Central Africa.

A further argument advanced by the advocates of Federation was that it would prevent Southern Rhodesia from being forced by economic necessity to join the Union of South Africa. Instead, it would create a great British bloc to stop the spread of Afrikaner influence in Africa. That did not convince me either, since it seemed only too likely that the proposed Federation would follow racial policies not fundamentally different from those of the Union. I did not like 'white domination' any better than 'baasskap', the Afrikaans original.

On the other hand, the economic arguments advanced in favour of Federation seemed to me to be very strong. Africa's great need is capital for development. The abysmally low standard of living, of skill and of productivity of the native peoples throughout Africa can only be raised by means of foreign capital. It was said that a larger and financially more secure Federation, not dependent on a single commodity, as Northern Rhodesia is dependent on copper, would be able to attract capital more easily. This was the argument that convinced many British politicians of both the big parties and with many of them it outweighed all the other considerations. They spoke of exciting plans for electrification and industrialization. 'Federation, is the road to greater prosperity, larger social services and political advancement,' said the Conservative Colonial Secretary, Oliver Lyttelton.

There seemed to me to be a lot of truth in the argument, but there was still the question, prosperity and greater political advancement for whom? And what sort of share of it would the Africans get? On the Copperbelt, for example, the informal industrial colour bar had not yet been breached and Africans were not allowed to acquire skills and earn high wages. In Southern Rhodesia an industrial colour bar was enforced by law. How would Federation affect this? I was afraid it would intensify it because the proposed Federal constitution handed the substance of political power over to the European settlers. Though the British Government had insisted conscientiously that the few existing African rights in the Northern territories be entrenched, it appeared to me that any future advance would be hindered severely. Africans had only a very small say in the running of their country. They could hardly be satisfied with guarantees that their rights would not be further reduced. The constitution should have ensured that as they became better-educated and more experienced politically, increases in their political power, even to the point where they controlled the parliament, would not be frustrated. But the Colonial Office was proposing to surrender to the settlers the right to initiate legislation over a wide range of subjects including franchise, citizenship and electoral laws. These were left to the first Federal parliament, dominated by settlers, to formulate. It seemed incredible that, so far as I knew, neither the British government nor the African MPs had ever contested this. Having been brought up among settlers I could hardly imagine (despite the loud protestations of 'partnership of the races' then fashionable among their politicians) that a settler-dominated parliament would design the franchise in any way but to perpetuate European domination. Once the British Government had accepted Federation it would not be able to do much to prevent this, despite the complicated veto clauses.

I lay no claim to have had prophetic powers. Sir Godfrey Huggins (now Lord Malvern) had said quite clearly, 'Could any sane person believe that representatives in the Federal Assembly would pass legislation which would enable Africans to hold all seats in the Legislature at any time?' Several years later the Federal Parliament passed a Constitutional Amendment Act and an Electoral Act which rigged elections as I had anticipated and the British Government submitted meekly.

I was opposed to the Federal proposals framed in 1952, but I strove not to let it influence my work. A civil servant must carry out the policies of his government, or resign.

I briefed our African announcers about the 'partnership idea' to which even some decidedly anti-African politicians seemed all of a sudden firmly dedicated. Keeping an eye on the British parliament which could still make or break their Federation scheme they protested, 'Europeans and Africans should pay due regard to each others' outlook, hopes and fears . . . each man must be free to rise to the level that his ability, energy, qualifications and character permit. . . .'

Our announcers listened in silence. Then one of them rummaged among his papers, handed me a press-cutting and said, 'Here, look at this. Why don't you put that in your news-bulletins?'

I looked at the article. It was the report on an assault-case against a European, Andrew James Botha, in Umtali, Southern Rhodesia. A number of African witnesses described how they went to attend a meeting about Federation to be addressed by the Prime Minister, Sir Godfrey Huggins. It was probably the first time that Africans had been admitted to a European political meeting at Umtali. They arrived early and found seats in the front of the cinema-hall before the speakers arrived. Then the hall filled up and there were cries from the audience that there were not enough seats for the Europeans and that the Africans should sit on the floor. Botha then went up to an African teacher, got hold of the lapel of his coat and dragged him out of his seat. The chairman intervened and asked the Africans to sit on the floor, which several proceeded to do, but Botha attacked an African who was slow to move and gave him a hard blow in the stomach. Then he moved up and down the front of the cinema shouting 'Why are the kaffirs sitting in seats while Europeans are standing?' There were cries of 'Throw out the kaffirs' and when the Prime Minister came on the stage the noise increased. Several other Europeans proceeded to pull Africans from their seats, grabbing them by the scruff of their necks and pushing them down the aisle. Outside the hall an African policeman was threatened. The magistrate, in summing up, said that the only thing he could say in Botha's favour was that he appeared to receive encouragement from other Europeans in the hall. For 'rank hooliganism', he fined Botha £10.

'There you are!' said our announcer ironically when I returned the paper. 'Partnership! Look, they even allow us to attend Huggins's meetings these days.'

'These are individuals,' I said lamely, 'it's not government policy.'

'But aren't these the people who'll control the Federation? They'll have a vote, but will we?'

.   .   .   .   .

I was recapitulating the contents of the various white papers that led up to Federation. There was one produced by a group of senior officials of the three territories and of Britain who had made a study of existing policies. With regard to native policies they came to the conclusion that the degree of similarity between the policies and the practices of the three Governments was much more striking than the differences.

'That's a lie,' said one of our Southern Rhodesian announcers. 'Haven't I told you before? Here in the North if I go to the district commissioner and he sees that I'm decently dressed and can speak English he gives me a chair and says "Now, how can I help you, Mr So-and-So?" But the native commissioner in my home district in Southern Rhodesia makes me squat on the floor and call him *mambo* as if he were a chief. Never mind what it says on paper.'

There was nothing I could say to this, but I thought that the Northern officials who had put their signatures to that document were either knaves or fools. I believed the latter.

The Northern Rhodesian officials were usually honest men, but hopelessly out of touch. District commissioners were given an advance summary of the proposed constitution and were asked by their superiors about likely African reactions. Almost all replied that there would be no objections, that possibly a few agitators might stir up trouble, but that if the DCs recommended the proposals, Africans would accept them without further ado. In the whole of the Western Province of Northern Rhodesia which as then delimitated contained the turbulent Copperbelt, only one district commissioner reported that Africans would regard the affair as a grave breach of trust and that there would be lots of trouble. This lone voice was not that of an old-timer with many years of experience of his district, but of a man recently returned from service in a part of Africa where there was no colour-bar. Back in Northern Rhodesia he shocked settlers and embarrassed his superiors by occasionally inviting Africans to his house for a drink and a chat. Only *he* foresaw that the Government was embarking on a dangerous course. Most of the others were insulated from the truth by employees and sycophants and the barrier of their own lack of receptivity. It was another case of not being adjusted to their times.

They still imagined themselves as kindly fathers and refused to believe that their 'children' might have a will of their own. Future events were to discredit them completely and to give a sort of post-facto justification to my own 'Rip van Winkle phobia', my ever-present fear of losing touch with our African audience.

What *were* Africans thinking? That was not so easy to find out, seeing how complicated it was to get true opinions about mere radio-programmes. Politicians, journalists and broadcasters flocked out to try and find out for themselves. All of a sudden our quiet backwater had become important. Among the visitors was Clement Attlee, then leader of the British Opposition. His Labour Party had not yet made up its mind whether to support the Federal scheme. In its original form the scheme had had the backing of Labour ministers before their electoral defeat of 1951 but some slight changes had been made since. A number of us followed Mr and Mrs Attlee on a visit to a 'typical African village'.

In my car I had a British journalist. 'I suppose it will be a model display village full of handpicked government stooges,' he said.

His remark irritated me, 'You're not in Soviet Russia,' I replied angrily. There was much to criticize in our administration, far more than this sort of reporter would see, but the administrators I knew were not dishonest. Still, as we drove on along the dusty bumpy track a slight worry crept into my mind. What if he were right? Under the stresses of the time, their honesty *was* wearing thin. Administrative pressure on us to suppress news was on the increase.

At last our column came to a halt at Mungule's village. I felt a slight relief as I saw that it was the usual squalid cluster of decaying huts with half-starved mongrel dogs sniffing about.

A *boma* messenger directed our party of about eight or ten to a row of chairs placed on a hillock, as if on a stage facing an audience, except that the audience had not arrived. There was great shouting and whistling and not long after Chief Mungule hastened along and was introduced. The party sat down, but it was discovered that Mr Attlee would have to talk across several other people to communicate with the chief. The district commissioner suggested a rearrangement. All sat down once more. Then the chief's interpreter arrived breathlessly. Seats were rearranged once again to accommodate him. The district commissioner asked where the villagers were. They were waiting in the shade of a big tree elsewhere, so the chief sent his messenger running off to call them.

There was a long pause.

'It is a bumpy road,' said Mr Attlee.

'Yes sir,' agreed the chief, 'I wish the Government would build a proper one. Would the big *bwana* not be so good as to tell the *bwana* governor?' Chief Mungule found the roles of government and opposition in the British constitution confusing. His interpreter intervened to brief him.

Another awkward pause. Mr Attlee was shifting his hat from one knee to the other. The district commissioner saw that he would have to get the conversation started:

'Chief Mungule!' he said, '*Bwana* Attlee, of whose fame you have heard, has come across the sea from England to see for himself how the subjects of the Queen are being cared for by her present advisers. He wishes to know how the crops and the cattle of the Lenje people are, and how the rains have been this last season.'

A few minutes of pleasantries ensued and at last Mr Attlee took the initiative.

'And do your people discuss the question of Federation, Chief Mungule?'

'Yes sir, they do.'

'And what do they know about Federation?'

'They do not know about it.'

'But they talk about it?'

'They talk very much.'

Mrs Attlee laughed and her husband cast her a quick glance. Then he continued,

'How can they talk about it if they do not know anything about it?'

'They are waiting for the big *bwana* to explain it to them.'

Another awkward pause, Mr Attlee was shifting his hat from knee to knee.

'May I take it from you, sir?' asked the district commissioner and placed the hat on an empty chair. Then he again intervened in the conversation.

'*Bwana* Attlee has not come to explain but to hear what the chief and the Lenje people have to say.'

'Sir,' said the chief, 'I and my people are against this thing. We do not want it. We do not want to hear about it. We have been happy and we do not want any change.'

'I see,' nodded Attlee, 'but what are your reasons?'

'We will lose our land if this thing comes. We are against it.'

At this point the villagers arrived, twenty or thirty toothless old men in discoloured greatcoats and torn trousers, behind them a handful of younger ones. They squatted down in front of our 'stage' and clapped their hands in greeting.

'We will lose our land if this Federation comes about,' said the chief raising his voice.

'But according to my reading of the constitutional proposals, African land-rights are entrenched firmly.'

'Maybe, maybe. But we do not want this Federation. We are afraid.'

'Afraid of what?'

'We are afraid of losing our land.'

The old men clapped their assent.

The following days, when Mr Attlee met African trade-union leaders and Congress leaders he was more in his element, but they were floundering. He questioned them astutely. Their case did not impress him. The African Trade Union Congress, among them the miners' leaders I had met on the Copperbelt, had framed various memoranda for visiting politicians. In them they claimed that the complete amalgamation of the three territories into one would result from Federation. But Attlee knew that all the skill of the constitutional advisers which his Labour government had set to work on the original draft had gone into preventing just that. The trade unionists claimed that Federation would result in increased immigration of South African artisans and therefore even fewer skilled jobs for Africans, but Attlee knew that the tacit intention behind the proposals was to reduce South African immigration. The trade unionists claimed that the security of African land-tenure was threatened, but Attlee had convinced himself that the draft constitution entrenched that firmly. They demanded universal adult suffrage on the one hand, and in the same document begged that the Colonial Office continue to rule them until they were ready for more political responsibility. Finally, hoping to arouse Attlee's ire against the Conservatives, they informed him that colonial governors were always chosen from the most reactionary elements. But Attlee knew that this was not true of the governors his party had appointed during their six years in office.

He told them he was 'not very impressed' with them. 'When you say that sort of thing it casts doubts on the other things you say.'

The African case was pathetically badly presented, but that did not mean that there was no case.

What *were* Africans thinking?

'Without land we shall be as wild pigs driven from place to place,' said one of my friends, a petrol-pump attendant.

This land-fear had become a real obsession. And yet except in one or two corners, there is no land-hunger in Northern Rhodesia. It is a vast, empty land with only seven people per square mile. One can drive for hours without coming upon a village. Any African may go to a headman, in some tribes another functionary, and ask to have a plot allocated to him. Only eight per cent of the land has been 'alienated' for the use of Europeans and of the Government, yet even this has produced a profound trauma. Was it the beginning of what had happened in South Africa and, to a lesser extent, in Southern Rhodesia? Hadn't Sir Godfrey Huggins said, before Federation was in the air and he had to keep an eye on the British House of Commons, that the allocation of most of Northern Rhodesia's land to natives condemned that country to perpetual backwardness and that a big influx of Europeans was essential to promote progress?

'Whatever he may have said,' I argued with our announcers, 'under this constitution he can't touch your land. It's as firmly safeguarded as is legally possible.'

'Europeans are too clever for us,' they replied, 'they always get the better of us. And all this new wealth that they say this Federation will bring, we don't believe in it. It's as if they were calling a dog but holding a stick behind their backs. They hate us, these settlers. Behind our backs they talk of us all as baboons.' They may not have been able to express their objections in European political concepts, but they did sense that political power was being handed to people hostile to their aspirations.

One of my illiterate friends complained, 'Change, change, always change! Why can't you whites ever leave us in peace?' He felt hurt, harried, hounded, overwhelmed, like Sichanda, our fictitious villager among the bus-queues of the Copperbelt. Such men had already seen enough complicated changes for one life-time. Land to them represented security, permanence, a haven from tensions and anxieties and from the humiliations of their urban life, and probably many things still deeper which as a European and a townsman I could not even contemplate.

At the beginning of the Federation campaign our broadcasting station confined itself to explaining the white papers and to offering to answer listeners' questions about Federation. But there were no questions. The great stream of letters about every subject under the sun contained only one or two about the subject that was agitating Africans most. It made me uneasy, were they losing faith in our impartiality? I suppose it should not have surprised me. They could not help noticing that the far-away BBC reported the pronouncements of the African Congress while we avoided almost all mention of them. They must have sensed that the pressure on us was becoming stronger. Advocates of Federation had started to claim that African opposition to Federation had only arisen because the Government had not given a 'firm lead'. It was quite untrue. Long before the first white paper came out there were already widespread fears of any form of association with the South. However, the officials now undertook in the Legislative Council to 'do everything in their power to ensure that Federation was not misunderstood.' That meant district commissioners and informa-tion services were now ordered to 'plug' it. For all his courage Kittermaster could not prevent this. In an effort to mellow it he demanded that broadcast debates be organized in which both sides could have their say. Now, the men in the Secretariat were essenti-ally decent people and embarrassed at the thought of suppressing opinions and using their broadcasting monopoly for partisan purposes. They agreed half-heartedly and started the complicated machinery of consultation between the three Governments who would have to approve, hoping maybe that others would turn it down and clear their consciences for them. To force the pace Kittermaster sent me off talent-scouting. In the whole of Northern

Rhodesia we could not find an African to defend the Federal proposals. There was one who had written to the papers pleading that Africans should not oppose it, but when we approached him we discovered that he was a Watchtower adherent who believed in passivity in the face of the corrupt governments of the world who would all be burnt up soon, very soon, on the great day of Armageddon. He was not the ideal advocate of Federation! We continued looking.

There was Moses Musale, who had been sent up to Northern Rhodesia from the South by the Capricorn Africa Society to persuade Africans that Federation was in their interests. This society was founded by Col. David Stirling, the 'Phantom Major' of Western Desert fame, who now lives in Africa. I have since got to know the colonel and his society and I have a high regard for them, as they are at present constituted. In 1953 however, their main concern was with the unification of the Rhodesias and Nyasaland. They had allowed their African propaganda to fall into the hands of a dubious 'expert' who sent up organizers like Musale. Musale sat in the Lusaka beer-hall offering free drinks to any African who signed a declaration in favour of Federation. After a few days of consuming his own bribes and making no converts he was called by Harry Nkumbula, the President-General of the African National Congress, for discussions, as a result of which Musale deserted the Capricorn Africa Society and joined the African National Congress. I got there too late to arrange for him to take part in our broadcast debates. I decided that this Nkumbula must be a man of great persuasive power.

The atmosphere was getting tenser. We decided to keep the back door of our studio shut, just in case. Then the Government published a new bill making it a criminal offence to issue statements dangerous to peace and good order at a meeting of over three people.

Harry Nkumbula had announced that he would burn the White Paper containing the draft constitution at a public meeting at Chilenje suburb, Lusaka. A British broadcaster visiting Rhodesia said he would like to attend and I offered to take him.

There were hostile murmurs as we pushed our way through the

crowd. The meeting was already fifteen minutes late in starting, but the speakers had not yet arrived. Most of the crowd were chattering in Bemba. I looked around and recognized some of the faces. They were not of the intelligentsia I had expected to see. I recognized no civil servants, but presumably they did not want to be seen, for Congress membership had almost become equated with treason in the eyes of their superiors. There was however, the 'garden-boy' of one of my acquaintances, then a rather bad carpenter I knew, and a driver I had once dismissed for drunkenness. It was not a pretty crowd, but ugly and frustrated, a rabble devoid of the sort of nobility with which our imagination endows Garibaldi's Thousand. Coarse remarks were made in our direction. An intolerant, suspicious crowd, spawned by our own Northern European intolerance, warped and degraded because we had spurned and rejected them. What a reservoir of pent-up fury, how easy to rouse to anger and violence!

There was applause as Harry Nkumbula arrived with several other leaders. They sat down at a table in the middle of the crowd. There was no platform, but a few stewards pushed back the audience to make a clearing. We had to stand on tip-toe to see Nkumbula. There was more waiting. Whispering. A poster 'Self-government our only ultimate goal' stood behind the speakers. A man edged through the crowd carrying a stool. He set it down among the front rank of the audience. Further waiting. Then the chairman stood up, raised his hand and called out 'Bayete,' the royal salute of the Zulu.

'Bayete,' replied some of the crowd a little self-consciously. Was this a new Congress salute? Then I noticed two chiefs' messengers push aside the crowd and make a path for a man I recognized as Mpezeni, Paramount Chief of the Ngoni, whose ancestors came from Zululand.

'Bayete,' called a few more onlookers half-heartedly. I smiled at the thought of this Bemba-dominated crowd saluting the chief of their arch-enemies. We were creating new loyalties; Bemba and Ngoni, chiefs and radical politicians were all getting together to oppose Federation.[1]

[1] Only remote Barotseland seemed to remain asleep. Of all the chiefs in the country, only Mwanawina III could be persuaded not to oppose Federation, to appeal to his people to avoid violence. He has since been knighted.

Mpezeni sat down, a poor shadow of his tyrant ancestors who had once been the scourge of Central Africa. His bloodshot eyes suggested how he found compensation.

The meeting began with prayers. Then Nkumbula adjusted his London School of Economics blazer and proceeded to read a speech in English. The audience would have been as clay in his hands, and had he been an orator he might have made their pent-up fury blaze into riot, but Nkumbula's address was dry and pedantic.

'Whatever criticisms may be launched against the African Congress, the Protectorate Government and the present British Government are alone responsible for the creation of the prevalent bitter violence and mistrust between black and white in Central Africa. . . .' He read on,

'The people really interested in Federation are the American and British capitalist interests who want to invest their money in Northern Rhodesia and get large profits. . . .'

After each sentence three interpreters interrupted his flow. The Bemba interpreter was Kenneth Kaunda. His more militant rendering occasionally drew a round of grateful applause, but the crowd was starved for fire and fury. Nkumbula droned on:

'After due deliberation regarding the proposals contained in the White Paper on Close Association we have decided that they are totally unacceptable to the African people and that we must voice our bitter opposition to them.'

I had expected a spell-binder, a fiery demagogue, but he spoke with all the detachment and mannerisms of touring district commissioners, and like them he spoke through interpreters. However, his style had more of the Blue Book than of Sanders of the River.

'. . . for these reasons it has been decided by the Supreme Council of the African National Congress to call upon our people to observe two days of prayer. During these two days no work shall be performed. Christian leaders are asked to conduct prayers for their Christian followers. Non-Christian elements are also asked to pray to God in their traditional way. It has also been provided that no drinking shall take place during the days of prayer. . . . I appeal to all anti-Federation elements to observe these days with solemnity and with great reverence.'

At long last we came to the burning of the white paper. I had expected a flaming bonfire, but Nkumbula merely brought out a few copies on a skewer. There was a delay as petrol was poured over them, then they were set alight and dropped on the earth.

But however badly staged the symbolic act roused the crowd. The passions they had not been able to release suddenly erupted in a roar. Women ululated shrilly, fists were clenched. 'Kill them! Kill them!' shouted a hoarse voice near me. We withdrew slowly towards the edge of the crowd. In the centre they were doing a war-dance around a tight-lipped European reporter. Nkumbula stepped between and waved the dancers away. A man near me set up a shout in English, to make sure we got his point, 'I don't care. Never mind f—— government! Put me in jail! I don't bloody care.' Then someone started to sing and within seconds the fierce poetry of their song seemed to unite the noisy rabble. It was another song of Kenneth Kaunda's, full of allegory about Northern Rhodesia's coat of arms, the fish-eagle holding a fish in its talons. The bird symbolized the Europeans, the fish the land, the beloved land:

> 'Vultures are flying high and low.
> Brothers, watch the vultures!
> What will they pick up next?
> What will they pick up next?
> A fish . . . or something bigger?
> Brothers, allow them no more!
> Allow them no more!
> They are cunning and armed with sharp beaks
> to frighten the live
> and to feast on the dead.
> Where are you, brothers?
> Are you watching?'

Public events are reported in the Press, but behind them are individual agonies that remain private.

The two days selected for strike and prayer approached. The African Congress strained its amorphous organization to mobilize 'mass action' and produce a 'national stoppage of work'. The Government grew jittery, a senior official addressed a warning to a meeting of African civil servants, but was shouted down. In European households the strike was discussed with apprehension, as soon as the servants were out of earshot.

A few days before the date Sunny Waluse telephoned me.

'Will you be in your office after four this afternoon?'

'Yes, I'm writing the news-bulletins, I'll be working late.'

'May I come and see you?'

'By all means. You know that I've moved? I now share an office at the Information Headquarters.'

'I know. Will you be alone?'

'I think so, why?'

'Well, I'll tell you this afternoon.'

I sat waiting uneasily later that afternoon. Maybe he only wanted to borrow money? But no, Waluse was not the type, unless he'd changed. I hadn't seen much of him in the last year or two, but we became very friendly when I was still working for the Registrar of Co-operatives. He was an agricultural demonstrator and his work had brought him to our offices frequently. He was a handsome man in his late thirties with a friendly smile. He had a temperament quite free of the dark fears and suspicions that so many Africans have. 'He is one of the few loyal ones,' said his employers, but that was only part of the truth. As a young boy Waluse had come under the influence of a truly Christian European. According to Waluse's descriptions there was something saintly about both the man and his wife. The knowledge that there were such Europeans made it easier for him to put up with the less saintly ones. As an adult he continued to judge all people by the standards they had set him:

'X is kind,' he would say. 'Y is unkind.' He divided all mankind into the kind and the unkind. I remember he used to disapprove of some agricultural extension officers who were doing valuable work energetically and efficiently. He preferred some notorious ditherers who had more charity in dealing with recalcitrant villagers. Being a brash youth with a materialistic bend, I used to think him obscurantist and told him so.

I thought back to our arguments as I waited for him. Now, several years later, I could see the seeds of our unkindness sprouting like weeds all around us, threatening to smother the crops of our efficiency. Co-ops and agricultural improvements, forestry and fisheries improvements were all met with fanatical opposition because of the hatred we had aroused. I began to doubt my original judgement.

Waluse came into my office. Some Africans, when agitated,

become a sort of dull grey and the shine leaves their dark skins. Waluse looked grey that afternoon.

'Sit down Sunny,' I said, 'what's up?'

He came to the point with un-African abruptness.

'What shall I do about the strike?'

I was afraid that would be what he wanted to talk about. I stalled.

'Sit down, let's talk about it.'

'What would you do if you were an African?'

I shrugged my shoulders, 'Tell me first, how do *you* feel about it?'

He was normally a soft-spoken man with a gentle sense of humour, but not that day.

'I feel I want to stand with my people, but I have a wife and children and two nephews to look after, and I have almost twenty years of government service. The Chief Secretary says they'll dismiss any civil servant who comes out on strike. I'm not a Congressman, you know that. I never have been. I've never had much time for them. Well you know them, some of them have been members of your co-op committees and all they ever did was steal the share-capital.'

'I know.'

'But they're right in this case. They're right!'

He was shouting. I gestured to him to lower his voice as I did not think he would want to be overheard by the press-officers who were still working next door.

Waluse had almost nothing in common with the frustrated and suspicious rabble who had danced around the burning white paper, but this issue united them all.

He continued more quietly. 'They are right. Every single African I know is with them in this, even the chiefs who have always feared them. It's easy for Nkumbula to call a strike of bricklayers or miners who're on daily pay, but I'm a civil servant. A civil servant has special duties and responsibilities. Besides, I've got a family to support and twenty years' pension-rights to lose.'

'It's very difficult,' I said.

'But civil servant or not, there comes a time when every African has to get up and speak the truth.'

'Maybe that doesn't only apply to Africans,' I ventured.

He looked at me and paused.

'But what are the others doing?' I resumed.

'Lots of them talk big, but they'll be scared when the day comes.'

'What proportion do you think will strike?'

'I don't know. Do you think they'll really dismiss us if we do?'

'I should think that depends on the proportion who come out. From what I hear of the Congress I can't imagine that they can organize very widespread stoppages. There are whole towns where they don't even have a branch. But if all the African civil servants were to come out, Government couldn't dismiss them. On the other hand, if there are only a few, they're sure to make an example of them.'

'Yes,' he nodded, 'and it will be the wrong ones, not the ones who hate Europeans most, but the most upright ones.'

Then I asked, 'And what will the Congress do if you go to work?'

'They'll ostracize us, and they'll call us traitors and police-spies and Capricornists and what-not. Some of their toughs have threatened to beat up anybody who goes to work, but that's all talk. It's not them I'm afraid of . . . though they can make life pretty unpleasant, especially for my wife. Even now, when she goes to the watertap some of the other women call after her, "There goes the wife of the *bwanas*' good boy." Oh, why did they have to bring in this Federation and all this trouble?'

He was quite exhausted and sat in front of me expectantly.

'What shall I do?'

I sat there looking at him. For the first time in all my years in Africa an African had really crossed the invisible barrier and had appealed to me as one human being to another, as a man in trouble to a fellow man. And on that singular occasion I did not know what to say. I was helpless and on the verge of tears.

'I don't know, Sunny. All I know is that I'm a bachelor and have few obligations and few years of service and I lack the courage of my convictions.'

In the House of Commons in London, half-empty as it always is for colonial debates, Mr Oliver Lyttelton, the Colonial Secretary, spoke:

M

'The use of phrases like "African opinion is solidly against the scheme" are far too definite and dogmatic to be accepted and find no general acceptance from those who are closely in touch with African opinion.'

And after the 'two days of prayer' had passed he denied that the overwhelming weight of African opinion was against Federation since the strikes and demonstrations had failed.

11. LEADERS?

THE STRIKES were a flop. Success or failure had depended on the only large and properly organized African trade union in the territory, the African Mineworkers Union, which had previously promised its support for Congress 'mass action'. At the last moment, however, the union leaders refused to call a strike. At one of the Copperbelt towns, Mufulira, the local branch defied the union leadership and came out, but at the other mines work continued as usual. Other Africans took their cue from the miners. Apart from Mufulira, the only town where there were large-scale stoppages was Lusaka, where Congress had its headquarters.

It was the Congress's first attempt at large-scale political action, and outside Lusaka the organization was far too chaotic to bring it off. The verbal support that Africans all over the territory gave to Harry Nkumbula was not enough.

Recriminations followed and the miners' leaders alleged that the Congress men had never consulted them and that they had only been asked to collaborate with this strike a day or two before it was due to start. At the time this seemed incredible to me, but some years later, when I got to know several of the Congress leaders, I came to see that it may well have been true.

I first met Harry Nkumbula at the inter-racial Kabulonga Club. I was then a member of the club committee and we admitted him to membership. For this we were subjected to vituperative attacks by the settlers' Press. They regarded him as the arch-fiend and said that admitting him to our club was condoning his crimes. Nkumbula, in turn, was denounced by many of his followers as going soft and selling out to the Europeans. The times were no longer favourable for black and white to get together.

When we were introduced, I said,

'We haven't met, but I came to see you burning the White Paper three years ago.'

He covered his face in mock horror and said, 'I think I must have been very cold that day.'

He was one of the first Africans I had met with a European-style sense of humour. His rather heavy and sinister features were quite deceptive, his personality was pleasant, easy-going. He was fond of liquor and of women and sometimes talked of his predilections with a wink. Politics he only discussed very rarely, and when he did it was with a tired resignation so that I felt he was sick to death of it all, sick of the years of living among the intense and politically-minded, sick of having to attend to a hundred details that could not be left to his entourage. He seemed happiest when talking of his undergraduate days in London. With his hangers-on he had a pleasant, jocular, unpatronizing relationship and they seemed devoted to him.

On one of the few evenings when, propping up the bar, he did hold forth about the state of the country, his speech full of the left-wing phraseology he had acquired in London, one of his lieutenants joked:

'Hey, Harry, that's seditious. They'll have you locked up again!'

'No,' he replied, 'no, they won't do that. Don't you realize, one of the basic principles of the British idea of government is that in a pub and under the influence a man may say anything he likes.'

One evening I tackled him about the goings-on in a remote area where Congressmen were opposing a cattle-inoculation campaign which he must have realized was in the interests of the Africans.

'I know,' he sighed wearily, 'I know. They're fools. What can I do? I just can't be everywhere at once. Our branches . . .!'

I believed him. He did not have the dynamism to control the loose, sprawling organization he was alleged to lead. There was no party-discipline of any sort in the Congress. Dozens of petty regional leaders, some of them barely literate, were all claiming to speak for Congress, but there was very little co-ordination. Over major issues they more or less agreed with Nkumbula and followed his example, but such a loose body was not a very effective political weapon and a general strike was beyond it. It seemed quite possible that before the two 'days of prayer' Nkumbula, Kaunda and company had overlooked the necessity of consulting the only properly organized union in the country, believing that it would follow their suggestions automatically. But as regards cattle inoculation, Nkumbula was certainly on the side of the Government. He did not strike me as the unscrupulous politician who would curry favour with the illiterates by opposing such measures. He was genuinely on the side of 'westernization'.

One evening he went so far as to suggest to me that our broad-casting station should stop playing traditional African music because this was 'reactionary and retrogressive'. I argued that the traditional music was often very good, so it would be philistine to suppress it. It would also be high-handed because the majority of Africans loved it. Then I took the opportunity to challenge him about the loin-cloth that his second-in-command, Kenneth Kaunda, once had worn at a demonstration. Wasn't this much more reactionary? He was embarrassed by the question and changed the subject quickly. I seemed to have touched on some source of internal dispute. I was certain that whatever influence Nkumbula had in the Congress was emphatically on the side of the university blazer as opposed to the loin-cloth. But among the heterogeneous crowd who made up the bulk of the Congress there were many who demanded to 'rebuild our destroyed shrines'. Many of them complained that Nkumbula was too moderate, too tired. They were probably right about the tiredness, but what they took to be moderation was more likely to be what Toynbee calls the Herodian approach as compared with their Zealotry. This is a conflict which may split the Congress in time, but to date Nkum-bula retains the leadership despite mounting criticism. Undoubt-edly he has some qualities which earn him devoted followers. When he stepped between the angry dancing mob and the European reporter at the White Paper burning one wave of his hand had been enough to make them withdraw.

Perhaps he remains in power because he is the one-eyed among the blind, most of the two-eyed being in government jobs, or perhaps it is because in his personal relations he has the common touch. Or could it be that it is his DC-ish personality that impresses his followers? I do not know.

Nkumbula never stood for any of the governmental councils in which Africans have some modicum of influence, preferring his freedom to criticize from outside. Among Europeans this helped to create a mystique around his name, which probably strengthened his position among Africans. The settlers and many officials imagined they saw his unscrupulous, secret machinations behind many minor regional agitations, like the one against inoculations, of which he often disapproved. They imagined him a daemonical rabble-rouser, a fiery champion of the Powers of Darkness. No wonder, few Europeans had met him and none but reporters ever attended his meetings. I too, never repeated the instructive experience because the day after the burning of the White Paper, the Special Branch of the police had descended on my bosses to ask what I had been doing there.

A very ugly atmosphere of suspicion was creeping over Central Africa.

Europeans created no mystique around Dauti Yamba, another Congress leader, who was one of the Northern Rhodesian African MPs. They had a chance to observe him in the Legislative Council.

Yamba looks like a dark caricature of a Midwestern senator and has the expansive manner attributed to such. Bloated with self-importance, he strings together long words which he speaks with emphasis and repetition, often quite ignorant of their meaning. Sometimes he attempts plays on words, but his command of English is not sufficient for acrobatics and they usually fall very flat.

To give a full idea of his speeches I would have to quote them *in toto*, pages and pages of Hansard. I shall, however, confine myself to some extracts from his speech about Federation during the most weighty debate ever to face the Northern Rhodesia legislature. Yamba summed up for the African opposition. He spoke for over half an hour, but only about three minutes of his speech actually dealt with the constitutional proposals.

'I will not hesitate, Sir, in giving to the House and the public a picture of the African opposition to this subject. Speaking as a member representing my people direct in this House, Sir, I have full authority to endorse what other Honourable Members representing African interests have already put forward. Sir, it is not my intention to launch my speech in such a manner of deliberate contravention, but the nature under which some of the Honourable Members expressed their views on this motion made it a justification to me and I hope, Sir, that you will grant me equal treatment as that extended to other Honourable Members of this House.

'In the first place, Sir, I will deal with the comments on

the points raised by the Honourable Member for Broken
Hill (Roy Welensky). The first point I would like to touch on
is the threat which I understood him to make during the
course of his speech. I understood the Honourable Member
for Broken Hill to mention these words, which can be corrected, and I think I might not be the only one who heard
him speaking so. I think the Honourable Members in this
House and the public understood the same. These are the
words which he said: "If the African does not come with us
he will face what happened to the Red Indians in America
and will disappear." Sir, that is a very important threat. I
am perfectly sure that this kind of words will not alter the
attitude of the Africans in the country and I should, with full
authority, say that I think under these circumstances all
Africans, if it is well suggested and intended that they
should disappear, would be prepared to disappear.

'Second point, Sir, the Honourable Member for Broken
Hill gave us a full picture of how Southern Rhodesia is facing
up to its national debt.' (Welensky had explained that the
apparently large debt of the Southerners was in fact profitably invested.) 'To this point, Sir, I must say how pleased I
have been to have been further educated on this particular
point. It is obviously understood in Northern Rhodesia that
it has come to the mind of Africans that Southern Rhodesia
is facing a tremendous financial disability and for this reason,
Sir, Southern Rhodesia would like to sell its dominating
power to Northern Rhodesia and Northern Rhodesia in
similar likeness, while it has a better chance of financial
standing, would like to offer cash for that dominating power
from Southern Rhodesia just to please a few of the gentlemen in power at the present time. This has been observed
and I think it is a fact. Well, Sir, I will put it to the House
and the public that we have no intention of running away
from our country in difficulties. We have no intention, even
if the copper-price went down, even if we are economically
badly pressed, we will stand to treat Northern Rhodesia
as our home.'

A European MP interjected, 'So do we.'

Yamba continued, 'I am glad to hear that, and therefore

we cannot have Federation, because Federation is going to improve something that one or two people wish to have in order to dominate the Africans in this country for ever.'

Yamba continued to ramble on for many minutes, then, at long last he got round to the failings of the constitutional document. This had listed the subjects for which the Federal Government would have responsibility and had left all the residual ones for the territorial governments. This is a constitutional device commonly used to avoid future disputes over subjects not listed. Of this Yamba said:

'Now, when I read the report, Sir, the page that they call the list of subjects in here, and I think I might have been very careless in reading it, I did not see a single list of territorial functions. I did not see them. Which are they? They are left in the air.

'They say that all matters affecting Africans remain territorial concerns. If we are to live happily here, and the Honourable Member for Nkana is very anxious about electric power in Kafue Gorge, we shall have to enjoy the lights which come from there on an equal basis. After all, Kafue is part of the African natural resources. That talk about all this secondary education and so on makes it possible that everything affects us, there is nothing that will not affect us, unless, of course, we are told to go somewhere else when this Federation comes. I would like to make it to be clearer that as long as we are human beings in this country, Federation will never fail to throw some effect on our lives in this country and we very much regret that if it might happen.'

And that was all that Dauti Yamba, MP had to say about the failings of the constitution. After that his speech petered out.

I remember listening to the speech with several of my African colleagues. They just shook their heads sadly.

I should, no doubt, make allowance for African conventions of oratory, but even by these he seemed a poor speaker. I found his speeches exasperating beyond description for I was gagged and would have wished him to say all the things that I had on the tip of my tongue.

Yamba's case was really rather tragic. He was a school-master who had come to the top in the nineteen-forties because he stood against white domination and had, apparently, been one of the best-educated men available at the time. But change had been rapid and ten years later there were so many abler, better-educated and younger men on the scene that he had become almost a figure of fun. He had to hang on to power by ever more pompous eye-wash designed to impress the illiterates.

When the first constitutional proposals for the Federation were advanced, neither Yamba nor any of the other Congress leaders made the slightest attempt to redraft or to counter them. They were convinced that they would be outwitted whatever happened. They could only refuse to have anything to do with them and to beg for the protection of London. His colleague, Mr Sokota said, 'We are not at present sufficiently advanced politically to defend ourselves against the European minority, without the assistance of the impartial officials of the British administration of the United Kingdom.'

Yet any astute politician might have seen that the settlers' leaders were only too keen to leave the franchise and citizenship clauses of the constitution vague until after the British House of Commons had approved of Federation. Such a politician might have waded in and produced a series of moderate counter-proposals for a non-racial, qualified franchise designed to appeal to Britain and in keeping with world-wide liberal ideas. Had he asked that these proposals be entrenched in the constitution, he would have provoked the violent opposition of the settlers and have shown them in their true colours. It would have driven a wedge between them and the British Government and might have re-sulted in the shelving of the Federation which Africans detested. But not one of the African leaders saw this possibility. They were having to fight in the arena of European culture, in which they felt lost. Perhaps this was inevitable. If there ahd been more astute leaders, better acquainted with European methods of diplomacy, the African masses might have disowned them. Any leader who asked for anything less than votes for all, a demand which both the British Government and the settlers regarded as ridiculous, ran the risk of being accused of selling out, of going soft.

There is a saying that the time calls the men, that leaders are produced in response to a challenge, almost automatically. In 1953 the seven million Africans of Central Africa produced no such leader. The challenge went unanswered.

The most prominent Africans in Southern Rhodesia were abler, but they did not provide this leadership for other reasons. I met several of them in connection with the Federation debates Kittermaster was still hoping to broadcast. We had not yet had a decision from the governments of Southern Rhodesia and Nyasaland, nor had we found any suitable Africans to speak in favour of Federation. But Kittermaster was determined to have his panel of speakers ready as soon as we received the 'Go ahead'. He sent me flying to Salisbury to interview possible speakers, including Mr Jasper Savanhu, one of the two Africans Sir Godfrey Huggins had taken with him to the constitutional conference in London. There Mr Savanhu had made a good personal impression, although it was realized that he was without any sort of mandate from the Africans. In fact, most heaped abuse upon his head. Settler papers spoke of him as 'a leader of capacity and character, not a seeker after easy and temporary popularity'. Mr Yamba, on the other hand, said of him, 'When one has lived under slavery for a long time his mind would be of a slave.'

Mr Savanhu was then the editor-in-chief of a European owned chain of newspapers catering for Africans. Following Rhodesian custom, I called on Mr Savanhu's employers first.

'What sort of a man is he?' I asked.

'Very able and sensible,' they replied and then added, 'He wasn't always so. When he was younger we had quite a bit of unpleasantness with him. He wrote some rather anti-European things and we parted company. He had a difficult year or two and then we agreed to take him back. Now we get on much better. He has become much maturer.'

I thought I knew what to expect. For once Yamba was likely to be proved right.

Mr Savanhu was enthusiastic about the proposed debates. He certainly gave the impression of an able man, intellectually head and shoulders above the Northern leaders, and much more realistic. He seemed to demonstrate that the more intense European contact in Southern Rhodesia could produce much more westernized

Africans, despite the lack of kindness. In the same way a dead-end kid may learn more about business than the well-educated heir to a banking-house. Things were not as clear-cut as Waluse imagined.

'Politics,' said Savanhu, 'is the art of the possible. For us Africans to cry for a Gold Coast government or for the paramountcy of native interests is to ignore reality. The reality is that the Europeans, because of their all-round superiority, seized the political initiative from the start and have held it ever since. The reality is that we've had complete European domination in the past. That's true in Southern Rhodesia and, to a lesser extent, it's also true in the Northern territories.'

He was undoubtedly right.

'There never was any paramountcy of native interests,' he continued, 'except on papers issued in London. Speaking for us in the south, these Federation proposals will give us certain advantages. They will give us two African MPs where we had none before. That's why I welcome them. Every advance is worthwhile.'

I was going to ask whether they meant any advance at all for the Northerners but refrained.

'Mr Savanhu,' I said, 'I'm looking for two speakers, one to take a strong pro-Federation line, the other pro-but-with-qualifications. I have various shades of antis lined up. Now where exactly do you stand?'

'I am entirely in favour.'

'So may I count on you to take that line in our discussions?'

'Mmmm, well now . . . wait a bit. I—I'd rather speak pro-but-with-qualifications. It will lead to less misunderstanding between myself and my African friends. You see, most of them are not quite so convinced of the benefits of Federation.'

I saw. I arranged to send him an airticket to come to Lusaka if and when the debates were held. But next day Mr Savanhu's realism had got the better of him. He went to the Southern Rhodesian Native Affairs Department and advised them that such debates on the air would have an unsettling effect on the native population, would exacerbate feelings and had better not be held. They did not need much persuading. The Nyasaland government too, felt that such debates would not serve any useful purpose, so they were never held. Our attempt to let both sides be heard on the air had been squashed.

Both Mr Yamba and Mr Savanhu are now members of the Federal Parliament. Yamba like certain of the African MPs from Northern Rhodesia and Nyasaland is elected by a series of all-African electoral colleges, so in his own inadequate way he does represent Africans. The situation in Southern Rhodesia is different, Mr Savanhu is elected by the entire 'common roll', that is by a roll which is almost entirely composed of Europeans and contains only a few thousand Africans. This constitutional device was designed, in the words of the then Southern Rhodesian Minister of Justice 'so that they will have to consider not merely the African voters but the interests of the country as a whole.' Most Africans dismiss him simply as a stooge. This is unkind and not strictly true. Mr Savanhu holds an invidious position with some skill and strives to do the possible. But very little is possible to him by the terms of the Federal constitution.

Pitted against the African politicians were several settlers' leaders of real ability. In Northern Rhodesia there was only one, Roy Welensky.

He is a great hulk of a man who carries his big body on a powerful bone-structure. He had been the heavyweight boxing champion of the Rhodesias in his youth and had come to his present eminence by way of engine-driving and the leadership of the Northern Rhodesian (European) Railway Workers' Union.

I used to watch him in the Legislative Council. He was then the leader of the Unofficial Members. Under our complicated colonial constitution he was thus rather like a leader of the Opposition, except that his opposition was also part of the coalition of three groups that ruled the country, the civil servants (all Europeans appointed by London); the members elected by the European settlers, and the handful of members representing Africans who held the balance of power.

Welensky sat in the cabinet, the Executive Council, without a portfolio. However, he resigned on one or two occasions when he felt the need to criticize the Government publicly rather than to influence it from within. During these periods of open opposition some life came into the little twenty-four man debating-chamber.

Normally it was deadly dull. The European population of Northern Rhodesia was then a mere forty thousand, the size of a small town in Europe or America, and the standard of the settlers' representatives was probably not unlike that of the town councillors of a small town—Welensky being the exception. The calibre of the African MPs I have already illustrated. The civil servants were the ablest group but usually restricted themselves to recitations of fact and seldom entered into controversy. After some of the most important debates they abstained from voting. I found it hard to write newsworthy bulletins about these sessions. In many ways they were merely public and edited re-stagings of the decision-making discussions in the cabinet.

But when Welensky was on the war-path the atmosphere changed.

A debate might start with the Chief Secretary, Mr R. C. S. Stanley, speaking with urbane, old-worldly wit, quoting Horace or an ancient African chief he had known in his remote, oh-so-remote bush-bashing youth. They were pleasant, competent speeches, as elegant as the speaker's bow-tie, but with little relevance to the sweat and the hatred of the land.

Then Roy Welensky would lever his bulky body in the creased tropical suit out of his arm-chair, glance at one or two notes he had made and launch into a quick-fire rebuttal, getting more insistent and aggressive as he warmed up. He thrust his forefinger in the direction of the officials. The Hansard palantypists strained themselves as his delivery became more rapid, his finger more pugnacious, more accusing. His every gesture seemed to express the self-confidence of the physically powerful. As he had once worried his boxing-opponents in the ring he now punched at the officials,

'I demand an answer. Yes or no? Yes or no?'

They seemed to shrink into their seats as he punched at them. He made shrewd, but by no means brilliant speeches. His colleagues may have praised them as 'statesmanlike' and 'superb', but in fact they were usually commonplace, repetitive and seldom contained an idea that was not widely current among settlers. Nevertheless before many minutes had passed, he had pushed the Chief Secretary, for all his knowledge of the classics, into the position of a reprimanded schoolboy and all the other officials looked more timid and flat-chested than ever. Once he went so far

as to rebuke a senior official for being too discursive in a parliamentary reply, as if he were correcting class compositions! By
these persistent attacks, session after session, he had won suc-
cessive victories over the Colonial Office and the British South
Africa Company.

I used to imagine that if the little men opposite him were to
cheek him he would stride across with big steps and bang their
heads together, while a startled Mr Speaker underneath the wig
would just sit there open-mouthed. It was not surprising: civil
servants are not renowned for being fighters!

African visitors crowding the public galleries in increasing
numbers must have observed the very physical undertones of the
debates and sensed a political factor that was not written into the
Federal constitution, but that Sir Godfrey Huggins later put into
words: that if ever there was a dispute between British officials and
the Rhodesian whites over the interpretation of the constitution,
it would not be the Rhodesians who would give way.

Off the war-path, Welensky had a warm, friendly, paternal
manner. He held out his big bear-like paws with genuine affection.
He liked people (white) and they in turn liked him. I certainly liked
him. I had seen quite a lot of him socially ever since my youth
and I believe I got a view of him denied to official biographers
and journalists.

When I was still an undergraduate I had a vacation-job at the
Government Secretariat. One day I was waiting for a bus when he
came along. It was the time when it was still a patriotic duty to
save petrol and travel by bus, and he came and waited with me,
asked about my studies, my family and so on. A few minutes later
one of the top civil servants, a foppish lawyer, joined us and
ignoring me started to engage Welensky in a conversation they
appeared to have broken off earlier in the day. Welensky turned
away, put out his large hand, pulled me into the circle by the
shoulder and introduced me,

'I want you to meet a friend of mine . . . he tells me that at the
universities in South Africa . . .'

This was not the baby-kissing politician. His interest was warm
and genuine. He knew that to be ignored hurts even an unknown
youth and he was going to teach the man manners. I could understand why it was that in his constituency at Broken Hill, married

couples brought their misunderstandings to him to sort out, and why his elections had been uncontested for years.

I used to see Welensky occasionally at the house of a friend of my family's where he came to relax from the cares of office and to hear records, mainly of operatic music. Host and visitors usually kept a deferential silence about political matters so that he could get away from it all. One evening however, a commercial traveller from Southern Rhodesia who did not know this unspoken rule started to hold forth about the qualifications for a Federal franchise.

'I suppose some way must be found to give Africans a vote. I reckon the minimum should be matric . . . the bare minimum, I think. Some have suggested Standard VIII but God, when I look at my driver . . .'

'You're probably right,' said Welensky, smiling his shrewd but engaging smile, 'but even on that Standard VIII minimum, I'm afraid I'd be disenfranchised. You see, I left school at the age of fourteen. I only got as far as Standard VI.'

Eight years of schooling! Less than most of the African leaders! But then he had a sharp and shrewd intellect, and he was playing on the home-ground of European culture.

Sometimes he spoke of the hardships of his youth, of the poor-white areas of Salisbury and Johannesburg where he had learnt to defend himself, and of the labour-troubles during which his brother, an active trade-unionist, had been framed and sentenced to imprisonment. Subsequently he had been black-listed as a troublemaker so that he could not get a job, Roy had to support him right through the depression. He spoke without very deep bitterness, rather with a sort of satisfaction that the bosses were now among his most ardent admirers. He had started out as the representative of the white workers only, fighting on two fronts, against the employers and against the rising African working-class. The task of a labour-leader in that situation is essentially conservative, to preserve the privileges which the industrial colour-bar, traditional in Southern Africa, gives to the European workers. But gradually he had come to regard the interests of all European settlers to be similar and he no longer spoke for the artisans alone. And of late he had even found that he got on extremely well with many of the financial Realpolitiker of the City of London. They saw in him a down-to-earth-and-no-nonsense-man, strong and

reliable. Under the government of men of his stamp their invest-
ments would be safe. He liked what he considered their realistic
approach to African racial problems, whereas he detested that of
the 'dangerous visionaries' of the Fabian Colonial Bureau. But
a minority of the magnates are far-sighted men who know that
there can be no future for Central Africa and its industries without
reasonably contented African masses. With this minority Welensky
cannot always see eye to eye. But the majority fêted him, so that
he has lost the bitterness of his youth.

He can adapt himself extremely well to the circles in which
he moves. Far too well. Over the years I observed how he expressed
liberal views when chatting in our circle of fairly liberal people,
but very different ones on the Copperbelt.

To us he said, 'We Jews'—he is half-Jewish himself—'we
Jews know about the suppressed aspirations of a people. We know
about frustration. That's something that must be avoided with
Africans. Mind you, the pace of African development is not easy
to regulate. You've got to admit that the present African members
of Legco are a pretty poor bunch.'

We had to admit it.

'But Rhodesia must find a way of absorbing them into society.
Discrimination will ruin the future of this country.'

However, a few days later he addressed a public meeting on the
Copperbelt, where the audience was composed largely of Afri-
kaners, his mother's people. He said that we who had been raised
in Africa knew that the native was not capable of greater political
participation now and would not be for a long time yet. The
Colonial Office was giving the native an inflated idea of his importance. If he continued to delude himself, there would be trouble
between white and black. The native needed to be treated justly
but firmly. This would be easy enough if it were not for the blun-
dering fools at Whitehall who encourage black agitators representing no one but themselves.

At the time I attributed the discrepancy to the hypocrisy I had
grown to expect from politicians, but over the years I decided that
this was an over-simplification. He was by no means a conscious,
calculating hypocrite. I started to understand when I observed
that he could not face a hostile meeting. During a period of
temporary unpopularity, the details of which are irrelevant, the

big aggressive bull of a man almost broke down under the onslaught of a hostile meeting. I decided that he only gave the
appearance of great strength when he knew himself loved and
approved of by his fellows. He could fight outsiders like the
Colonial Office, but not the people among whom he had grown
up. His chief quality as a politician was not his strength at all,
but his sensitivity and intuition. He sensed what people thought,
believed, wanted to hear and he adapted himself with great skill.
It was not hypocrisy, but an emotional necessity. His sad youth in
the hostile slums had left its scars.

I used to think he can be a powerful and able spokesman for the
European settlers, but not a leader. He knows how to express their
feelings, but he will never guide them along paths which they
may, at first, not want to take. Huggins, yes. Sir Godfrey Huggins
is a cocky, impish little man who delights in shocking his public,
who enjoys diverting the political stream. But Welensky is only
formidable when he is swimming with it.

In this way he is not unlike Nkumbula; both are spokesmen
rather than leaders. But with Nkumbula it is easily recognized
because he is tired and lacks dynamism, whereas Welensky seems
tough, aggressive, persistent and is infinitely more able. Nkumbula
yearns for the easy life, Welensky for power. This, and the looks
and mannerisms of the prize-fighter have made him look deceptively
like a leader.

What then, is Welensky's real attitude towards African advancement, the chief problem of the Federation of which he is
now the Prime Minister? That is difficult to ascertain in so adapt-
able a politician. I believe it is basically the attitude of the European
workers among whom he grew up, the attitude of my sporting
acquaintances on the Copperbelt, 'Mustn't run them down . . .
royal game these days! The raw kaffir underground, he's a damn'
fine fellow. It's the educated ones, they're the bad eggs.'

He told his biographer Don Taylor, how as a young man, when
he was managing a 'kaffir-store' far away from other white men,
he once offered sixpence to a huge African to be his sparring-
partner. The African had never heard of such easy money. He
put on the gloves and all went well for a brief period of decorous
sparring. Then Welensky forgot himself and crossed with a
tremendous right flush to the jaw. '*Ikona, baas!*' howled the

N

African, scrambling off the floor. 'No more! Take your sixpence back.'

It is just the sort of anecdote that would have delighted my Copperbelt acquaintances, but this primitive attitude towards Africans is one that a man of Welensky's ability might have overcome, as he overcame his class-rancour. If he has not done so, it is because the all-European milieu in which he lives does not pay serious regard to Africans, and he is not the man to challenge the values prevalent among his fellows.

I am not suggesting that it would have been easy or even possible for a settler's champion to win the affection of Africans. There are very real cleavages of interest which personal charm alone cannot bridge. But with his human warmth and understanding of people and his intuitive adaptability it should have been possible for him to avoid becoming the most hated of Europeans. But Welensky plays entirely to a white audience. He cultivates the bluff, forthright manner of the frontiersman which Rhodesian whites value highly. He believes in straight, tough talking, 'I call a spade a spade . . . Don't mollycoddle Africans, don't spoonfeed them. They've got to earn their passages.'

But Africans traditionally, value the reverse, politeness and respect towards elders, wisdom, 'speaking well'. Waluse valued above all one quality, kindness. If Rhodesian Africans have to say an unpleasant truth, they take care to cloak it in conciliatory compliments. Only at moments of uncontrollable anger and hatred will they call a spade by that name. So to them every speech of Welensky's on racial matters sounded loaded with venom and loathing. It was not always what he said, but his pugnacious delivery that upset them.

I have quoted some of Yamba's reactions. One remark Welensky made in that debate on Federation was of particular significance because it travelled beyond the debating chamber into the compounds and locations and then was whispered in ever more garbled form in almost every village of Northern Rhodesia and beyond. Exactly what Welensky said of the Africans was this:

> 'If they do not come with us, and I do not mean it as a threat, if they do not come with us they will meet with the same fate which came to the Indians in the USA, they

disappeared. We have got to become part of the industrial civilization that the western world insists upon. If we do not do that, we will disappear.'

Despite the disavowal, Yamba and other Africans saw this as a threat. In fact, it was no more than a tactless remark, born of Welensky's ignorance of Africans. Few races have fitted themselves to industry so rapidly. But he should have known that to them it would mean one thing: he wants to murder us. He wants to wipe us out like the Americans wiped out the Red Indian.

I think I remember that I had uncomfortable forebodings as I included his words in our news-bulletin. Africans were so hurt, so much on edge. I did not think they could bear that sort of remark. But a newswriter must not censor the tactless remarks of politicians, however much he may fear their consequences.[1]

---

[1] The predicted split in the African Congress occured while this book was in the press. Kaunda led the more extreme breakaway Zambia Congress which called for a boycott of the elections for the Northern Rhodesian Legislative Council. His organization appeared to be gaining ground when it was proscribed in March 1959 and Kaunda and other leaders were 'rusticated', ie banished to villages. Nkumbula stood for and was elected to the Legislature.

In March 1959 Mr Savanhu was appointed parliamentary secretary to the Federal Ministry of Home Affairs.

12. VAMPIRE-MEN

NEVER BEFORE had so many British politicians made an attempt to understand Central African conditions. Many agreed with Stanley Evans, the Labour member, who informed the House of Commons that ninety-five per cent of the African population lacked political consciousness, knew nothing and cared less about Federation.

But then the inarticulate spoke.

On the Copperbelt the sale of sugar dropped suddenly. Rumours said that the Europeans were poisoning it, that Roy Welensky had ordered a massacre. Within a day or two this had spread to Broken Hill, then to Lusaka, then Livingstone. But the news had not yet penetrated to my office. I knew nothing of all this, nothing until late one afternoon when I was putting the finishing touches to the day's news-bulletin. Next door, in the press-office, they were also still working. There was nothing unusual in this. When the Legislative Council was in session they often issued late press-communiques. I went next door to collect my copy. The orderly who normally worked the duplicator was busy there now. With him was the photo-department's darkroom assistant.

'More press-comms?' I asked.

They stood as if paralysed. I took one from their large pile. It was headed, 'Private Circular to Africans only!' It was a leaflet being duplicated in secret. It said that on the 28th October the 'House of Laws' in London had decided to put poisoned sugar on sale to Africans, commencing on February 8th of next year, 1953. This would have the effect in the case of women, of causing their children to be born dead, and with men of making them impotent. The sugar would be recognized by the letters LPS on the packets. All Africans were warned to beware of such sugar.

I took the amazing leaflet next door to read it at my leisure. The two Africans followed me, blocked the door and asked menacingly, 'What do you want this for?'

'I'm interested,' I replied.

They stood around undecidedly, then said, 'Can we have it back now?'

'No,' I said, 'I'm keeping it.'

I picked up my other papers and pushed my way through them. They stepped aside. I walked over to the broadcasting studios to deliver my news-bulletin and to ask the Africans on duty about this leaflet. They said they had heard the rumour the previous day but had never seen such pamphlets. The matter was serious and I could not close my eyes to it. I took it to the home of one of the senior men of the Information Department. He nearly went through the roof before I had finished telling him my story.

'The police came and told me about this thing this very morning,' he said, 'they're ransacking the whole country for the machine on which they were typed.'

'Well, they can stop looking,' I said.

'No, they come from at least four different sources,' he told me, 'some from the Copperbelt. That's where it seems to have started. Anyway, they can make an example of these chaps . . .'

A day or two later I stood in court as the crown-witness. The two accused had the look of hunted animals in their eyes. They did not have a lawyer and the chase was easy, almost unsporting. The Congress who might have briefed a lawyer either forgot about it or wanted to make sure they were not identified with the deed. The public prosecutor was a keen young huntsman.

'Where did you get this from? . . . Who asked you to duplicate it? . . . When did you first see it? . . . Where?'

The accused never split on whoever had asked them to make these leaflets. Maybe they had done it on their own initiative after seeing some copies from the Copperbelt. They invented a fantastic tale: they had picked up a leaflet in the street and thinking that the Director of Information ought to be informed about such a dangerous matter they had decided to make copies to give to him.

They struggled pathetically, but their every movement enmeshed them more. I too was in on the kill. I had said in evidence that I had seen about fifty leaflets on the duplicator.

'How many copies did you want to give the director?' the prosecutor demanded to know.

'Two or three,' said the darkroom assistant.

'Mr Fraenkel said that you made about fifty. Why?'

'No we didn't. He's lying. He has always hated us.'

'Another witness has said that he found some two hundred copies in the incinerator, partly destroyed. So you made two hundred copies?'

'The first few weren't neat.'

'Does it need two hundred to get two or three neat copies?'

'My friend had never seen a duplicator working. I wanted to show him . . .'

They had very little understanding of European court-procedure. The magistrate tried to explain, but his legal terms and concepts meant nothing to them, either in English or in translation. When he told them that they now had the right to cross-examine me, the dark-room assistant only asked me why it was that I hated him, he had done me no harm. Why had I denounced him?

Later the prosecutor asked the accused whether they had believed what the leaflets said.

'No, sir, I didn't,' replied the dark-room assistant.

To me it was only too obvious that he was lying, but he probably thought that it would infuriate the whites still more if he now insisted that it was true. I felt like shouting across the court-room,

'Admit it, you idiot, admit it!'

But the prosecutor was already in for the kill.

'So you made these pamphlets knowing that they contained a lie which would cause great fear and alarm among ignorant people?'

'Yes sir.'

The magistrate, in his judgement, preached at length about how nonsensical such a rumour was and how dangerous. Then he sentenced the dark-room assistant to three years imprisonment, the orderly to two.

The sentence was fully justified, but I did not relish my own part in the hunt, and I doubted whether the example would have much effect. However, it did succeed in stopping the spread of leaflets. But that made little difference, this was the sort of rumour that had started by word of mouth among the illiterates and among them it continued to spread like an epidemic, to Nyasaland and to parts of Southern Rhodesia. We put all our persuasive skill into discrediting it in our broadcasts, but without success. I sought out some of my old acquaintances, simple, uneducated

Africans I had known since I was a child. For the first time they seemed embarrassed by my visits. It was no longer good to be seen being too friendly with a European. We discussed the rumour and I tried to explore their beliefs to find some way of dispelling them. Time and again they brought up the name of Welensky. Didn't I know that he had said that he would kill all natives? Didn't I know that the same had been done in America? I tried to explain what he had really meant, all to no avail.

From sugar the rumour turned to tinned meat. Recently a low-grade meat had come on the market, labelled 'For African consumption'. The rumour said that this was human meat, poisoned to break African opposition to Federation. A district commissioner on the Copperbelt held a public meat-eating demonstration at which he and his senior African clerk opened some of these tins and braved the inferior cuts that the Rhodesias reserve for black men. But the majority of the audience merely decided that the DC had a strong medicine to resist the poison and the fear was unabated. More than at other times, Africans turned to look behind them as they walked, and avoided paths through the tall grass. One never knew what might lurk there.

The rumours were most widely believed by the illiterate, but not only by them. Like witchcraft beliefs these rumours too had a much wider influence. One member of Alick Nkhata's Quartet, a nervous young man with about eight years of schooling behind him got into such a state of anxiety that he would not touch any food for a week. At the week-end he cycled many miles out of town to a village where all food was grown locally and was undefiled by Europeans. There he ate and then bought supplies. After that he made the long trip there every week-end.

Europeans read about the court-case in their papers, grumbled that the Government did not lock up their offices properly and laughed at the ignorant *munts*. Perhaps they observed that some of their servants, previously honest, had started to steal sugar bought by and for Europeans, but few inquired any deeper. If they sensed that there was more to know, they shut out the realization. They refused to see what was uncomfortable for them, just as Germans I had known in the days of Hitler had refused to see things that it was more comfortable not to know. But to me all this was no laughing matter. I knew that the Mau Mau in Kenya

had been launched with the 'ridiculous' rumour that the award of
city-status to Nairobi presaged further alienation of African land.
What more was facing us?

One evening, some weeks later, I drove home just as it was
getting dark. The streets seemed strangely deserted, but I paid
no special attention to it. When I reached home my mother asked
me to speak to Senti, our cook. She could not make out what was
troubling him. I found him sitting in the kitchen, grey with fear.
He clutched at my hand and begged me to drive him home. There
was terror in his eyes.

'But for God's sake, Senti, why?'

'I am afraid.'

'Afraid of what?'

'They're all over.'

'Who, man, who?'

'*Banyama!*'

Banyama! Kamupila! Vampire-men! So the atavistic myth was
going around again. Several times during my years in Africa it had
come up, the story that there were vampire-men abroad, that they
caught children and gave them an injection so that they lost the
power of speech and became docile creatures of their captors who
led them away to some far-away place, then sucked their blood
and feasted on their flesh. Other variants had it that adults too,
were caught, that a rubber ball was forced into their mouths so
that they could not shout and they were marched off to the Belgian
Congo for slave-labour. Unlike the vampires of European myth-
ology, the *banyama* are not dead men who have returned to walk
the earth, but living men. Anyone may be a *munyama* (singular),
European or African, you or I or our best friend. One cannot
trust anybody. A *munyama* need not even be a free agent of evil,
he may have been captured by another and then turned loose to
catch more victims for cannibalistic orgies.

Just what episodes in Africa's past, human sacrifices or slave-
raiding, had given rise to the superstition I could never establish,
but I had observed that the rumour always reared its head at
times of crisis and insecurity. One of the worst scares I remember
was a few months after the war when the Northern Rhodesian
troops had not yet returned and their families could not understand
why. The rumour that one of my own broadcasts had set off about

the Northern Rhodesian Regiment drowning on the way to
Malaya may well have had a similar undercurrent.

But now a new version of the *munyama*-belief appeared, the
victims lost their will-power and were made to support Federation!
The agents of the Capricorn Africa Society were accused of being
vampire-men. Obviously they had themselves been caught and
then turned loose to catch others. Why else would any African
say he supported Federation?

I tried to talk Senti out of it, but he swore that half a dozen
people in his suburb had been caught by *banyama* and had disappeared without a trace. I phoned the compound-manager whom
I knew, and he told me that the previous week a woman had, in
fact, reported that her husband was missing. A day or two later
however, he had been found to have spent the time in the embraces
of another. But Senti was quite unconvinced. I took him home
that evening and, seeing how upset he was, drove between the
rows of concrete huts along unmade tracks, right up to his house.
He called his wife from the car, she opened her door a little, he
dashed out of the car and disappeared, bolting the door behind
him. I returned through the dark and silent compound, but since
all the thousands of houses look identical I lost my way. I stopped
to ask, calling outside several houses where a candle was still
showing, but got no response. Behind the barred doors people
were sitting in silence. At long last I found my own way out of the
maze.

The fresh rumour again travelled all over the country like a
bush-fire. *Bacapricorn* became synonymous with *banyama*, vampire-men. Children were kept away from school and every day
around dusk the streets emptied.

Any unusual event became the focus of rumours. On the
Copperbelt a soap-company gave away free samples to Africans.
This had never happened before and Africans threw away the
samples, believing the soap would make them lose their will-
power and accept Federation.

In Nyasaland the rumour had it that the vampires used a grey
Land Rover with a shiny metal back which looked a little like a
bully-beef tin blown up, to transport away their human cargo.
When the Central African Film Unit, which happened to use just
such a camera-truck, turned up at a school-ground, children fled

in terror and one little boy fainted and collapsed at the feet of the startled camera-men.

Then the whole vast terror found a new focus: us! The Central African Broadcasting Station and its announcers. How could the announcers broadcast 'bad news', news which displeased Africans, unless they had lost all their will-power? How else could they be made to read pro-Federation propaganda on the air?

We alone of Lusaka government departments sent our staff home by car, because our announcers worked late and unusual shifts. Our green van moved about the silent compounds at night, after even the noise of the radio had ceased. This gave grounds for further suspicion. Obviously this was the truck in which the vampire-men transported away their human cargo. But where to? Recently a labour recruiting agency had opened a transit-camp outside Lusaka. That must be the place. Years later I discovered that an *ad-hoc* committee of African Congressmen had, unbeknown to their leaders, hired a taxi and sent men to keep this camp under observation.

Then the rumour found yet another unusual thing to focus on, unusual courage, the courage of our Falstaffian radio-comic Edward Kateka, 'he from whom words pour unceasingly like water down a waterfall'. He had been a sergeant-major in the army and had learnt to stand on his own feet and disregard community pressure in a way that is very unusual among such gregarious people as the Africans. The rumours did not cow him. They affected him less than any other member of our African staff and he defied the rumour-mongers openly. When he heard some men whisper behind him in the street he did not run away and lock himself in. He turned and confronted them, demanding that they repeat to his face what they had whispered behind his back. Obviously such a man must have strong medicine, he must be the most potent of the vampire-men. Kateka continued to go out at night, and even went to a sparsely attended dance. Again he heard himself abused in whispers. Such a man as he, they said, should not be allowed to live. Later, as he was about to leave, he turned around and called into the hall, 'I'm going home now, along the main-road to Chilenje. Those of you who want to kill me, come and get me. I shall be alone.'

It was against Kateka above all that the hatred and suspicion broke. A few days later he was awakened in the morning by a crowd around his house who threatened to burn it down and to kill him. He opened the door and faced them. They recoiled and shouted,

'A child is missing! You have abducted it. *Munyama!*'

'That's a serious charge,' he replied. 'If I have committed this crime I should be punished.'

'Yes, yes,' they shrieked.

'If what you say is true I should be reported to the police and tried and put into prison.'

'Yes, yes.'

'In that case let us all go to the police-station and you can lay a charge against me.'

The ignorant mob agreed and with Kateka striding at their head they marched to the nearest police-station. Once there he asked for protection which was immediately granted.

Kateka could take all this, but his wife could not. She was terrified, and while he was at work she took refuge in our offices. She sat in a corner all day long, quietly suckling her baby, miserable and fearful.

Deprived of their prey the mob sent Kateka and our other announcers anonymous letters:

'. . . you wanted to kill Nkumbula you even received revolvers from your Master the General Prisedent of Capricornists. You see now nine people missed in Lusaka here. But mind out We are still on the meeting, you shall see one of you he will be killed you are nine in number you are all civil servants here is your names Kateka, Nkata, Elieli Piri and Mwanakatwe and so on.

'Your huts will be burnt to ashes all of you and we can't tell the time of burning them you are the people pretending to become mans eater, *kamupila*, even your wives . . .'

The atmosphere was becoming ever more like that of Mau-Mau-ridden Kenya. Nkhata and Zulu too, were accused. It seemed that the better-loved the broadcaster had been, the greater the hatred that was now turned on him.

'My best friends are afraid to come and see me,' complained Nkhata, 'I am quite alone. They don't even greet me in the street.

They cross over to the other side to avoid me. It is not they that believe this nonsense, but they're afraid. They think they too will be accused if they are seen with me.'

I nodded, 'Like being a Jew in Nazi Germany. Even those who knew better were afraid to be seen with us.'

He did not know the circumstances and continued,

'I have only one friend who still comes to see me.'

'That takes courage,' I said, 'who is it?'

'Waluse.'

I nodded. Waluse: not only did he value kindness in others, he also knew when others needed it most. He was a man of rare qualities.

Pepe Zulu seemed to me on the verge of a nervous breakdown. He had committed himself entirely to the side of rationalism and westernization, had dismissed the past. 'It has nothing to teach us.' But now Africa's past was catching up with him. He did not have the emotional resources to cope with the onslaught.

'Why us?' he begged to know, 'why us? They've always trusted us. I know they've mistrusted other departments, but then people like the Forestry officers do bully them to stop them cutting wood. But we, we've always been popular. We bring them education and entertainment and we don't even ask a licence-fee. Why pick on us now?'

'There's so much suspicion around,' said Kittermaster, 'that they probably fear the Greeks especially when they bear gifts.'

The Africans looked mystified and Kittermaster told them the story of Troy. At other times they would have laughed and asked questions and responded with Bantu legends, but now they listened miserably. The laughter had gone out of our studios.

'But there must be some way of fighting this thing,' I said.

'I'll try,' said Nkhata, 'I'll compose a song about it. I'll poke fun at it. I'll say that everybody is a *munyama* now. We're all *banyama* together.'

Kittermaster was worried, 'In their present frame of mind they're likely to believe it.'

'We'll have to test it out on some guinea-pigs before we put it on the air,' I suggested.

'I'm hoping to give a concert later this month,' said Nkhata, 'I could try it on the audience.'

'But will anybody turn up for a concert of yours?' I asked incredulously.

'I hope so,' he said. 'When there are many of them together I can't very well suck their blood!'

I shook my head and looked at Kittermaster. We'll never understand these people properly, I thought.

For weeks on end we moved in a strange twilight world in which the nightmare and cannibalistic orgies had assumed a fearful reality and all the ugliness of the old Africa lay exposed. 'Open sore of the world', Dr Livingstone had called Africa. It was still far from healed.

But the great majority of Europeans knew nothing of all this. They continued to play bridge and to give cocktail parties where they told jokes about the African miner who had refused a better job in the Ventilation Department because 'Congress he say ventilation no good for we Africans.'

Nkhata proved to have been right about his concert. A large audience turned up, paid their entrance-fee and applauded his amusing songs about modern town-life just as of old. The new song about vampire-men went down fairly well and caused some laughter. But during the interval when he went to get some fresh air, members of the audience strolling around outside shrieked when they noticed him among them and fled in terror.

I have never been able to understand this strange juxtaposition of terror and gaiety, of tragedy and laughter, in the make-up of so many Central Africans. On first acquaintance they strike the visitor as happy, laughing, singing people. But should he stay and make an effort to get to know them better, he will be overwhelmed by their dark fears and morbid superstitions and their deep sadness. He looks at their legends and starts to shudder. There is one of the Tonga tribe, transcribed by Torrend, which is fairly typical of hundreds I have recorded on tape. It tells of a father who killed his pregnant wife with a spear for eating some fruit that he wanted for himself. The unborn child then emerges from the womb and, trailing its umbilical cord, it follows the father, weeping and accusing him until he turns and slays the child also. Eventually the mother-in-law traps him in a deep hole, pours boiling water over him and he dies in agony. In other similar tales told to children, fathers kill babies by forcing red-hot irons up their

anuses. I sometimes think that the laughter is only a veil to cover
the terror-stricken soul, but maybe that is not the whole story
either.

We put Nkhata's song about the vampire-men on the air, but it
did not have very much effect. The rumour took a long time to die.

All these danger-signs went unheeded by the politicians in
London. But then, how could they be expected to see political
expression in the symbolism of the voiceless fear of the fish for the
circling birds of prey, in the nightmare of the monster that strikes
men dumb and sucks their blood, in the dread of sexual impotence?
How could they be expected to translate such expression into the
blue books and white papers with which they are familiar?

Few of the Africans knew much about the constitutional proposals. In that respect the politicians were right. But Africans were
most certainly not unconcerned. They feared the domination of the
Southern settlers with an intensity greater than any I have ever
seen.

We few who were close enough to see this either did not have
the courage to speak out, or were ignored by the old hands in the
Secretariats. The handful of missionaries who did speak out were
dismissed as 'impractical visionaries'.

In Nyasaland the tension burst into riot on a large scale in one
district. Court-houses were destroyed, telephone wires cut, 'loyal'
chiefs beaten, bridges wrecked. In Northern Rhodesia violence
was very near the surface, but only erupted in less spectacular
incidents, the stoning of European-owned cars, chiefs refusing to
obey orders and threatenening civil servants, the boycott of
European stores and pickets beating would-be purchasers. On the
Copperbelt there started a series of strikes over petty grievances,
elsewhere chiefs ordered their tribesmen to resist unpopular laws,
and were dismissed by the Government. The actions were often
apparently unconnected with Federation but were the product of
the general malaise.

On June 24th, 1953, the House of Commons voted by a hundred
and eighty-eight to a hundred and sixty-four in favour of Federation. The Conservatives voted for it, a group of Labour MPs
defied the party leadership and abstained, the Liberals and the
majority of Labour MPs voted against it.

Many politicians then predicted that Africans would come to

accept Federation once they saw that it did not bring serious changes into their daily lives. However, five years after the event they still harbour as passionate a hatred of it as ever, and countries that were reasonably happy backwaters a few years ago are now full of suspicion and political violence.

The faith that our audience had once had in our broadcasting station had collapsed completely. Our announcers were threatened. Our recording-vans had their tyres punctured in remote villages. People refused to record for us. If they could be persuaded to do so, many of their songs had the refrain, 'We don't want Federation.'

We had reached rock-bottom.

The African masses expressed themselves in primitive and irrational ways, but their fears were real and rational and, in my view, to a large extent justified. They could see that power was being handed to people who were hostile to their aspirations and that their future advancement would be hindered. However, the form that their opposition took and the morbid intensity of their fears seemed to me to have struck some very deep root. One would have to pry into the infantile experiences and into the subconscious life of the Africans to lay it bare, but that is a task for a psychiatrist. I am not suggesting that African behaviour was emotional rather than rational and that it can therefore be discounted. The distinction is false. It is generally acknowledged that the political behaviour of all peoples, however apparently rational, has a substructure of subconscious motivation.

European settlers often say that it will take Africans a thousand years to reach our state of development. This is nonsense. We Europeans are not so far from believing such myths. Ernest Jones relates in his book *The Nightmare* that the age of the Encyclopaedists and of Voltaire was also the age of some of the worst vampire-scares to sweep Europe. A great one arose in Danzig as late as 1855, and in the eighteen-seventies at Chicago and Rhode Island there were instances of corpses being exhumed and parts burnt, to stop 'vampiric visitations'. I myself can bear witness that German Nazis spread with all the means of modern propaganda, stories about Jews committing ritual murder and using the blood of Christian children, which were every bit as absurd as the *banyama* stories. Nevertheless they obtained some credence. No, it is not likely take Africans a thousand years to reach our state of development.

In 1950 Sir Godfrey Huggins spoke about the difficulties of transplanting democracy to Africa. He said, 'It is irresponsible to place such a dangerous weapon as the vote in the hands of people who still seek the solution to their problems by studying the entrails of a goat.'

This is a sentiment with which I agree. But such men as Waluse and Kateka and many others I have written about have freed themselves from their past and had the courage to withstand enormous social pressures. They have proved themselves equal and superior to most Europeans. They seem to have accomplished that thousand year transition already. Yet they do not have an the equal vote, and a dozen times a day they are lumped together with the uneducated majority.

To the majority, to the lads in Barotseland who in 1953 asked me about the results of World War II, to John Square, the cowboy, and to Amon Chapusha, the Watchtower adherent, I too would not give the vote. Not yet. They need more education and more experience in dealing with imported political concepts. However, this is no justification for treating them as sub-human, for denying them the right to acquire industrial skills, for humiliating them by curfews or by making them shop through hatches, for inventing a hundred devices designed to deny that they were created in the image of God, for making no attempt to understand them.

Sir Godfrey's statement is a case in point: had he ever tried to get to understand the Africans he ruled for over twenty years he might have known that the tribes of the Rhodesias did divining by means of bones and of axes, by hunting, through poison-ordeals on chickens and on humans, by medicated horns, boiling water and by smelling out, but *none* of them ever sought a solution to their problems by studying the entrails of a goat. That practice was indulged in by the highly civilized, and enfranchised, rulers of ancient Rome.

13. UP-HILL STRUGGLES

OUR GOODWILL and prestige seemed damaged beyond repair. Many of our most enthusiastic listeners had been alienated. The country was seething with hatred.

No doubt that was the time I should have resigned, but I hung on to my job. I found it too interesting to give up. I tried to delude myself that maybe things would get better, that possibly Federation might not be such a bad thing, that there might turn out to be some truth in the liberal protestations of the settler-politicians.

Our team set to work to try and regain the confidence of our public all over again. 'We've got to catch the genuine *vox populi*,' said Kittermaster, 'we've got to go out and get the men in the street. We're not yet exploiting the full possibilities of these little portable recording-machines. Studio-discussions and brains-trusts are all very well, but we ought to have a crack at discussion programmes in which the speakers are ordinary men literally in the street, people shooting their mouths off about everyday problems. I'd produce them myself if I didn't have so much paper-work. I'm weighed down with all this paper.'

I offered to try a programme in Bemba, collaborating with an African producer. Kittermaster suggested Nkhata the guitarist.

I insisted that we would have to tackle some real live problems like the colour-bar in shops, juvenile delinquency, the bad treatment of patients in hospitals and low wages. Kittermaster agreed although he realized that sooner or later we would come in for the criticism of the settler Press which had of late, become very much more noisy. He knew that we would never regain the confidence of Africans without running the risk of settler criticism.

I think we both regarded these programmes as a sort of atonement for past weaknesses, as a gesture to show that even if we had had to compromise, we had not knuckled under for good. We were still determined to run an honest unbiased broadcasting service.

Nkhata and I got down to the series. We called it '*Imikalile Yesu*', 'The Way We Live'. We decided that for the discussion on juvenile delinquency he should try and contact a social worker, a

o

well-known young thug, a tribal elder, a young prostitute, a drunkard at the beer-hall, a villager, a Congress official . . .

It was easy to plan, but difficult to get the speakers. Most of the people Nkhata asked, refused to record. After a day or two spent tramping the compounds, he came back and reported that the only people who would collaborate were some of the *bwanas'* good boys', and there weren't many of those. Most of the people had shouted, 'You want us to support Federation. You are all Government spies and *banyama*. If we say what we really think you'll never broadcast it anyway. You'll just report us to the police.'

So in the first few programmes we had to call upon personal friends of Nkhata's and mine. Amon the Watchtowerman, and Senti my cook, made their debuts as broadcasters, voicing their own strange, untutored views on the issues of the day. We edited down the recordings, full of long rambling opinions, into short, controversial programmes. Since our choice of speakers was restricted, these first programmes were not as good as they might have been, but they produced an effect. People no longer claimed that if they really said what they thought, we would never broadcast it anyway. They were hearing some views on the air that most emphatically did not sound like Government hand-outs.

Gradually others came forward to record. Often the first was some bold ruffian who merely yelled into the microphone that the Government were a bunch of bastards. We recorded it dutifully, knowing that we would edit it out later. But the onlookers were encouraged by the boldness and others came forward and made more original observations. After a few weeks we had broken the ice and could usually count on getting a sufficient number of interesting speakers. After a month or two we had queues wherever Nkhata appeared with his recording-machine.

Most of the views we heard were misinformed, abusive and primitive, but we allowed speakers to let off steam and tried to incorporate many of them in our programmes, balancing them against better-informed and more rational opinions.

It defeats one's purpose to be too far out of step with an audience. It is permissible to be one step ahead, or two, but the ideas and facts accepted as commonplace by most Europeans often seem quite novel and highly improbable to Africans. One cannot teach if one gets too many steps ahead. I had observed this repeatedly. At the Namushakende Development Team for example, peasants newly converted to soil conservation, who spoke in their own lively, homely but seldom accurate way, were far more persuasive than expert lecturers.

But it was difficult work trying to re-establish a reputation for impartiality in that tense political climate. Not that there was any shortage of subjects for frank discussion; for instance, at the time there was a great wave of resentment among Africans against the police, who had used tear-gas to disperse rioting women with babies. 'They'd gas their own mothers, the ——,' said an African I spoke to. I decided to take the bull by the horns and choose as my subject for the next week's programme the police, and why they were unpopular.

This would have been an obvious decision for a broadcaster in happier countries, but in Central Africa it meant bracing oneself for a possible onslaught from one's fellow-Europeans for 'letting down the side'. We braced ourselves.

There seemed no point in having anyone lecture about the tensions that arise from the imposition of an unfamiliar system of law, when this imposition is in the hands of European-appointed policemen with qualifications quite different from those demanded by Bantu society of its traditional holders of authority. We had to keep the argument to concepts familiar to our audience: whether or not the police accepted bribes, whether or not they showed polite-ness.

In our editing, Nkhata and I strove to preserve the distinctly African flavour of the arguments.

'I hate policemen,' said a man whom we recorded at Broken Hill, 'they are my enemies. If I made friends with one and he spots a stolen article in my house, he'll arrest me. Even if I'm his friend, he'll arrest me. Or maybe if he's too embarrassed he'll report me to another and the other one will come for me.'

Next we brought in a speaker who said that this was high praise indeed, that it was a policeman's duty to be impartial and to report all law-breakers, even friends and relatives. But this was probably not anything like as convincing as the story told by a labourer who praised a policeman. 'He helps to catch that thief for you, but does not ask any money from you. He only does work for you but is paid by the Government at the end of the month.'

Before the broadcast we showed a transcript of the programme to senior police-officers. I was pleased and relieved when they read peaceably all the abuse heaped upon the heads of their men, then remarked that since their own point of view was also presented fairly they had no objections. Even in our climate something of the British tradition of tolerance still managed to grow. But not everywhere.

Next we tackled hospitals. Why were Africans still resisting going to Government hospitals after so many years of intensive propaganda? Why were mission and mine hospitals less suspect?

We reaped a great crop of grievances, some ridiculous, many justified. To each we gave a patient hearing, then brought in African dressers and male nurses to give their views. We avoided doctors. They might have been more accurate, but less convincing. Despite the many grievances they expressed, the programme amounted to a very formidable case for the advantages of hospitals.

Among the grievances vented there were many that were commonplace among Africans, for example, that women feared hospitals because they did not trust the morals of the African male nurses, and that the nurses secretly sold drugs prescribed for patients.

There is a measure of truth in both. There had been a serious number of cases of adultery against male nurses, and there is an active black market in stolen drugs which almost every African knows about. During the very week of my broadcast there was a *cause célèbre* of the first sort, when one of the male nurses tried to commit suicide. But since this case only involved Africans, it was never reported in the European papers. I thought it right and proper to ventilate such grievances, and to get some facts and figures to show that they were not as widespread as the rumours would have it.

This broadcast brought upon my head the long-expected attack of the local paper. 'For the Witchdoctors an Official Boost' ran the headline. The paper suggested that by allowing such grievances to be broadcast, we had seriously damaged the reputation of the hospitals.

'In our opinion contradiction was not enough. They should have been deleted from the script because the suspicion and distrust the stating of these views will have caused could be removed by no amount of contradiction.'

As if in that land of distrust and suspicion the venting of a few commonplaces would have any serious effect!

But what really roused the editor to fury was that while speakers were discussing why African herbalists had no cures for syphilis, I had allowed it to be said that this was because the disease had only come into the country recently, with the coming of the Europeans. In fact, it is not certain whether the Arabs or the Europeans qualify for this doubtful distinction, but certainly its great spread dates from the coming of the Europeans and the beginnings of the towns. But the paper was not arguing about facts. I had touched upon a deeper emotion.

'It can only substantiate the worst lies spread about Europeans by African nationalist extremists.' It was suggested that the producer be fired immediately.

My superiors gave me their backing, but what gave me even more pleasure were some of the letters of support that African listeners wrote. Above all they seemed to appreciate the respect that our programmes showed for simple, uneducated people, allowing them a hearing almost as if we regarded them as human beings! One of the letters came from Stephen Mpashi, Northern Rhodesia's first African novelist. It expressed much more graphically what we were trying to do, than we had been able to say ourselves.

'People are airing off their views quite freely, in other words they are emptying their minds freely hence making it easy for those who know how to refill the minds of people with good knowledge.

The best way I know of changing a man to your way of thinking is to start off by saying "yes, yes" and then adding a little "but" after he has spoken himself out.'

We certainly added our little 'but'. At the end of each programme, however, we left the decisions to our listeners. We summed up the various views briefly and then put it to the public: what do you think?

The approach worried Nkhata a little. He thought we should end on a more definite note, but I insisted that one could only create responsible citizens by making them think for themselves. Nkhata was not alone in worrying. Many of our listeners wrote in to ask 'But which is right?'

A few weeks later Kittermaster launched a second, similar series in the Nyanja language. This was called '*Kabvulumvulu*', the 'Whirlwind', because the producer swept all over the country like a whirlwind, recording opinions. The producer was Sylvester Masiye, the African who had organized army educational broadcasts at Nairobi and who had been insulted in the airways bus at Ndola. Massiye's approach differed from mine in one important respect. Instead of summing up for all sides at the end of the programme, he gave his own decisions without any embarrassment.

'Now, Tom Nyirenda who said that wives should eat at table together with their husbands was right. This encourages civilized family life. How can a wife share her husband's problems if he regards her as a servant who eats outside after he has finished? Further, Blackson Phiri who said that your man-visitors will take liberties with your wife if she sits at table is talking nonsense. You should not invite such people to your home.'

Masiye's programmes were an enormous success, attracting ten times the correspondence of 'The Way We Live'. Masiye was right and I was wrong. That was the exciting thing about our job, one was ever learning, discovering. The majority of our listeners were still at the stage where they wanted a measure of parental guidance. Weaning had to be gradual.

Not that all listeners always followed Masiye's advice without demur. When he claimed that there was no such thing as witchcraft, bagfuls of letters arrived to convince him of his folly. One even wrote from remote Nyasaland,

> 'Confirm that you still deny the existence of witchcraft and I shall turn up one night at your house to convince you . . . "If the child wants to play with fire, give it to him so that he learns from experience." I am the dreadful one!'

But this new threat to our announcers caused us no worry! We had other problems to face.

In 1954 Kittermaster resigned. It is not for me to discuss his reasons, but maybe they were not entirely unlike those of Marriot,

'The District Officer' in a novel of that name he has since had published. Marriot leaves his district frustrated by racial tensions that destroy his life's work and by time-serving officials who are too weak-kneed to resist settler politicians.

African members of the Legislative Council paid Kittermaster high tribute and one of the local papers noticed that this was the very first time that African legislators had paid spontaneous tribute to a European official.

When his furniture was sold by auction, one of my acquaintances in the crowd asked a European farmer there what it was he was hoping to buy. 'Oh, nothing,' the farmer replied, 'I've just come to gloat . . . to gloat that at long last we shall be rid of this man.'

The Colonial Office in London did not want to lose so talented a broadcaster and persuaded Kittermaster to reconsider, to take over the running of a broadcasting station in a very different sort of country, a quiet island in the Mediterranean with sunny beaches and cool forests, an island where there was no tension between black and white. Its name? Cyprus!

A fortnight after his arrival it burst into rebellion and not long after his fine new transmitters were blown to smithereens. But all that seems to have caught the administrators as unawares as the Mau Mau rising in Kenya and as the African reaction to Federation. This lack of simple human contact seems to be much more than a local Rhodesian problem.

To me Kittermaster's departure was a serious personal blow, but I decided to try and carry on. The administration revealed its utter lack of interest by appointing as acting Broadcasting Officer the very first district officer who happened to come back from overseas leave and had not yet been assigned to a district. He was a conscientious and honest man, but totally without experience, flair or even interest in the exciting job that had been thrust upon him. On the stroke of four he drove home, leaving behind him a startled staff used to seeing every member of the team working many hours overtime, not for money but for the love of the work.

I was confirmed in my appointment as second-in-charge, and tried desperately to keep alive some of the enthusiasm for honest forthright broadcasting. This resulted in frequent brushes over news policy. Sometimes I got my way, sometimes I did not.

Then, after what seemed an interregnum of years, Sapper, who had been my predecessor as second-in-charge, returned to our station as head. It was good to have an enthusiast at the helm again. But times had changed: things were never to be what they had been before Federation.

Physically however we grew. The planning of years before now started to bear fruit. Money voted and architects' drawings made several years before now started to become brick and mortar, new studios, transmitters, offices. We launched a second programme, so that we could now broadcast in two of our nine languages simultaneously. The vast record-library that we had accumulated, the largest library of African music in the world, now served to fill our great increase in broadcasting hours. We took on more staff.

Sapper saw that the happy-go-lucky cameraderie of former days could no longer cope with our growing task. Regretfully he reorganized us. Instead of the informal discussions which everybody from office-orderly to boss, plus any visiting friends, had joined, we now had weekly meetings of senior staff at which minutes were taken. A hierarchy of responsibility was built up.

I knew that it was an inevitable and probably overdue development, but I could not help regretting it. It meant more responsibility for me, as second-in-charge, but it gave me little pleasure.

Instead of working in a little control-room with the open door crowded with eavesdroppers, our men now broadcast from beautifully-pannelled studios, air-conditioned and without windows. Two foot six of cavity-wall, literally the thickest walls in the country, separated us from the world outside. It was much more professional, but did it make for better results?

My own position was changing also. I now worked on budgets rather than broadcasts. Instead of recording African music in remote villages, canoeing over flooded plains or climbing down mines, I now seemed to get no closer to the folk-singers of Africa than a weekly session of listening to the tapes and discs recorded by our units in the field. At these sessions we threw out the musically bad or excessively obscene. I no longer worked in the entrance-room, but had a large office to myself. Instead of my seeing all who came through, there were now receptionists and there was a visitors' book for them to sign. Often I was overcome with frustration, as when making a weekly check of the book I found that someone I had long wanted to meet, a famous singer, politician or a chief had been shown over our studios and had gone without my knowing it.

I had come to believe that the only real contribution I could make in Central Africa was by establishing close human contact with Africans in every walk of life. If at all then only by personal example could I help break down colour-bars and tensions. I tried to find as much time as possible for listener research investigations, to meet as many people as possible and to study African folksongs, but the trend was against me. Our growing organization and my own rise in status made it ever more difficult. Two foot six of cavity-wall stood between me and human contact.

It was an inevitable development, but I was only 30 and felt far too young and adventurous to remain behind a desk for the rest of my life. There were worlds to discover all around me, vast bare patches on the map.

There were other reasons for frustration. Even two foot six of cavity-wall were no protection against the new sort of world that was forcing its way in on us. It was no longer so easy to work as we saw fit, to preserve that 'island of sanity' which overseas journalists had remarked upon. The settler Press was becoming increasingly worried in case we were 'giving the natives ideas'. They were in an odd situation, on the one hand they were flattered by our world reputation and reprinted the complimentary words of John Gunther and of Unesco publications, but on the other hand they were becoming increasingly suspicious and my series of plays on constitutional history came in for another round of hysterical abuse from the local paper. But then, the constitutional history of Britain is full of 'dangerous ideas'. Again I was backed by my superiors. Our minister waved aside my defence with the words, 'We ignore that rag automatically.' But how much longer could he?

The criticism of one's audience, even if it hurts, is healthy and useful. But in the Central African situation the criticism that had to be heeded increasingly was not that of our African audience, but of the European settlers and their press, whose views often clashed with those of the Africans we broadcast to.

For example, ever since our station had been functioning we had ended the evening's programme with two anthems, 'God Bless Africa', the mission-inspired Bantu anthem, and 'God Save the

Queen'. All of a sudden one of the European legislators complained about this, 'because we have only one loyalty and that is to Her Majesty the Queen.' There was no widespread agitation. He was one of the two independent right-wing MPs. The majority party remained indifferent. Nevertheless this one insignificant voice brought about our climb-down, we had to change the position of playing the Bantu anthem, thereby offending hundreds of thousands of Africans.

They were all petty incidents and I cannot claim that any one of them caused me much worry. But they were typical of the changing atmosphere which did.

I felt worst of all about the African resentment of Europeans. Despite the confident predictions of British politicians, Africans did not settle down happily under Federation. The tensions and the hatreds of the land did not diminish. They grew worse every day.

Sapper saw my acute frustration and suggested that I go off to Nyasaland for a few months to launch a new venture, the reopening of a small studio at Zomba which we had had to abandon for lack of staff. I accepted with gratitude and for several months worked in Nyasaland, setting up an organization resembling in miniature, the small enthusiastic band I had known at Lusaka.

I loved the job. The country is of breath-taking scenic beauty. It was good to sit, not at an office-desk, but at the wheel of a Land Rover, fording rivers at speed, labouring up mountain-passes that looked like landscapes of the moon, driving in relays through the night covering the length and breadth of that placid backwater of a territory.

It felt good to use my persuasive talents, not to wrangle in smoky committee-rooms, but to talk my way, microphone in hand, into initiation ceremonies that few white men had ever seen.

I recorded the rhythms of the boatmen as they sang and stamped on the metal ferry that they pulled across the Shire river, the masked dancers of the Vinyau society and the chant of the *muezzins* in Islam's southernmost outpost. I watched dances that were imitations of the German goose-step which Africans had seen and delighted in up north, in Tanganyika. I helped with campaigns to reclaim the eroded slopes of tall mountains. I interviewed an octogenarian who in his youth had been a slave, dragged as far as the Gulf of Persia. I recorded cowboy youngsters strumming the saucy songs of the new towns. And then, in the steaming South, I came upon one of the last of the blind minstrels.

It was good to be out on the road again!

But even in that exotic backwater one could no longer escape. On the northern beaches of idyllic Lake Nyasa a villager said to me, 'You betrayed us. Why did you impose Federation on us?' In a village in the Shire highlands I came upon an itinerant agitator preaching that Nyasaland must withdraw from the Federation, that the two African MPs should resign immediately. And everywhere I heard the hoary myth that the labourers who had gone to build the white man's dam at Kariba would never return for they were being fed to vampire-men.

There was no escaping the hatred and suspicion we had triggered off. We stopped at a remote ferry, and an African who saw the initials on our recording-van came up to inform us that a state of emergency had been declared on the Copperbelt, that most of the trade union leaders had been arrested. The news reached me in a remote part of the country within a quarter of an hour of its first announcement. What changes we had brought in Central Africa!

As soon as I got back to my base at Zomba, I was handed a spate of telegrams from Sapper, 'Keep me informed of your movements. Stay near telegraph-line.' and 'Be ready to return if necessary. Make provisional bookings on all planes.' There was no escaping!

But they managed to handle the emergency without me, while I was more profitably employed doing broadcasts on agricultural improvement schemes. When eventually I got back to Lusaka I could no longer settle down to the administrative routine, nor the steadily worsening political atmosphere.

Every traffic accident involving an African sparked off stone-throwing and a small riot. To repress these, collective punishment was made legal. Shrieking women charged administrative offices demanding the right to brew beer. A series of boycotts of stores practising racial discrimination brought more violence, black-shirted Congress strong-men beat up boycott breakers. European storekeepers who had apparently paid protection-money had pickets withdrawn. African colour-bar breakers marched into European restaurants and were assaulted by European customers. Legislation was passed against picketing. There were undignified

scenes as 'European' churches were invaded by Africans. A series
of industrial disputes broke out which were meaningless economically. There was one about the wearing of protective leggings by
Africans. These leggings are designed to protect the miners and
they are no serious inconvenience, but for some reason or other,
European miners were not forced to wear them, so Africans came
to look upon them as a symbol of inferiority, of degradation. They
refused to put them on. A dozen things were assuming symbolic
importance far beyond their apparent significance.

The whole state was sliding down a slippery slope towards more
violence and repression and yet more violence. The situation was
bringing out the ugliest traits in men on both sides.

In that atmosphere the triumphant settlers might have tried to
tread softly, tried to give African wounds a chance to heal. 'Peace
would have been nourishing,' said Dauti Yamba. But instead, they
insisted on forcing through laws to strengthen their political
position. For once Yamba spoke sense when he quoted an old
Bemba proverb: if you have knocked a hole in a man's head and
meet him just as it has healed, you don't start by drawing his
attention to the scar! But the Federal Government introduced
legislation to rig the franchise so that Africans should always
remain with very little influence and they further changed the
constitution so as to increase the number of MPs and to bring in
more African stooges elected by a predominantly European roll.
This was designed to dilute the influence of the African radicals.

Although the African Affairs Board, which had been written
into the Federal constituion for just such contingencies, reserved
these bills for the British veto, the Government in London again
lacked courage. Africans felt that twice more they had been
betrayed.

That year there were five hundred convictions for crimes of
political violence in Northern Rhodesia alone. Late that year a train
was derailed by Congress supporters.

It is a fearful thing to see a catastrophe approaching and to be
able to do nothing about it.

The only reaction of the Government was to increase police
expenditure with every budget. A mobile striking-force with steel
helmets and shields was becoming a familiar sight. We were
governing with ever less consent.

They were demoralizing, disheartening days. I was far from alone in feeling this. One day a senior official turned to me and said: 'Tell me this, you have lived under the Nazis in a police-state. Tell me, was it like this?'

I was glad that I could say truthfully that it was not, that the comparison was preposterous. In Rhodesia the judiciary was fair and the administrators not murderers, but comparatively well-meaning men, who were unequal to their difficult task. No, it was not like Nazi Germany, but that was not saying much. I still did not like the way things were going.

I often thought of Germany, when debating with myself whether to stay or not. I had long been saying to myself that the increasing illiberalism could only be fought from inside, that it was people with views and contacts like mine who ought to stay. But in the end I decided that the argument was false, as false as history has shown up the 'inner emigration' to have been, the justification that many German non-Nazis made for carrying on the administration for a régime repugnant to them. They said to themselves that they were helping to mellow the régime. It was a comforting lie, but a lie. The régime became no more mellow.

I felt that unlike Waluse I had few responsibilities, so I should face up to the truth, that I wasn't doing enough good to justify my staying on. I could see that the higher I rose, the less freedom I would have, the more I would be compelled to conform, and the less I would have of that human contact with Africans which I needed and which I thought they needed too. 'Kindness', Waluse had asked for. But how much kindness can you write into a draft-budget or a programme-schedule?

It was then that I decided to leave Central Africa.

14. WHITE MEN HAVE NO SYMPATHY

ONE OF MY last acts with the CABS was to stand in for Alick Nkhata the musician, who was away on tour, and to give a hearing to all the musicians who assembled every Wednesday to record. Our old airless converted tin hut which served as recording-studio was still in use. The new recording-suite was not yet completed. A number of musicians sat on the grass outside, waiting.

First I heard a few cowboy youths who were strumming indifferently songs that better artists had recorded already. I refused to record them. Then there was a choir of girls dragging their way through some dreary mission-tunes. They too were turned down, with apologies. It was an unprofitable afternoon. Finally there was a mediocre combination of guitar, banjo and rattle. I knew that Nkhata or Sapper with their discriminating ears would have sent them away too, but I enjoyed the words so I recorded them. They sang about a lad who regretted never having gone to school. Now he did not know any English and when his smart friends spoke he thought they might be swearing at him!

I was about to go back to my office when a ragged old man was led into the studio by a boy of ten. Where the eyes had been there were only cavities. Nkhata had mentioned that he had tried to arrange for him to come. He was one of the last few blind minstrels remaining in Central Africa. In all my years I had recorded only one other, some months before in Nyasaland. These men are composers, singers, instrumentalists, choirmasters and sometimes tribal archivists all in one. This one moved from village to village in the Eastern province of Northern Rhodesia, playing the *kalimba*, a plucking instrument with a calabash resonator. He was two hours late and another producer was due to take over the studio. First I thought of telling the blind man to come back again next week, but then I changed my mind. I got on to the phone and persuaded the producer to hold back his recording for half an hour. He had his office full of Europeans waiting to act in a play for our European programmes, but agreed reluctantly to have a preliminary rehearsal in his office.

I set to work. The minstrel spoke a dialect I did not know, so I called an interpreter and through him explained the procedure. The boy was to watch my green signalling-lamp. When I flicked it, he was to touch the old man's shoulder as a sign for him to start. When I flashed it a second time, he was to touch the musician again. That was the sign that recording-time was coming to an end. The musician should then finish his verse properly. On no account was he to stop abruptly. I gave demonstrations of good and bad endings. Then I guided the old man's hand over the microphone and explained that this was the ear of the recording machine, that he would have to sing straight in this direction if he wanted the machine to hear him properly. I repeated these explanations several times, slowly and clearly as I had learnt to do with villagers. Then we rehearsed one or two songs, but time was short and I decided to record without further ado. Anything this man sang was likely to be of interest for our archives. I took up my position at the control-desk outside, the technician started the disc-cutter, I signalled with the lamp, the boy touched the old man's shoulder gently. He paused for a moment, then asked, 'Is it now you want me to sing?'

The disc was spoilt and time running out. While the technician set up another, the interpreter and I went back into the studio and I explained the instructions over again as patiently as I could. The old man listened dully. I began to suspect that he was drunk or drugged. We made a second start, but this time he spoilt it by an unrehearsed beating of the rhythm on the calabash-resonator which was so loud that it dominated the recording. I had to stop him and change the position of the microphone. Once more I went over the instructions, trying to keep back my acute irritation, for I knew that if I raised my voice even a little he would get frightened and sing badly. We started a third time, but now the boy missed his cue.

'Christ, give me patience!' swore the technician. I went in again to go over the instructions. The producer and the actors for the next programme arrived and started to gesticulate through the glass window, but by now I had my man all set and to avoid time-wasting arguments I stayed in the studio with him. The technician started the recording machine. I touched the naked shoulder protruding through the old man's ragged shirt and this time, yes, he started correctly, and plucking the metal prongs of his *kalimba* and beating the rhythm on the calabash resonator with his knees, he sang a melody strange to European ears, but which in my eighteen years in Central Africa I had grown to love, a weird, haunting chant. He was quite carried away by his singing. He sang with such intensity he looked as if he were in pain. I forgot my irritation, but not quite, for he bungled the ending.

We led the minstrel away and paid him off and he left, but the interpreter stayed with me for a moment and said: 'It is an interesting song . . . Wouldn't you like it for your private collection?' I suggested that we listen to it again and that he translate it for me. He took the disc and placed it delicately on a gramophone in our listening-cubicle, and the words of the dirty, ragged, blind old man filled the little room.

> 'I do not know the way to God,
> Else I would have gone to complain.
> Oh, Jesus, what clothes shall I wear on this earth?
> White men have no sympathy.
>
> I do not know the way to God,
> Else I would have gone to complain:
> Their voices are harsh and their eyes are not kind.
> White men have no sympathy.
>
> I should have asked for eyes,
> but I do not know the way to God.
> Oh, Jesus, what clothes shall I wear on this earth?
> White men have no sympathy.'

I wanted to rush after him, but he had gone, supported by his little boy. And anyway, had I found him, I would not have known what to say.

WAYALESHI

Peter Fraenkel

...roud when I switch on my saucepan special
...he whole world in my hut.' These
... a Rhode... ...ger to the